tantric transformation

Extemporaneous talks given by Osho at
the OSHO International Meditation Resort, Pune, India

tantric transformation

When Love Meets Meditation

ON *THE ROYAL SONG OF SARAHA*

OSHO

Previously published as *Tantra Vision,* Vol. 2
This title is also available as an eBook ISBN-13: 978-0-88050-410-2

Volume 1 is published as *The Tantra Experience – Evolution Through Love*
Book ISBN-13: 978-0-9836400-3-5
eBook ISBN-13: 978-0-88050-321-1

This book is a series of original talks by Osho, given to a live audience. All of Osho's talks
have been published in full as books, and are also available as original audio recordings.
Audio recordings and the complete text archive can be found via the online OSHO Library
at www.osho.com/library

Osho comments in this work on excerpts from: *The Royal Song of Saraha: A Study in the
History of Buddhist Thought,* translated and annotated by Herbert V. Guenther (1968).
All rights reserved. Permission granted by Dr. Ilse Guenther.

OSHO MEDIA INTERNATIONAL

New York • Zurich • Mumbai
an imprint of
OSHO INTERNATIONAL
www.osho.com/oshointernational

Distributed by Publishers Group Worldwide
www.pgw.com

Library of Congress Catalog-In-Publication Data is available

Printed in India by Manipal Technologies Limited, Karnataka

ISBN-13: 978-0-9836400-6-6

contents

preface

These songs of Saraha are of great beauty. They are the very foundation of Tantra. You will first have to understand the Tantra attitude towards life, the Tantra vision of life. The most basic thing about Tantra is this – and very radical, revolutionary, rebellious – the basic vision is that the world is not divided into the lower and the higher, but that the world is one piece. The higher and the lower are holding hands. The higher includes the lower, and the lower includes the higher. The higher is hidden in the lower – so the lower has not to be denied, has not to be condemned, has not to be destroyed or killed. The lower has to be transformed. The lower has to be allowed to move upwards and then the lower becomes the higher. There is no unbridgeable gap between the Devil and God: the Devil is carrying God deep down in his heart. Once that heart starts functioning, the Devil becomes God.

That is the reason why the very root of the word *devil* means the same as *divine*. The word *devil* comes from *divine*; it is the divine not yet evolved, that's all. Not that the Devil is against the divine, not that the Devil is trying to destroy the divine – in fact the Devil is trying to find the divine. The Devil is on the way towards the divine; it is not the enemy, it is the seed. The divine is the tree fully in bloom, and the Devil is the seed – but the tree is hidden in the seed, and the seed is not against the tree. In fact the tree cannot exist if the seed is not there. The tree is not against the seed; they are in deep friendship, they are together. Poison and nectar are two phases of the same energy, so are life and death – and so is everything: day and night, love and hate, sex and superconsciousness.

Tantra says: never condemn anything – the attitude of condemnation is a stupid attitude. By condemning something you are denying yourself the possibility that would have become available to you if you had evolved the lower. Don't condemn the mud, because the lotus is hidden in the mud; use the mud to produce the lotus. Of course the mud is not the lotus yet, but it can be. The creative person, the religious person, will help the mud to release its lotus so that the lotus can be freed from the mud.

Saraha is the founder of the Tantra vision. It is of tremendous import – and particularly for the present moment in human history because a new man is striving to be born, a new consciousness is knocking on the doors, and the future is going to be that of Tantra because now dual attitudes can no longer hold man's mind. They have tried for centuries; and they have crippled man and they have made man guilty They have not made man free; they have made man a prisoner. They have not made man happy either, they have made man very miserable. They have condemned everything: from food to sex they have condemned everything, from relationship to friendship they have condemned all. Love is condemned, the body is condemned, the mind is condemned. They have not left a single inch for you to stand on; they have taken away all, and man is hanging, just hanging. This state of man cannot be tolerated any longer.

Tantra can give you a new perspective; hence I have chosen Saraha. Saraha is one of my most-loved persons; it is my old love affair. You may not even have heard the name of Saraha, but Saraha is one of the great benefactors of humanity. If I were to count on my fingers ten benefactors of humanity, Saraha would be one of those ten. If I were to count five, then too I would not be able to drop Saraha.

Osho
The Tantra Experience

CHAPTER 1

the tantra map

For the delights of kissing the deluded crave,
declaring it to be the ultimately real –
like a man who leaves his house and standing at the door
asks a woman for reports of sensual delights.

The stirring of biotic forces in the house of nothingness
has given artificial rise to pleasures in so many ways.
Such yogis from affliction faint for they have fallen
from celestial space, inveigled into vice.

As a brahmin, who with rice and butter
makes a burned offering in blazing fire
creating a vessel for nectar from celestial space,
takes this, through wishful thinking, as the ultimate.

Some people, who have kindled the inner heat
and raised it to the fontanel,
stroke the uvula with the tongue in a sort of coition
and confuse that which fetters with what gives release,
in pride will call themselves yogis.

T antra is freedom – freedom from all mind constructs, from all mind games; freedom from all structures, freedom from the other. Tantra is a space to be. Tantra is liberation.

Tantra is not a religion in the ordinary sense. Religion is again a mind game, religion gives you a certain pattern. A Christian has a certain pattern, so has a Hindu, so has a Muslim. Religion gives you a certain style, a discipline. Tantra takes all disciplines away.

When there is no discipline, when there is no enforced order, a totally different kind of order arises in you. What Lao Tzu calls Tao, what Buddha calls *dhamma,* arises in you. This is not anything done by you; it happens to you. Tantra simply creates a space for it to happen. It does not even invite, it does not wait; it simply creates a space. And when the space is ready, the whole flows in.

I have heard a very beautiful story, a very ancient one...

In a province, no rain had fallen for a long time – everything was dried up. At last the citizens decided to fetch the rainmaker. A deputation was sent to see him in the distant town where he lived, with the urgent request to come as soon as possible and make rain for their parched fields.

The rainmaker, a wise old man, promised to do so on condition that he was provided with a solitary little cottage in the open country where he could withdraw by himself for three days – no food or drink would be required. Then he would see what could be done. His requests were met.

On the evening of the third day abundant rain fell, and full of praise, a grateful crowd made a pilgrimage to his house and exclaimed, "How did you do it? Tell us."

"It was quite simple," the rainmaker answered. "For three days all I did was to put myself in order. For, I know that once I am in order, then the world will be in order, and the drought must yield place to the rain."

Tantra says that if you are in order, then the whole world is in order for you. When you are in harmony, then the whole existence is in harmony for you. When you are in disorder, then the whole world is disorder. And the order must not be a false one, it must not be a forced one. When you force some order upon yourself, you simply become split; deep down the disorder continues.

You can observe it: if you are an angry person you can force your anger, you can repress it deep down in the unconscious, but it is not going to disappear. Maybe you become completely unaware of it, but it is there – and you know that it is there. It is running underneath you, it is in the dark basement of your being, but it is there. You can sit smiling on top of it, but you know it can erupt any moment. And your smile cannot be very deep, and your smile cannot be true, and your smile will be just an effort you are making against yourself. A man who forces order from the outside remains in disorder.

Tantra says there is another kind of order. You don't impose any order, you don't impose any discipline; you simply drop all structures, you simply become natural and spontaneous. It is the greatest step a man can be asked to take. It will need great courage because the society will not like it, the society will be dead against it. The society wants a certain order. If you follow the society, the society is happy with you. If you go a little bit astray here and there, the society is very angry – and the mob is mad.

Tantra is a rebellion. I don't call it revolutionary because it has no politics in it. And I don't call it revolutionary because it has no plans to change the world, it has no plans to change the state and the society. It is rebellious, it is individual rebellion. It is one individual slipping out of the structures and the slavery. But the moment you slip out of the slavery, you come to feel another kind of existence around you which you have never felt before – as if you were living with a blindfold and suddenly the blindfold has become loose, your eyes have opened and you can see a totally different world.

This blindfold is what you call your mind – your thinking, your prejudices, your knowledge, your scriptures; they all make up the thick layer of the blind-fold. They are keeping you blind, they are keeping you dull, they are keeping you unalive.

Tantra wants you to be alive – as alive as the trees, as alive as the rivers, as alive as the sun and the moon. That is your birthright. You don't lose anything by losing the blindfold; you gain all. And if everything is to be lost in gaining it, nothing is lost. Even a single moment of utter freedom is enough to satisfy. And a long life of a hundred years, yoked like a slave, is meaningless.

To be in the world of Tantra needs courage: it is adventurous. Up to now, only a few people have been able to move on that path. But the future is very hopeful. Tantra will become more and more important. Man understands more and more what slavery is, and man also understands that no political revolution has proved revolutionary. All political revolutions finally turn into anti-revolutions. Once revolutionaries are in power they become anti-revolutionary. Power *is* anti-revolutionary. So there is a built-in mechanism in power: give anybody power and he becomes anti-revolutionary. Power creates its own world. So up to now there have been many revolutions in the world and all have failed, utterly failed; no revolution has helped. Now man is becoming aware of it.

Tantra gives a different perspective. It is not revolutionary; it is rebellious. Rebellion means individual. You can rebel alone, you need not organize a party for it. You can rebel alone, on your own. It is not a fight against society, remember; it is just going beyond society. It is not anti-social, it is asocial; it has nothing to do with society. It is not against slavery, it is for freedom – freedom to be.

Just look at your life. Are you a free man? You are not: there are a thousand and one bondages around you. You may not look at them, it is very embarrassing; you may not recognize them, it hurts. But it doesn't change the situation: you are a slave. To move into the dimension of Tantra you will have to recognize your slavery. It is very deep-rooted; it has to be dropped, and being aware of it helps you to drop it.

Don't go on pacifying yourself, don't go on consoling yourself, don't go on saying, "Everything is okay." It is not. Nothing is okay, your whole life is just a nightmare. Have a look at it! There is no poetry and no song and no dance and no love and no prayer. There is no celebration. Joy? – it is just a word in the dictionary. Bliss? – yes, you have heard about it, but you have not known anything about it. God? – in the temples, in the churches. Yes, people talk about it. Those who talk, they don't know; those who hear, they don't know. All that is beautiful seems to be meaningless, and all that is meaningless seems to be very, very important.

A man goes on accumulating money and thinks that he is doing something very significant. Human stupidity is infinite. Beware of it, it will destroy your whole life; it has destroyed millions of people's lives down the ages. Take hold of your awareness – that is the only possibility to get out of stupidity.

Before we enter today's sutras, something has to be understood about the Tantra map of inner consciousness. I have told you a few things about it, but a few more things have to be said.

First: Tantra says that no man is just man, and no woman is just woman. Each man is both man and woman, and so is each woman – woman and man. Adam has Eve in him, and Eve has Adam in her. In fact, nobody is just Adam and nobody is just Eve, we are Adam-Eves. This is one of the greatest insights ever attained.

Modern depth psychology has become aware of it; they call it bisexuality. But for at least five thousand years Tantra has known it, preached it. It is one of the greatest discoveries of the world because with this understanding you can move in your inner direction; otherwise you cannot move in your inner direction. Why does a man fall in love with a woman? – because he carries a woman inside him, otherwise he would not fall in love. And why do you fall in love with a certain woman? There are thousands of women, but why, suddenly, does a certain woman become most important to you, as if all other women have disappeared and that is the only woman in the world? Why? Why does a certain man attract you? Why at first sight does something suddenly click?

Tantra says you are carrying an image of a woman inside you, an image of a man inside you. Each man is carrying a woman and each woman is carrying a man. When somebody on the outside fits with your inner image, you fall in love – that is the meaning of love.

You don't understand it; you simply shrug your shoulders and say, "It has happened." But there is a subtle mechanism in it. Why did it happen with a certain woman, why not with others? Your inner image fits somehow, the outer woman is similar in a way. Something just hits your inner image. You feel, "This is my woman," or "This is my man"; this feeling is what love is. But the outer woman is not going to satisfy, because no outer woman is going to completely fit with your inner woman. The reality is not that way at all. Maybe she fits a little bit – there is an appeal, a magnetism, but it will be worn out sooner or later. Soon you will recognize that there are a thousand and one things that you don't like in the woman. It will take a little time to come to know about those things.

First you will be infatuated. First the similarity will be too much, it will overwhelm you. But by and by you will see that there are a thousand and one things, details of life, that don't fit – that you are aliens, strangers. Yes, you still love her, but the love has no more infatuation, that romantic vision is disappearing. And she will also recognize that something appeals in you, but your totality is not appealing. That's why each husband tries to change the wife and each wife tries to change the husband. What are they trying to do? Why? Why does a wife continuously try to change the husband? For what? She has fallen in love with this man, then immediately she starts changing him? Now she has become aware of the dissimilarities. She wants to drop those dissimilarities; she wants to take a few chunks off this man so that he completely fits with her idea of a man. And the husband also tries – not so hard, not so stubbornly as women try because the husband becomes tired very soon – the woman hopes longer.

The woman thinks, "Today or tomorrow or the day after tomorrow – some day he will change." It takes almost twenty, twenty-five years to recognize the fact that you cannot change the other. By the age of fifty, when the woman has passed her menopause and the man too, when they are getting really old, then they become alert by and by that nothing has changed. They have tried hard, they have tried every way; the woman remains the same and the man remains the same. Nobody can change anybody. This is a great experience to come to, a great understanding.

That's why old people become more tolerant: they know that nothing can be done. That's why old people become more graceful: they know that things are as they are. That's why old people become more accepting. Young people are very angry, nonaccepting; they want to change everything: they want to make the world the way they would like it. They struggle hard, but it has never happened. It cannot happen, it is not in the nature of things. The outer man can never fit with your inner man, and the outer woman can never be absolutely the same as your inner woman. That's why love gives pleasure and also pain, love gives happiness and also unhappiness. And the unhappiness is much more than the happiness.

What does Tantra propose about it, what has to be done then? Tantra says that there is no way to be satisfied with the outer; you will have to move inward. You will have to find your inner woman and inner man; you will have to attain to a sexual intercourse inside. That is a great contribution.

How can it happen? Try to understand this map. I have talked about seven chakras, the Yoga-Tantra physiology. In man the *muladhar* is male and *svadhishthan,* female. In woman the *muladhar* is female and the *svadhishthan,* male, and so on and so forth. In seven chakras, up to the sixth, the duality remains; the seventh is nondual.

There are three pairs inside you: the *muladhar-svadhishthan* have to have to marry; the *manipura-anahata* have to have to marry; the *vishuddha-agya* have to have to marry.

When the energy moves outside, you need a woman outside. You have a little glimpse for a moment – because coition with a woman outside cannot be permanent, it can be only momentary. For a single moment you can lose yourself in each other. Again you are thrown back to yourself, and thrown back with a vengeance. That's why after each lovemaking, there is a certain frustration: you have failed again, it didn't happen the way you wanted it to happen. Yes, you reached to a peak, but before you had even become aware of it, the decline, the fall began. Before the peak was achieved, the valley. Before you had met the woman or the man, the separation. Divorce comes so fast with marriage that it is frustrating. All lovers are frustrated people: they hope much, they hope against their experience, they hope again and again – but nothing can be done. You cannot destroy the laws of reality. You have to understand those laws.

The outer meeting can only be momentary, but the inner meeting can become eternal. And the higher you move the more eternal it can become. The first chakra, the *muladhar*, in man is male. Even while making love to a woman outside, Tantra says, remember the inner. Make love to the woman outside, but remember the inner. Let your consciousness move inward. Forget the outer woman completely. In the moment of orgasm forget the woman or the man completely. Close your eyes and be in, and let it be a meditation. When energy is stirred, don't miss this opportunity. That is the moment when you can have a contact – an inward journey.

Ordinarily it is difficult to look in; but in a love moment there is some gap, you are not ordinary. In a love-moment you are at your maximum. When orgasm happens, your whole body energy is throbbing with dance; each cell, each fiber dancing in a rhythm, in a harmony, that you don't know in ordinary life. This is the moment, this moment of harmony; use it as a passage inward. While making love, become meditative, look in.

A door opens at that moment – this is the Tantra experience. A door opens in that moment, and Tantra says that you feel happy only because that door opens and something of your inner bliss flows to you. It is not coming from the outer woman, it is not coming from the outer man; it is coming from your innermost core. The outer is just an excuse.

Tantra does not say that to make love to the outer is sin, it simply says that it is not very far-reaching. It does not condemn it, it accepts its naturalness, but it says that you can use that love wave to go far inside. In that moment of thrill, things are not on the earth: you can fly. Your arrow can lead the bow toward the target. You can become a Saraha.

If while making love you become meditative, you become silent, you start looking in, you close your eyes, you forget the outer man or woman, then it happens. The *muladhar*, your male center inside, starts moving towards the female center – the female center is the *svadhishthan* – and there is a coition, there is an intercourse inside.

Sometimes it happens without your knowing it. Many sannyasins have written me letters; I have never answered before because it was not possible to answer. Now I can answer; you will be able to understand. One sannyasin writes to me again and again, and he must be wondering why I do not answer. The map was not available up to now, now I am giving you the map. Listening to me he always feels as if he is going into orgasm. His whole body starts throbbing, and he has the same experience as he has while making love to a woman. He becomes very puzzled – naturally so. He loses track of what he was listening to – he forgets, and the thrill is so much and the joy is so much that he is worried. What is happening? What is this inside him?

This is happening: the *muladhar* is meeting with the *svadhishthan*, your male center is meeting with your female center. This is the joy when you move into meditation, when you move into prayer; this is the mechanism of your inner celebration. And the moment the *muladhar* and *svadhishthan* meet, the energy is released. Just as when you love your woman energy is released, when the *svadhishthan* and *muladhar* meet, energy is released and that energy hits the higher center, the *manipura*.

The *manipura* is male, the *anahata* is female. Once you have become attuned to the first meeting of your man and woman inside, one day the second meeting suddenly happens. You do not have to do anything about it; just the energy released from the first meeting creates the possibility for the second meeting. And when energy is created by the second meeting, it creates the possibility for the third meeting.

The third meeting is between the *vishuddha* and *agya*. And when the third meeting happens, the energy is created for the fourth, which is not a meeting, which is not a union, but unity. The *sahasrar* is alone; there is no male-female. Adam and Eve have disappeared into each other totally, utterly. Man has become the woman, the woman has become the man; all division disappears. This is the absolute, the eternal meeting. This is what Hindus call *sat-chit-anand*. This is what Jesus calls "the Kingdom of God."

In fact the number seven has been used by all the religions. Seven days are symbolic and the seventh day is the holiday, the holy day. Six days God worked and on the seventh day he rested. You will have to work on six chakras, the seventh is the state of great rest, utter rest, absolute relaxation – you have come home.

With the seventh you disappear as part of duality; all polarities disappear, all distinctions disappear. Night is no longer night, and day is no longer day. Summer is no longer summer, and winter is no longer winter. Matter is no longer matter, and mind is no longer mind – you have gone beyond. This is the transcendental space Buddha calls nirvana.

These three meetings inside you, and the achievement of the fourth, have another dimension too. I have talked to you many times about four states: sleep, dream, waking, *turiya*. *Turiya* means "the fourth," "the beyond." These seven chakras, and the work through them, have a correspondence with these four states also.

The first meeting between the *muladhar* and *svadhishthan* is like sleep. The meeting happens, but you cannot be very aware of it. You will enjoy it, you will feel a great freshness arising in you. You will feel great rest, as if you have slept deeply; but you will not be able to see it exactly – it is very dark. The man and woman have met inside you, but they have met in the unconscious; the meeting was not in the daylight, it was in the dark night. Yes, the result will be felt, the consequence will be felt. You will suddenly feel a new energy in you, a new radiance, a new glow. You will have an aura. Even others may start feeling that you have a certain quality of presence, a vibe. But you will not be exactly alert to what is happening, so the first meeting is like sleep.

The second meeting is like dreaming: when the *manipura* and *anahata* meet, your meeting with the inner woman is as if you have met in a dream. Yes, you can remember a little bit of it, just as in the morning you can remember the dream that you had last night – a little bit here and there, a few glimpses.

Maybe something has been forgotten, maybe the whole is not remembered, but still you can remember. The second meeting is like dreaming. You will become more aware of it, you will start feeling that something is happening. You will start feeling that you are changing, that a transformation is on the way, that you are no longer the old person. And with the second, you will start becoming aware that your interest in the outer woman is lessening or your interest in the outer man is not as infatuating as it used to be.

With the first there will also be a change, but you will not be aware of it. With the first you may start thinking that you are no longer interested in *your* woman, but you will not be able to understand that you are not interested in *any* woman at all. You may think you are bored with your woman and you will be happier with some other woman; some change will be good, a different climate will be good, a different quality of woman will be good. This will be just a guess. With the second you will start feeling that you are no longer interested in the woman or the man, that your interest is turning inward. With the third you will become perfectly aware; it is like waking. The *vishuddha* meeting the *agya*: you will become perfectly aware, the meeting is happening in the day-light. Or you can say it in this way: the first meeting happens in the dark middle of the night, the second meeting happens in a twilight time between the night and the day, the third meeting happens in full noon – you are fully alert, every-thing is clear. Now you know you are finished with the outer. It does not mean you will leave your wife or your husband, it simply means that the infatuation is no more. You will feel compassion. Certainly the woman who has helped you so far is a great friend, the man who has brought you so far is a great friend; you are grateful. You will start being grateful and compassionate to each other.

It is always so: when understanding arises it brings compassion. If you leave your wife and escape to the forest, that simply shows you are cruel and compassion has not arisen. It can be only out of nonunderstanding, it cannot be out of understanding. If you understand you will have compassion.

When Buddha became enlightened, the first thing he said to his disciples was, "I would like to go to Yashodhara and talk to her" – his wife.

Ananda was very much disturbed. He said, "What is the point of your going back to the palace and talking to your wife? You have left her – twelve years have passed." And Ananda was also a little bit disturbed because how can a buddha think about his wife? Buddhas are not expected to think that way.

When the others had left, Ananda said to Buddha, "This is not good. What will people think?"

Buddha said, "What will people think? I have to express my gratitude to her, and I have to thank her for all the help she gave me. And I have to give something of that which has happened to me – I owe that much to her. I will have to go."

He went back, he went to the palace, he saw his wife. Certainly Yashodhara was mad; this man had escaped one night without even saying anything to her. She said to Buddha, "Couldn't you have trusted me? You could have said that you wanted to go, and I would have been the last woman in the world to prevent you. Couldn't you have trusted me even that much?" And she was crying – twelve years of anger! And this man had escaped like a thief in the middle of the night – suddenly, without giving a single hint to her.

Buddha apologized. And he said, "It was out of nonunderstanding. I was ignorant, I was not aware. But now I am aware and I know; that's why I have come back. You have helped me tremendously. Forget those old things; now there is no point in thinking about spilt milk. Look at me – something great has happened. I have come home. And I felt my first duty was towards you, to come and to convey and to share my experience with you."

The anger gone, the rage subsided, Yashodhara looked out through her tears. Yes, this man had changed tremendously; this was not the same man she used to know. This was not the same man, not at all. He looked like a great luminosity: she could almost see the aura, a light around him. And he was so peaceful and so silent; he had almost disappeared, his presence was almost absence. And then, in spite of herself, she forgot what she was doing. She fell at his feet and she asked to be initiated.

When you understand, there is bound to be compassion. That's why I don't say to my sannyasins to leave their families. Be there.

Rabindranath has written a poem about this incident – when Buddha goes. Yashodhara asked him one thing: "Just tell me one thing," she said. "Whatever you have attained – I can see you have attained, whatsoever it is, I don't know what it is – just tell me one thing: Was it not possible to attain it here in this house?"

And Buddha could not say no. It *was* possible to attain it there in the house. Now he knew, because it has nothing to do with forest or with town, with the family or with an ashram. It has nothing to do with any place; it has something to do with your innermost core. It is available everywhere.

First, you will start feeling that your interest in the other is loosening. It will be a dim phenomenon, dark – looking through a dark glass, looking through a very foggy morning. Second, things become a little clearer, like a dream, the fog is not so much. Third, you are fully awake – it has happened, the inner woman has met the inner man. The bipolarity is no longer there: suddenly you are one. Schizophrenia has disappeared, you are not split.

With this integration you become an individual. Before that you were not an individual, you were a crowd, you were a mob, you were many people, you were multi-psychic. Suddenly you fall into order. That's what this ancient story says.

The rainmaker had asked for three days... If sometimes you look into these small stories you will be wonderstruck; their symbols are great. The man had asked for three days to sit silently. Why three days? Those are the three points: in sleep, in dream, in waking; he wanted to put himself in order. First it happens in sleep, then it happens in dreams, then it happens in waking. And when you are in order, the whole existence is in order. When you are an individual, when your split has disappeared and you are bridged together, then everything is bridged together.

It will look very paradoxical, but it has to be said: the individual is the universal. When you have become an individual, suddenly you see that you are the universal. Up to now you have been thinking that you were separate from existence; now you cannot think that. Adam and Eve have disappeared into each other. This is the goal that everybody is trying to find in some way or other. Tantra is the surest science for achieving it; this is the target.

A few more things: I told you that the *muladhar* has to be relaxed, only then can the energy move upward, inward. And inward and upward mean the same; outward and downward mean the same. Energy can move inward or upward only when the *muladhar* is relaxed. So the first thing is to relax the *muladhar*.

You are holding your sex center very tight. The society has made you very aware of the sex center; it has made you obsessed with it, so you are holding it tight. You can simply watch. You are always holding your genital organism very tight, as if you are afraid that something will go amiss if you relax. Your whole conditioning has been to keep it uptight. Relax it; leave it to itself. Don't be afraid – fear creates tension. Drop the fear. Sex is beautiful; it is not a sin, it is a virtue. Once you think in terms of its being a virtue you will be able to relax.

I have talked about how to relax the *muladhar* before. And I have talked about how to relax the *svadhishthan*; it is the death center. Don't be afraid of death. These are the two fears which have been dominating humanity: the fear of sex and the fear of death. Both fears are dangerous; they have not allowed you to grow. Drop both the fears.

The third chakra is the *manipura*; it is loaded with negative emotions. That's why your stomach becomes disturbed when you are emotionally disturbed; the *manipura* is affected immediately. In all the languages of the world we have expressions like, "I cannot stomach it." It is literally true. Sometimes when you cannot stomach a certain thing you start feeling nauseous, you would like to vomit. In fact sometimes it happens – a psychological vomit. Somebody has said something and you cannot stomach it, and suddenly you feel nausea: you vomit, and after vomiting you feel very relaxed.

In Yoga they have methods for it. The yogi has to drink a large amount of water in the morning – a bucketful of water with salt; the water has to be luke-warm – and then he has to vomit it. It helps to relax the *manipura*. It is a great process, a great cleansing process.

You will be surprised: now many modern therapies have become aware of that vomiting helps. Action Analysis is aware of the fact that vomiting helps. Primal Therapy is aware of the fact that vomiting helps. It releases the *manipura*. Tantra and Yoga have always been aware of it.

The negative emotions – anger, hatred, jealousy and so on and so forth – have all been repressed. Your *manipura* is overloaded. Those repressed emotions don't allow the energy to go up; those repressed emotions function like a rock: your passage is blocked. Encounter, Gestalt and therapies like that, all function unknowingly on the *manipura*. They try to provoke your anger, they try to provoke your jealousy, your greed; they provoke your aggression, your violence, so that it bubbles up, surfaces. The society has done one thing: it has trained you to repress all that is negative and pretend all that is positive. Now, both are dangerous. To pretend the positive is false, hypocrisy, and to repress the negative is dangerous; it is poisonous, it is poisoning your system.

Tantra says to express the negative and allow the positive. If anger comes, don't repress it; if aggression comes, don't repress it. Tantra does not say go and kill a person – but Tantra says that there a thousand and one ways to express the repressed emotions. You can go into the garden and chop wood. Have you watched woodcutters? They look more silent than anybody else. Have you watched hunters? Hunters are very good people. They do a very dirty thing, but they are good people. Something happens to them while they are hunting. Killing animals, their anger, their aggression is dissolved. The so-called non-violent people are the ugliest in the world. They are not good people because they are holding down a volcano. You cannot feel at ease with them; something is dangerously present there – you can feel it, you can touch it, it is oozing out of them.

You can just go into the forest and shout, scream. Primal Therapy is just scream therapy, tantrum therapy. And Encounter and Primal, Gestalt, are of tremendous help in relaxing the *manipura*.

Once the *manipura* is relaxed there arises a balance between the nega-tive and the positive. And when the negative and positive are balanced, the passage is open; then the energy can move higher. The *manipura* is male. If the *manipura* is blocked, then energy cannot go upward. It has to be relaxed.

Polarity Balancing can be of great help in bringing about the balance between positive and negative. That's why I am allowing all sorts of methods from all over the world in this ashram. Anything that can be of help has to be used, because man has been so damaged that all sources of help should be made available. You may not even be able to understand why I am making available all the methods to you: Yoga, Tantra, Tao, Sufi, Jaina, Buddhist, Hindu, Gestalt, Psychodrama, Encounter, Primal Therapy, Polarity Balancing, Rolfing, Structural Integration – why I am making all these things available to you. You have never heard of these things being done in any ashram anywhere in the East at all. There is a reason for it: man has been damaged so much that all sources should be tapped. Help should be taken from every source possible; only then there is hope. Otherwise man is doomed.

The fourth chakra is the *anahata*. Doubt is the problem with the fourth chakra; if you are a doubting person, your fourth chakra will remain unopened. Trust opens it. So anything that creates doubt destroys your heart. The *anahata* is the heart chakra. Logic, logic chopping, argumentativeness, too much rationality, too much of Aristotle in you, destroy the *anahata*. Philosophy, skepticism, destroy the *anahata*.

If you want to open the *anahata*, you will have to be more trusting. Poetry is more helpful than philosophy, and intuition is more helpful than reasoning, and feeling is more helpful than thinking. So you will have to shift from doubt to trust, only then does your *anahata* become open, does your *anahata* become capable of receiving the male energy from the *manipura*. The *anahata* is female; it closes with doubt, it becomes frigid with doubt, it becomes dry with doubt – it cannot receive the male energy. It opens with trust: with trust, moisture is released in that chakra and it can allow the penetration of the male energy.

Then the fifth: the *vishuddha*. Noncreativity, imitativeness, parroting, monkeying – these are damaging.

Just the other day I was reading a small anecdote...

A schoolchild was asked, "Ten copycats are sitting on a fence. One jumped off and went away. How many are left?"
And the child says "None."
The teacher says "None? Only one has left!"
And the child says "They are copycats. When one jumps, all jump."

The *vishuddha* is destroyed by copying. Don't be an imitator, don't be just a carbon copy. Don't try to become a Buddha and don't try to become a Christ. Beware of books like Thomas à Kempis' book *Imitation of Christ*

– beware. No imitation is going to help. The *vishuddha* is destroyed by non-creativity, imitation; and it is helped by creativity, expression, finding your own style of life, being courageous enough to "do your own thing." Art, song, music, dance, inventiveness are all helpful. But be inventive – whatsoever you do, try to do it in a new way. Try to bring some individuality into it, bring some authentic signature. Even cleaning a floor, you can do it in your own way; even cooking food, you can do it in your own way. You can bring creativity to everything that you do; it should be brought. In as much as you are creative the *vishuddha* will open. And when the *vishuddha* opens, only then can the energy move into the *agya*, the third-eye center, the sixth center.

This is the process: first cleanse every center, purify it, beware of what damages it, and help it so that it becomes naturally functioning. Blocks are removed, energy rushes.

Beyond the sixth is the *sahasrar*, the *turiya*, the one-thousand-petaled lotus. You bloom. Yes, that's exactly what it is. Man is a tree: the *muladhar* is the root and *sahasrar* is the blooming of it. The flower has bloomed, your fragrance is released to the winds. That is the only prayer; that is the only offering to the feet of the divine. Borrowed flowers won't do, stolen flowers from the trees won't do; you have to flower and offer your flowers.

Now the sutras. The first sutra:

> For the delights of kissing the deluded crave,
> declaring it to be the ultimately real –
> like a man who leaves his house and standing at the door
> asks a woman for reports of sensual delights.

Kissing is symbolic – symbolic of any meeting between yin and yang, between male and female, between Shiva and Shakti. Whether you are holding hands with a woman – this is a kissing, hands kissing each other – or you are touching her lips with your lips, that is kissing; or your genital organs together – that too is a kiss. So the kiss is symbolic in Tantra of all meetings of opposite polarities. Sometimes you can kiss just by seeing a woman. If your eyes meet and touch each other there is a kiss, the meeting has happened.

For the delights of kissing the deluded crave, declaring it to be the ultimately real... Saraha says that the deluded – the people who are not alert at all to what they are doing – go on hankering for, missing, the other: man, the woman; woman, the man. They are continuously hankering to meet the other – and the meeting never happens. The absurdity of it is this: you hanker and hanker and desire and desire, and nothing but frustration comes into your hands. Saraha says this is not the ultimately real meeting. The ultimately real meeting is that which happens in the *sahasrar*. Once it has happened, it has happened forever. That is real. The meeting that happens outside is unreal, momentary, temporal – just a delusion.

It is *...like a man who leaves his house and standing at the door asks a woman for reports of sensual delights*. A beautiful simile. Saraha says that holding the hand of a woman outside, while the woman inside is waiting to be yours and forever yours, is just *...like a man who leaves his house and standing at the door asks a woman for reports of sensual delights.*

First *...leaves his house...* You are leaving your house, your innermost core, in search of a woman outside – and the woman is within. You will miss her wherever you go; you can go on running all over the earth and chasing all sorts of women and men. It is a mirage, it is a rainbow search, nothing comes into your hands. The woman is inside, and you are leaving the house.

And then *...standing at the door...* That too is symbolic. You are always standing at the door, by the senses – those are doors. Eyes are doors, hands are doors, genital organs are doors, ears are doors – these are doors. We are always standing at the door. Looking through the eyes, hearing through the ears, trying to touch with the hands, a man continuously remains at the door and forgets how to go inside the house. And then the absurdity of it – you don't know what love is and you ask a woman about the delights, about her experience. You think that by listening to her experience you will become blissful. It is taking the menu for the food.

Saraha is saying that first you go out of yourself – stand at the door – and then you ask others what delight is, what life is, what joy is, what God is. And God is waiting all the time within you. He resides in you, and you are asking others. And do you think that by listening to them you will come to any understanding?

> The stirring of biotic forces in the house of nothingness
> has given artificial rise to pleasures in so many ways.
> Such yogis from affliction faint for they have fallen
> from celestial space, inveigled into vice.

First: sex is not the ultimate in pleasure, it is just the beginning, the alpha, the *ABC* of it; it is not the omega. Sex is not the ultimately real, it is not the bliss supreme, but just an echo of it; the *sahasrar* is far away. When your sex center feels a little happiness, it is just a faraway echo of the *sahasrar*. The closer you come to the *sahasrar*, the more happiness you feel.

When you move from the *muladhar* to the *svadhishthan*, you feel happier – the first meeting of the *muladhar* and the *svadhishthan* is of great joy. Then the second meeting is of even greater joy. Then the third meeting and you cannot believe that more joy can be possible; but more is still possible because you are still far away – not very far but still at a distance – from the *sahasrar*. The *sahasrar* is just incredible. The bliss is so much that you are no more, only bliss is. The bliss is so much that you cannot say, "I am blissful," you simply know that you *are* bliss.

At the seventh you are just a tremor of joy – naturally so. Joy happens in the *sahasrar* and then it has to pass six layers. Much is lost, it is just an echo. Beware: don't mistake the echo for the real. Yes, even in the echo something of the real is there. Find the thread of reality in it. Catch hold of the thread and start moving inward.

The stirring of biotic forces in the house of nothingness has given artificial rise to pleasures in so many ways. And because of this delusion that sex is the ultimate in pleasure, so many artificial things have become very important. Money has become very important because you can purchase anything for money: you can purchase sex. Power has become important because through power you can have as much sex as you want; a poor man cannot afford it. Kings used to have thousands of wives – even in the twentieth century, the Nizam of Hyderabad had five hundred wives. Naturally, one who has power can have as much sex as he wants. Thousands of other problems have arisen because of this delusion that sex is the ultimately real: money, power, prestige.

The stirring of biotic forces in the house of nothingness... It is just imagination; it is just imagination that you are thinking it is pleasure. It is autohypnosis, autosuggestion. And once you autosuggest to yourself it looks like pleasure. Just think: holding the hand of a woman, and you feel such pleasure: it is just autohypnosis. It is just an idea in the mind.

The stirring of biotic forces... Because of this idea in the mind, your bio-energy is stirred. It is stirred sometimes even while looking at a *Playboy* picture; there is nobody, just lines and colors – and your energy can be stirred. Sometimes just an idea in the mind and your energy can be stirred. Energy follows imagination.

The stirring of biotic forces in the house of nothingness – you can create dreams, you can project dreams onto the screen of nothingness – *has given artificial rise to pleasures in so many ways.*

If you watch the pathology of man, you will be amazed: people have such ideas that you cannot believe what is happening. Some man cannot make love to his woman unless he looks at pornography first. The real seems to be less real than the unreal; he becomes excited only through the unreal. Have you not seen it again and again in your own life – that the real seems to be less exciting than the unreal?

Rushma is sitting just there. She has come from Nairobi. The other day she asked, "I hanker so much for you, Osho, in Nairobi. I dream about you, I fantasize about you; and I have come from so far. And now my heart is not fluttering that way. What has happened?" Nothing has happened; it is just that we are more in love with the imaginary than with the real. The unreal has become more real. So in Nairobi you have "your" Osho. That is your imagination; I have nothing to do with it, that is your idea. But when you come to me, I am here; and then suddenly your imaginary ideas are no longer relevant. You come with a dream in your mind; my reality will destroy the dream.

Remember to change your consciousness from the imaginary to the real. Always listen to the real. Unless you are very, very alert you will remain in the trap of the imaginary.

The imaginary seems to be very satisfying for many reasons. It is under your control. You can have Osho's nose as long as you want – in your imagination. You can think whatsoever you want to think; nobody can hinder it, nobody can enter your imagination, you are utterly free. You can paint me as you want, you can imagine me, you can expect, you can make whatsoever you want of me. You are free; the ego feels very good.

That's why when a master is dead he finds more disciples than while he is alive. With a dead master, disciples are completely at ease; with a living master, they are in difficulty. Buddha never had as many disciples as he has now, after twenty-five centuries. Jesus had only twelve disciples; now, half of the earth. Just see the impact of the absent master: now Jesus is in your hands, you can do whatsoever you want to do with him. He is no longer alive, he cannot destroy your dreams and imaginations. If the so-called Christians had seen the real Jesus, their hearts would stop fluttering immediately. Why? – because they would not believe. They have imagined things, and Jesus is a real man. You could have found him in a pub, drinking with friends and gossiping. Now, this doesn't look like the "only begotten son of God." It looks very ordinary: maybe he is just the carpenter Joseph's son. But once Jesus is gone, he cannot interfere with your imagination. Then you can picture and paint and create images of him as you like.

Far away it is easier: the imagination has full power. The closer you come to me, the less and less power your imagination will have. And you will never be able to see me unless you drop your imagination. So is the case with all other pleasures.

The stirring of biotic forces in the house of nothingness has given artificial rise to pleasures in so many ways. Such yogis from affliction faint for they have fallen from celestial space, inveigled into vice. If you imagine too much, you will lose your celestial space. Imagination is samsara, imagination is your dream. If you dream too much, you will lose the celestial space, you will lose your divinity, you will not be a conscious being. Imagination will outweigh you, it will overburden you, you will be lost in a fantasy. You can faint in your fantasy and you can think that it is *samadhi*. There are people who faint and then they think they are in *samadhi*. Buddha has called such *samadhis* "wrong *samadhis*." So too Saraha says that it is a wrong *samadhi*. Imagining about God, going on into your imagination, feeding your imagination, nurturing it more and more, fantasizing more and more – you will faint, you will lose all consciousness; you will have beautiful dreams of your own creation.

But this is falling from the celestial space. And Saraha says that to fall from your purity of awareness is the only vice. What does he mean by the "celestial space"? Space without any dreams. Dreaming is the world; without dreaming you are in nirvana.

> *As a brahmin, who with rice and butter*
> *makes a burned offering in blazing fire*
> *creating a vessel for nectar from celestial space,*
> *takes this, through wishful thinking, as the ultimate.*

In India, the brahmins have been doing *yagnas*. They have been offering rice and butter to the fire, the blazing fire, and imagining that the offering is going to God. Sitting around a fire, fasting for many days, doing certain rituals, certain mantras, repeating certain scriptures, you can create a state of autohypnosis. You can be fooled by yourself and you can think that you are reaching God.

Saraha says that those who really want to enter godliness will have to burn their inner fire; the outer fire won't do. And those who really want to attain will have to burn their own seeds of desire; rice won't do. And those who really want to attain will have to burn their ego; butter won't do. Butter is just the most essential part of milk, the most purified part of milk. So is ego the most purified dream; it is ghee, purified butter. Offering ghee to the fire is not going to help. You have to burn your inner fire.

And sexual energy moving upward becomes a fire, it becomes a flame. It is fire! Even when it moves outward, it gives birth to life; sex energy is the most miraculous thing. It is through sex energy that life is born. Life is fire, it is a function of fire; without fire life cannot exist. Without the sun there will be no trees, no men, no birds, no animals. It is transformed fire that becomes life.

While making love to a woman, the fire is going outward. While moving inward, the fire is going in. And when you throw your seeds of desire, seeds of thought, seeds of ambition, seeds of greed into this fire, they are burned. And then, finally, you throw your ego – the most purified dream; that too is burned. This is real *yagna*, real ritual, real sacrifice.

As a brahmin who with rice and butter makes a burned offering in blazing fire creating a vessel for nectar from celestial space, takes this, through wishful thinking, as the ultimate. And he thinks, through wishful thinking, that this is the ultimate. The man who is making love to a woman and thinks that it is the ultimate is throwing into the outer fire in exactly the same way; he is pouring into something outside. And so is the woman who thinks she is making love or moving into a great space of bliss and benediction by just making love to a man, just throwing out her fire.

The fire has to move inward; then it gives a rebirth to you, it rejuvenates you.

> *Some people, who have kindled the inner heat*
> *and raised it to the fontanel,*
> *stroke the uvula with the tongue in a sort of coition*
> *and confuse that which fetters with what gives release,*
> *in pride will call themselves yogis.*

And a very important thing: just as I explained to you the map, you have to remember that the *vishuddha*, the fifth chakra, is in the throat. *Vishuddha*, the throat chakra, is the last point from which you can fall. Up to that point there is a possibility of falling back. With the sixth chakra, the third eye, attained, there is no possibility of falling back. You have gone beyond the point from which one can return. The point of no return is the third eye. If you die at the third-eye center, you will be born at the third-eye center. If you die at the *sahasrar*, you will not be born again. But if you die at the *vishuddha*, you will slip back to the first, the *muladhar*. In the next life you will have to start from the *muladhar* again.

So up to the fifth there is no certainty; there is promise, but no certainty. Up to the fifth there is every possibility of falling back. And one of the greatest possibilities that has caused many people in India to fall back is, this sutra says: *Some people, who have kindled the inner heat and raised it to the fontanel...*

You can create the inner heat – the flame starts moving upward and it comes to the throat; then there arises a great desire to tickle the throat with the tongue. Beware of it. In India they have devised great techniques for tickling it with the tongue. They have even cut the roots of the tongue so that the tongue becomes long and can easily move backwards – you will find many yogis doing that. The tongue can move backwards and it can tickle the fifth center. That tickling is masturbatory because the sex energy has come there.

Just as I told you, the fifth chakra, *vishuddha*, is male. When the male energy comes to the throat, your throat becomes almost a genital organ – of more superiority, of more finesse than the genital organ. Just a little tickle with the tongue and you enjoy greatly. But that is masturbatory, and once you start doing that... And it is very, very great pleasure, sex is nothing compared to it. Remember it: sex is just nothing compared to it. Tickling with your own tongue, you can enjoy it so much. So in Yoga there are methods...

Saraha is making it clear that no Tantrika should do that. It is a deception and a great failure because the energy has come up to the fifth, and now the desire arises to tickle it; that is the last desire. If you can keep yourself alert and can move beyond that desire, then you will reach to the sixth center, the *agya*; otherwise you will start falling back. That is the last temptation. In fact, in Tantra that is the temptation which you can say that Jesus had when Satan came and tempted him, or Buddha had when Mara came and tempted him. This is the last temptation, the last effort of your desire-mind, the last effort of your dream world, the last effort of the ego before it is lost utterly. It makes a last effort to tempt you. And the temptation is really great: it is very difficult to avoid it. It is so pleasurable, infinitely more pleasurable than sex pleasure.

When people think that sex pleasure is the ultimate, what to say about this pleasure? And it loses no energy. In sex you have to lose energy; you feel frustrated, tired, weak. But if you tickle your sex energy when it has come to the throat, there is no loss of energy. And you can go on tickling the whole day – that's what Delgado has attained through mechanical devices.

Some people, who have kindled the inner heat and raised it to the fontanel, stroke the uvula with the tongue in a sort of coition and confuse that which fetters with that which gives release... This is again samsara – falling back into samsara. *...and confuse that which fetters with that which gives release, in pride will call themselves yogis.* But they are not, they have missed. In fact the right word for them is *yogabrashta*, "one who has fallen from Yoga."

The fifth center is the most dangerous center. You cannot tickle any other center – that is the danger of it. You cannot tickle the *svadhishthan*, you cannot tickle the *manipura*, you cannot tickle the *anahata*; they are beyond you, there is no way to reach them and tickle them. You cannot tickle the third eye. The only point which can be tickled is the *vishuddha*, your throat center, because it is available. The mouth is open, it is available, and the easiest way is to turn your tongue backwards and tickle it. In Yoga treatises you will find it described as something great; it is not, beware of it.

This is the inner map of Tantra alchemy. The energy can start moving any time; you just have to bring to your lovemaking a little meditation, a little inwardness. Tantra is not against lovemaking, remember; let it be repeated again and again. It is all for it, but not just for it; it is the first rung of the ladder, a seven-runged ladder.

Man is a ladder. The first rung is sex and the seventh rung is the *sahasrar* – *samadhi*. The first rung joins you with samsara, the world, and the seventh rung joins you with nirvana, the beyond. With the first rung, you move in a vicious circle of birth and death again and again; it is repetitive. With the seventh rung, you go beyond birth and death. Life eternal is yours – the kingdom of God.

Enough for today.

freedom is a higher value

The first question:

Osho,
The love in me is dependent on the outside world. At the same time I see what
you say about being complete within. What happens to love if there is nothing
and nobody to recognize and taste it? Who are you without disciples?

The first thing: there are two kinds of love. C. S. Lewis has divided love into these two kinds: "need-love" and "gift-love." Abraham Maslow also divides love into two kinds. The first he calls "deficiency-love" and the second he calls "being-love." The distinction is significant and has to be understood.

The need-love or deficiency-love depends on the other; it is immature love. In fact it is not truly love – it is a need. You use the other, you use the other as a means; you exploit, you manipulate, you dominate. But the other is reduced, the other is almost destroyed. And exactly the same is being done by the other: he is trying to manipulate you, to dominate you, to possess you, to use you. To use another human being is very unloving, so it only appears like love; it is a false coin. But this is what happens to almost ninety-nine percent of people because the first lesson of love that you learn is in your childhood.

A child is born; he depends on the mother. His love towards the mother is a deficiency-love: he needs the mother, he cannot survive without the mother.

He loves the mother because she is his life. In fact there is no love; he would love any woman, whosoever would protect him, whosoever would help him to survive, whosoever would fill up his need. The mother is a sort of food that he eats. It is not only milk that he gets from the mother, it is love too – and that too is a need.

Millions of people remain childish all their lives; they never grow up. They grow in age, but they never grow in their minds. Their psychology remains juvenile, immature – they always need love, they hanker for it like food.

Man becomes mature the moment he starts loving rather than needing. He starts overflowing, sharing; he starts giving. The emphasis is totally different. With the first, the emphasis is on how to get more. With the second, the emphasis is on how to give – how to give more and how to give unconditionally. This is growth, maturity, coming to you.

A mature person gives. Only a mature person can give because only a mature person has it. Then love is not dependent, then you can be loving whether the other is or is not. Then love is not a relationship, it is a state.

What would happen if all the disciples disappeared and only I was here? Do you think there would be any change? What happens when a flower blooms in the deep forest with nobody to appreciate it, nobody to know its fragrance, nobody to pass a comment and say "beautiful," nobody to taste its beauty, and its joy, nobody to share – what happens to the flower? It dies? It suffers? It becomes panicky? It commits suicide? It goes on blooming, it simply goes on blooming. It does not make any difference – whether somebody passes by or not is irrelevant. It goes on spreading its fragrance to the winds, it goes on offering its joy to existence, to the whole.

If I am alone, then too I will be as loving as when I am with you. It is not you who are creating my love. If you are creating my love then, naturally, when you are gone my love will be gone. You are not pulling my love out, I am showering it on you: it is gift-love, it is being-love.

And I don't really agree with C. S. Lewis and Abraham Maslow because the first love that they call "love" is not love, it is a need. How can a need be love? Love is a luxury. It is abundance, it is having so much life that you don't know what to do with it, so you share. It is having so many songs in your heart that you have to sing them – whether anybody listens or not is not relevant. If nobody listens, then also you will have to sing it, you will have to dance your dance.

The other can receive it, the other can miss it, but as far as you are concerned it is flowing, it is overflowing. Rivers don't flow for you, they are flowing whether you are there or not. They don't flow for your thirst, they don't flow for your thirsty fields – they are simply flowing there. You can quench your thirst, you can miss; that's up to you. The river was not really flowing for you, the river was just flowing. It is accidental that you can get the water for your field, it is accidental that you can get water for your needs.

A master is a river, the disciple is accidental. The master is flowing; you can partake, you can enjoy, you can share his being. You can be overwhelmed by him, but he is not *for* you; he is not flowing for you in particular, he is simply flowing. Remember this. And this I call mature love, real love, authentic love, true love.

When you depend on the other, there is always misery. The moment you depend you start feeling miserable because dependence is slavery. Then you start taking revenge in subtle ways because the person you have to depend upon becomes powerful over you. Nobody likes anybody to be powerful over them, nobody likes to be dependent because dependence kills freedom. And love cannot flower in dependence, love is a flower of freedom: it needs space, it needs absolute space. The other must not interfere with it. It is very delicate.

When you are dependent, certainly the other will dominate you, and you will try to dominate the other. That's the fight that goes on between so-called lovers: they are intimate enemies, continuously fighting. What are husbands and wives doing? Loving is very rare: fighting is the rule; loving is exceptional. And in every way they try to dominate; they even try to dominate through love. If the husband asks the wife, the wife denies, she is reluctant, she is very miserly. She gives, but very reluctantly; she wants you to wag your tail around her. And so is the case with the husband. When the wife is in need and asks him, the husband says that he is tired. In the office there was too much work – "really overworked" – and he would like to go to sleep.

I have read a letter written by Mulla Nasruddin to his wife. Listen to it…

To my dear, ever-loving wife,

During the past year I have tried to make love to you 365 times, an average of once per day, and the following is a list of the reasons you gave for rejecting me:

Wrong week, 11 times
It will wake the children, 7 times
It is too hot, 15 times
It is too cold, 3 times
Too tired, 19 times
Too late, 16 times
Too early, 9 times
Pretending to sleep, 33 times
The window is open, neighbors might hear, 3 times

Backache, 16 times
Toothache, 2 times
Headache, 6 times
Not in the mood, 31 times
Baby restless, might cry, 18 times
Watched late show, 15 times
Mud-pack, 8 times
Grease on face, 4 times
Too drunk, 7 times
Forgot to visit the chemist's, 10 times
Visitors sleeping in the next room, 7 times
Just had hair done, 28 times
"Is that all you think about?" 62 times
Dearest, do you think we can improve on our record during the forthcoming year?
Your ever-loving husband,
Mulla Nasruddin.

These are ways to manipulate, to starve the other – to make him more and more hungry so that he becomes more and more dependent.

Naturally, women are more diplomatic about it than men because man is already powerful. He need not find subtle and cunning ways to be powerful; he *is* powerful. He manages the money – that is his power. Muscularly he is stronger – that is his power. Down the centuries he has conditioned the mind of the woman that he is more powerful and she is not powerful. In every way he has always tried to find a woman who is in every way less than him. A man does not want to be married to a woman who is more educated than him because then the power is at stake. He does not want to marry a woman who is taller than him because a taller woman looks superior. A man does not want to marry a woman who is too much of an intellectual because then she argues, and argument can destroy power. A man does not want a woman who is very famous because then he becomes secondary. And down the centuries man has asked for a woman who is younger than him. Why? – why can't the wife be older than you? What is wrong? But an older woman is more experienced; that destroys power.

So man has always asked for a woman who is less in every way. That's why women have lost their height. There is no reason for them to be shorter than men, no reason at all; they have lost their height only because the smaller woman was always chosen. By and by it has entered in their minds so deeply that they have lost their height. They have lost their intelligence because an intelligent woman was not needed: an intelligent woman was a freak. You will be surprised to know that just in this century their height is increasing again. And you will be surprised, even their bones are becoming bigger and their skeleton is becoming bigger. Just within fifty years – particularly in America. And their mind is also growing and becoming bigger than it used to be, their skull is becoming bigger. With the idea of freedom, some deep conditioning has been destroyed.

Man already has power so he need not be very clever, need not be very indirect. Women don't have power. When you don't have power, you have to be more diplomatic; that is a substitute. The only way they can feel powerful is that they are needed, that the man is continuously in need of them. This is not love; this is a bargain. And they are continuously haggling over the price: it is a continuous struggle.

C. S. Lewis and Abraham Maslow divide love in two. I don't divide in two. I say that the first kind of love is just a name, a pseudo coin, it is not true. Only the second kind of love is love.

Love happens only when you are mature. You become capable of loving only when you are a grown-up. When you know that love is not a need but an overflow – being-love or gift-love – then you give without any conditions.

The first kind, the so-called love, derives from a person's deep need for another, while gift-love or being-love flows or overflows from one mature person to another out of abundance. One is flooded with it – you have it and it starts moving around you, just as when you light a lamp, rays start spreading into the darkness. Love is a by-product of being. When you *are,* you have the aura of love around you; when you are not, you don't have that aura around you. And when you don't have that aura around you, you ask the other to give love to you.

Let it be repeated: when you don't have love and you ask the other to give it to you, you are a beggar. And the other is asking you to give it to him or to her. Now, they are two beggars holding out their hands before each other, and both are hoping that the other has it. Naturally both feel defeated finally and both feel cheated.

You can ask any husband and any wife, you can ask any lovers, they both feel cheated. It was your projection that the other had it. If you have a wrong projection, what can the other do about it? Your projection has been broken; the other did not prove according to your projection, that's all. But the other has no obligation to prove his being according to your expectations.

And you have cheated the other: that is the feeling of the other because the other was hoping that love would be flowing from you. You both were hoping love would be flowing from the other, and both were empty. How can love happen? At the most you can be miserable together. Before you used to be miserable alone, separate; now you can be miserable together. And remember, whenever two persons are miserable together, it is not a simple addition – it is a multiplication.

Alone you were feeling frustrated; now you feel frustrated together. One thing is good about it: now you can throw the responsibility on the other, that the other is making you miserable. That is the good point. You can feel at ease: "Nothing is wrong with me. The other... What to do with such a wife – nasty, nagging? One has to be miserable." "What to do with such a husband? – ugly, a miser." Now you can throw the responsibility on the other; you have found a scapegoat. But misery remains, becomes multiplied.

Now, this is the paradox: those who fall in love don't have any love – that's why they fall in love. Because they don't have any love they cannot give. And one thing more: an immature person always falls in love with another immature person because only they can understand each other's language. A mature person loves a mature person, an immature person loves an immature person.

You can go on changing your husband or your wife a thousand and one times, but you will again find the same type of woman and the same misery – repeated in different forms, but the same misery repeated. It is almost the same; you can change your wife, but you are not changed. Now who is going to choose the new wife? *You* will choose. The choice will come out of your immaturity again. You will choose a similar type of woman again.

The basic problem of love is to first become mature; then you will find a mature partner, then immature people will not attract you at all. It is just like that. If you are twenty-five years of age you don't fall in love with a baby two years old. Exactly like that: when you are a mature person psychologically, spiritually – you don't fall in love with a baby. It does not happen, it *cannot* happen. You can see that it is going to be meaningless.

In fact, a mature person does not fall in love; he rises in love. The word *fall* is not right. Only immature people fall; they stumble and fall down in love. Somehow they were managing and standing, but now they cannot manage and they cannot stand – they find a woman and they are gone, they find a man and they are gone. They were always ready to fall on the ground and to crawl. They don't have the backbone, the spine, they don't have the integrity to stand alone.

A mature person has the integrity to be alone. And when a mature person gives love, he gives without any strings attached to it: he simply gives. And when a mature person gives love, he feels grateful that you have accepted his love, not vice versa. He does not expect you to be thankful for it – no, not at all. He does not even need your thanks. He thanks you for accepting his love.

When two mature persons are in love, one of the greatest paradoxes of life happens, one of the most beautiful phenomena: they are together and yet tremendously alone. They are together so much so that they are almost one, but their oneness does not destroy their individuality. In fact, it enhances it: they become more individual. Two mature persons in love help each other to become freer. There is no politics involved, no diplomacy, no effort to dominate. How can you dominate the person you love? Just think over it.

Domination is a sort of hatred, anger, enmity. How can you even think of dominating a person you love? You would love to see the person totally free, independent; you would give him more individuality. That's why I call it the greatest paradox: they are together so much so that they are almost one, but still in that oneness they are individuals. Their individualities are not effaced; they have become more enhanced. The other has enriched them as far as their freedom is concerned.

Immature people falling in love destroy each other's freedom, create a bondage, make a prison. Mature persons in love help each other to be free, they help each other to destroy all sorts of bondages. And when love flows with freedom there is beauty. When love flows with dependence there is ugliness.

Remember, freedom is a higher value than love. That's why, in India, we call the ultimate *moksha*. *Moksha* means freedom. Freedom is a higher value than love. So if love is destroying freedom, it is not of worth. Love can be dropped, freedom has to be saved; freedom is a higher value. And without freedom you can never be happy; that is not possible. Freedom is the intrinsic desire of each man, each woman – utter freedom, absolute freedom.

So one starts hating anything that becomes destructive to freedom. Don't you hate the man you love? Don't you hate the woman you love? You hate: but being with someone is a necessary evil, you have to tolerate it. You have to manage to be with somebody because you cannot be alone, and you have to adjust to the other's demands. You have to tolerate, you have to bear them.

Love, to be really love, has to be being-love, gift-love. Being-love means a state of love. When you have arrived home, when you have known who you are, then a love arises in your being. Then the fragrance spreads and you can give it to others.

How can you give something which you don't have? To give it, the first basic requirement is to have it.

You say, "The love in me is dependent on the outside world." Then it is not love; or if you want to play with words like C. S. Lewis and A. H. Maslow, then call it need-love, deficiency-love. It is like calling a disease a healthy-disease

– it is meaningless, it is a contradiction in terms. Deficiency-love is a contradiction in terms. But if you are too attached to the word *love* it is okay; you can call it deficiency-love or need-love.

You then say, "At the same time I see what you say about being complete within." No, you cannot see it yet. You hear me, you understand it intellectually, but you cannot see it yet. In fact, I am speaking one language and you understand a different language. I am shouting from one plane and you are listening on a different plane. Yes, I am using the same words you use, but I am not like you so how can I give those words the same meaning as you give them? You can understand intellectually and that will be a misunderstanding. All intellectual understanding is a misunderstanding.

Let me tell you a few anecdotes...

A Frenchman who was visiting Ireland entered a compartment of a train, and in the carriage were two Irishmen who were commercial travelers. One of these asked the other, "And where have ye been lately?"

Came the reply, "Sure and haven't I just been to Kilmary and now I am off to Kilpatrick. What about yerself?"

To which the first replied, "I have been to Kilkenny and Kilmichael and now I am off to Kilmore."

The Frenchman listened in amazement. "Murdering scoundrels!" he thought, and got out at the next station.

Now listen: Kil-mary, Kil-patrick, Kil-kenny, Kil-michael and Kil-more. Kill more... The Frenchman must have got frightened. "Murdering scoundrels!"

Something exactly like this continuously goes on happening. I say something, you understand something else. But it is natural; I am not condemning it, I am simply making you aware of it.

There were three boys, one called Trouble, one called Manners, and one called Mindyourownbusiness. Their father was a philosopher so he had given them very meaningful names. Now, it is very dangerous to give people meaningful names.

Trouble got lost, so Manners and Mindyourownbusiness went to the police station. Mindyourownbusiness said to Manners, "Now you wait here outside," and in he went.

Inside he said to the copper at the desk, "My brother's lost."

The copper said, "What's your name?"

"Mindyourownbusiness."

"Where's your manners?" said the copper.

"Outside on the doorstep."

"Are you looking for trouble?"

"Yes, have you seen him?"

This goes on continuously. I say that until you are total within yourself, love will not flow. Of course you understand the words, but you give those words your own meaning. When I say, "Unless you are total within yourself..." I am not proposing a theory, I am not philosophizing at all; I am simply indicating a fact of life. I am saying: "How can you give if you don't have? How can you overflow when you are empty?" Love is an overflow. When you have more than you need, only then can you give; hence it is a gift-love.

How can you give gifts when you don't have any? You hear this and you understand, but then the problem arises because the understanding is intellectual. If it has penetrated your being, if you have seen the facticity of it, then the question will not arise. Then you will forget all your dependent relationships and you will start working on your own being: clearing, cleansing, making your inner core more alert, aware; you will start working that way. And the more you start feeling that you are coming to a certain totality, the more you will find that side by side love is growing; it is a by-product.

Love is a function of being total – then the question will not be there. But the question is there, so you have not seen the fact. You have listened to it as a theory and you have understood it; you have understood the logic of it. To understand the logic is not enough; you will have to have the taste of it.

"The love in me is dependent on the outside world. At the same time I see what you say about being complete within. What happens to love if there is nothing and nobody to recognize and taste it?" It need not be recognized; it needs no recognition, it needs no certificates, it needs nobody to taste it. The recognition of the other is accidental, it is not essential to love; love will go on flowing. If nobody tastes it, nobody recognizes it, nobody feels happy, delighted, because of it, love will go on flowing because in the very flow you feel tremendously blissful. You rejoice tremendously when your energy is flowing. You are sitting in an empty room and the energy is flowing and filling the empty room with your love. Nobody is there; the walls will not say, "Thank you" – nobody to recognize, nobody to taste it. But that doesn't matter at all. Your energy releasing, flowing – you will feel happy. The flower is happy when the fragrance is released to the winds. Whether the winds know about it or not is not the point.

And you ask: "Who are you without your disciples?" I am that I am. Whether disciples are there or not is irrelevant; I am not dependent on you. And my whole effort here is that you can also become independent of me.

I am here to give you freedom. I don't want to impose anything on you, I don't want to cripple you in any way. I want you just to be yourselves. And the day it happens that you are independent of me, you will be able to really love me – not before it.

I love you. I cannot help it. It is not a question of whether I can love you or not – I simply love you. If you are not here, this Chuang Tzu auditorium will be full of my love; it will not make any difference. These trees will still get my love, these birds will go on getting it. And even if all the trees and all the birds disappear, that doesn't make any difference; the love will still be flowing. Love *is*, so love flows.

Love is a dynamic energy; it cannot be stagnant. If somebody partakes, good. If nobody partakes, that too is good. Do you remember what God said to Moses?

When Moses encountered God, of course God gave him a few messages to deliver to his people.

And Moses was a true Jew, he asked, "Sir, but please tell me your name. They will ask, 'Who has given you these messages?'" – they will ask God's name. "So what is your name?"

And God said, "I am that I am. Go to your people and say 'I am that I am' says so. It is a message from 'I am that I am.'"

It looks very absurd but is of tremendous significance: I am that I am. God has no name, no definition, just being.

The second question:

Osho,
I don't go anywhere. Why is a map needed? Isn't being herenow enough?

Yes, there is no goal and nowhere to go. And the map is not needed if you have understood me. But you have not understood me, and the map is needed. The need for a map is not because there is a goal, there is no need to go anywhere. The map is needed because you have gone somewhere and you have to come back to the herenow. There is no need to go anywhere, but you have dreamed that you have gone somewhere. The map is needed to come back home. You have gone astray, you have moved in your imagination, in your desire, in your ambition; you don't look at yourself. Your being is behind you and you are rushing away. The map is needed to look back, to meet your being, to encounter yourself.

But if you understand me – that here and now is all that is – you can burn the map, you can throw away the map; then a map is not needed for you. For one who has arrived home, the map is not needed. But don't burn the map until you have arrived home.

There is a famous painting of a Zen monk burning Buddhist scriptures. Somebody asks him, "Master, what are you doing? You have always taught these scriptures, and you have always been commenting on and reflecting upon these scriptures – why are you burning them?"

And the master laughs and he says, "Because I have come home, so the map is not needed."

But you should not burn them unless and until you have come home. You carry a map: it is meaningful while you are away. When you have arrived, you throw it away. If you throw it before you have arrived, you will be in danger.

Yes, here and now is more than enough – not enough, more than enough. It is all that there is. But you are not herenow, so all these maps are needed to bring you home. You have not gone anywhere really, but you are dreaming that you have gone somewhere. These maps are also dream maps. Remember, these maps are dream maps; these maps are as false as your samsara, as your world.

The ultimate scripture has no word in it. The Sufis have a book, *The Book of the Books*. It is simply empty, not a single word written in it. Down the centuries it has been given from one master to another, handed over from the master to the disciple, and has been kept with tremendous respect. That is the ultimate in scriptures. The Vedas are not so beautiful, the Bible is not so beautiful, Gita is not so beautiful, the Koran is not so beautiful, because something is written there. The *Book of the Books* is really of tremendous value – but will you be able to read it? When, for the first time in the West the Sufis wanted it to be published, no publisher was ready. "What? There is nothing to publish!" they would say. "It will be just an empty book. What to publish it for?"

The Western mind can understand the word: the black ink spread on the white page; it cannot see the white page directly. The white page does not exist for the Western mind, only the black ink. The clouds exist for the Western mind, not the sky: mind exists for the Western mind, not consciousness. Content exists, but they have completely forgotten the container.

Thoughts are just like black ink on white paper; thoughts are just the written message. When thoughts disappear, you will become *The Book of the Books* – empty. But that is the voice of existence.

You say: "I don't go anywhere. Why is a map needed? Isn't being herenow enough?" Just because you ask the question, you will still need the map: a question is a question for the map. If you have understood me, there is no question left. Then what is there to be asked? Here and now is enough. What is there to ask? What can you ask about the here and now? All asking is asking about the goals of somewhere else, then and there.

The third question:

Osho,
I have been married for twenty years already and that "Why can't she understand?" feeling is there. And then I have never seen her in my life, and then I am in the middle of a honeymoon, and then... My mind goes bananas!

Mind always goes bananas – that is the way of the mind. The mind is a flux, it continuously changes. It is not the same for any two consecutive moments; each moment it is different. Yes, one moment you feel that you have not seen your wife in your whole life, you have not met her yet, although you have been living with her for twenty years. Another moment you see yourself just in the middle of a honeymoon: you have seen her beauty, her grace, her joy, her innermost core. And then it is gone and the scene goes on changing.

The mind is very slippery. It goes on slipping, it cannot stay anywhere. It has no capacity to stand; it is a flux. With the mind, everything is like that: one moment you are happy, another moment you are unhappy. One moment you are so joyful, another moment you are so sad – it goes on and on, the wheel of the mind goes on moving. One moment one spoke is on top, another moment another spoke has come to the top, and it goes on this way. That's why in the East we call it samsara, the wheel. The world is a wheel, it goes on moving – the same wheel, again and again and again, and it is not stable for a single moment.

It is like a movie: if the movie stops for a single moment, you will be able to see the screen. But the movie goes on moving, and it is moving so fast and you are so engrossed in it, so occupied with it, that you cannot see the screen. And the screen is the reality. The pictures projected upon it are just dreams. Mind goes on projecting.

I have heard...

A millionaire entered a post office and saw an elderly couple standing at the counter drawing their old-age pensions. He was in a good mood and he felt very sorry for the old couple and he thought they should be given a week's holiday to know the beauties and the joys of life. He was in a charitable mood. Going up to them he said, "How would you like to spend a week at my residence? I will give you both a wonderful time."

Well, the old couple agreed, and so the millionaire took them off to his house in his Rolls and, as he had promised, saw that they had a really good holiday with excellent food, color television and many luxuries which they never dreamed they would ever have. At the end of the week he walked into the library where the old boy was enjoying a quiet time with a glass of wine and smoking a cigar. "Well," he said, "have you enjoyed yourself?"

"Indeed I have," the old boy replied. "But can I ask you a question?"

"Certainly," replied the millionaire.

"Then," said the other, "who's the old woman I have been sleeping with all week?"

This will be the situation of people who have lived with their wives, with their husbands, their whole lives. Who is the woman you have been sleeping with for twenty years? There are moments when you feel you know. There are moments when suddenly there is a Wall of China, opaque, dark – you cannot see anything, you don't know who this stranger here is.

All our knowing is so superficial; we remain strangers. You can sleep with the woman for twenty years – that doesn't make much difference, you remain strangers. And the reason is that you don't even know yourself. How can you know the other? – it is impossible, you are hoping for the impossible. You don't even know yourself! You don't know the man you are and you have been here in existence for eternity. You have been here for millions of lives and you don't know yet who you are. So what to say about twenty years?

And how can you know the other, the woman who is far away from you? You cannot enter into her dreams, you cannot enter into her thoughts, you cannot enter into her desires – how can you know her being? You cannot even know her dreams. You may be sleeping in the same bed with the same woman for twenty years, but she dreams her dreams, you dream your dreams; your subjectivities remain worlds apart.

Even while you are making love to a woman and holding her in your arms, are you really holding the woman who is there or are you holding just an imagination, a projection, a shadow? Are you really holding the real woman in your hands, or just a mind image, a ghost? Do you love this woman who is there, or do you have certain ideas that you love and you find those ideas reflected in this woman? When there are two persons in a bed, my feeling is that there are always four persons: two ghosts lying just in between the two – the woman's projection of the husband and the husband's projection of the wife.

It is not accidental that the husband goes on trying to change the wife according to some ideal, and the wife goes on changing – trying, at least, to change – the husband according to some ideal. Those are the two ghosts. You can't accept the woman as she is, can you? You have many improvements to make, many changes. And if it were really possible, if one day God came to the world and said, "Okay. Now all wives are allowed to change their husbands as they want," or, "All husbands are allowed to change their wives as they want," do you know what would happen? The world would simply go crazy. If women were allowed to change their husbands, you would not find a single man left that you could recognize. All the old people would be gone. If husbands were allowed to change their wives, then no single woman here would be left as she was. And do you think you would be happy? You would not be because then the woman that you had changed, and made according to your ideas, would not appeal to you; she would not have a mystery in her.

Look at the absurdities of the mind, the demands of the mind – suicidal demands. If you were able to change your husband and you really became powerful enough to change him totally, would you love that man? He would be just something put together by you. He would not have any mystery, he would not have any soul, he would not have any integrity of his own, and he would not have anything to be explored by you. You would lose interest, you would be bored by him; he would be just "homemade." What interest? Interest arises only because there is something unknown to be explored, a mystery, an invocation challenging you to move into the unfamiliar.

The first thing: you have not known yourself, so how can you know your wife? – it is not possible. Start by knowing yourself. And this is the beauty of it: the day you know yourself, you will know all. Not only your wife, you will know the whole existence; not only man, but trees and birds and animals, and the rocks and the rivers and the mountains. You will know all because you contain all; you are a miniature universe.

And another beauty, another incredible experience, is that the moment you know yourself, the mystery is not finished. In fact for the first time, the mystery becomes tremendous. You know, and yet you know that much is still there to be known. You know, and yet you know that this knowledge is nothing. You know, and yet the boundary is far away. You only enter into the ocean of knowledge – you never reach the other shore.

In that moment the whole existence is mysterious: your wife, your child, your friend. And your knowledge is not destructive of the magic, of the poetry of life; that knowledge enhances the poetry, the magic, the miracle, the mystery.

"I have been married for twenty years already, and that 'Why can't she understand?' feeling is there." Do you understand yourself? Have you not been doing things for which you repent later on? And you say you have done it in spite of yourself. Do you understand yourself? Do you do things through understanding? When somebody hits you and you become angry, are you becoming angry with understanding? – or just because he has pushed your button?

Your knowledge about yourself is so superficial: it is just like the driver of a car. Yes, he knows a few things: he can manage the steering wheel, he can manage the accelerator, he can manage the clutch, he can manage the gearbox, he can manage the brake – that's all. Do you think he knows everything about the car? What is hidden under the bonnet is not known at all, and that is the real car; that is where the action is, that is where the real thing is happening. What he is pushing and pulling are nothing but buttons. Sooner or later those things are going to disappear from cars. They *should* disappear, they are very primitive – this steering wheel, this accelerator, this brake. They should disappear, they are not needed; a computer can do all that. And then even a small child can drive the car – there is no need for a license really.

But do you understand what is happening inside? When you push a button and the electric light comes on, do you understand electricity? You simply know how to push the button, that's all.

I have heard a story...

When for the first time electricity came to Vienna, a friend of Sigmund Freud came to visit him. He had never seen electricity. At night Freud left him in his room to rest. The friend was very worried: he had never seen electricity and he could not find how to turn the light off. He tried hard: he stood on the bed, he tried to blow out the light, but he could not find any way to blow it out. And he was afraid to go back and ask Freud because that would be too foolish. "What will these people think? You cannot even blow out a light? You don't know even that much." That would look too ignorant. He was from a small village so they would laugh, and that would not be good. So he covered the lamp with a towel and went to sleep.

He couldn't sleep well; again and again he thought about it: there must be some way... He got up; again and again he tried – and the light was still there and it was difficult to sleep. And worse than the light was this pricking, a continuous pricking: "I don't know even such a small thing."

In the morning, when Freud asked him, "Did you sleep well?" the friend replied, "Everything was good. Just one thing I have to ask: how to turn this light off?"

And Freud said, "It seems you don't know electricity at all. Come here.

Just on the wall is the switch; you push the switch and the light is off."

Then the villager said, "So simple! Now I know what electricity is."

But do you know what electricity is? Do you know what anger is? Do you know what love is? Do you know what happiness, joy is? Do you know what sadness is? Nothing is known. You don't know yourself. You don't know your mind. You don't know your inner being. You don't know how this whole life happens. From where? Where does anger come from? Where does joy come from? From where? One moment you are celebrating and the next moment you are ready to commit suicide.

That feeling of, "Why can't she understand?"... This feeling is natural about your wife. How can you understand her? You have not even understood your mind. The day you understand your mind and your being, you have understood all minds and all beings because the fundamental law is the same. If you can understand a single drop of seawater, you have understood all the seas – past, present, future – of this earth, of other planets, because once you have understood that it is H_2O, you have understood water. Wherever water exists, it will be H_2O. Once you have understood your anger, you have understood all the anger of all the human beings ever: past, present, future. If you have understood your sexuality, you have understood all sex.

Please don't try to understand the other; that is not the way. Try to understand yourself – that is the way. You are a miniature universe. In you is the whole map of existence.

The fourth question:

Osho,
I love my husband but I hate sex, and that creates conflict. Isn't sex animalistic?

It is. But man is an animal – as much of an animal as any other animal. When I say that man is an animal, I don't mean that man finishes with animality; he can be more than the animal, he can be less also. That is the glory of man, the freedom and the danger, the agony and the ecstasy. A man can be far lower than the animals, and a man can be far higher than the gods. Man has infinite potentiality. A dog is a dog: he remains a dog. He is born a dog and he will die a dog. A man can become a buddha, and a man can become an Adolf Hitler too. So man is very open-ended on both sides – he can fall back. Can you find any animal more dangerous than man, madder than man?

Just think of a scene: fifty thousand monkeys sitting in a stadium, killing small children, throwing them into a fire. What will you think about them?

Thousands of children are being thrown into a fire – a great fire is burning just in the middle of the stadium, and fifty thousand monkeys enjoying, dancing, and children are being thrown – their own children. What will you think about these monkeys? Will you not think that the monkeys have gone mad? But this has happened in humanity. In Carthage it happened: fifty thousand men burning children. They burned three hundred children at one time as an offering to their god – their own children!

But forget about Carthage, it is long past. What did Adolf Hitler do in this century? Of course, this is a far-advanced century, so Adolf Hitler was capable of doing greater things than were done in Carthage. He killed millions of Jews; thousands at a time would be forced into a chamber and gassed. And hundreds of people would be looking from the outside, watching through one-way mirrors. What will you think about these people? What type of men? People being gassed, burned, evaporated, and others are watching? Can you think about animals doing such a thing?

In three thousand years man has been through five thousand wars – killing and killing and killing. And you call sex animalistic? Animals have never done anything more "animalistic" than man. And you think man is not an animal?

Man *is* an animal. And the idea that man is not an animal is one of the hindrances for your growth. So you take it for granted that you are not animals, and then you stop growing. The first recognition has to be this: "I am an animal and I have to be alert and go beyond it."

It happened...

A man wrote to a country hotel in Ireland to ask if his dog would be allowed to stay there. He received the following answer:

Dear Sir,

I have been in the hotel business for over thirty years. Never yet have I had to call in the police to eject a disorderly dog in the small hours of the morning. No dog has ever attempted to pass off a bad cheque on me. Never has a dog set the bedclothes alight through smoking. I have never found a hotel towel in a dog's suitcase. Your dog is welcome.

P.S. If he can vouch for you, you can come too!

Animals are beautiful, whatsoever they are; they are just innocent. Man is very cunning, very calculating, very ugly. Man can fall lower than the animals because man can rise higher than man, higher than the gods.

Man has an infinite potentiality: he can be the lowest and he can be the highest. He has the whole ladder in his being, from the first rung to the last rung.

So the first thing I would like to say to you: don't call sex just animalistic because sex can be just animalistic – that is possible – but it need not be. It can rise higher: it can become love, it can become prayer. It depends on you. Sex in itself is nothing like a fixed entity; it is just a possibility. You can make it as you like it, as you want it.

That is the whole message of Tantra: sex can become *samadhi*. That is the vision of Tantra: sex can become *samadhi*, through sex the ultimate ecstasy can enter in you.

Sex can become the bridge between you and the ultimate.

You say: "I love my husband but I hate sex, and that creates conflict." How can you love your husband and yet hate sex? You must be playing with words. How can you love your husband and hate sex?

Just try to understand it. When you love a man you would like to hold his hand too. When you love a man you would like to hug him sometimes too. When you love a man you would not only like to listen to him, you would like to see his face too. When you hear only the voice of your beloved, the beloved is far away, the sound is not enough; when you see him too you are more satisfied. When you touch him, certainly you are even more satisfied. When you taste him, certainly you are even more satisfied. What is sex? It is just a meeting of two deep energies.

You must be carrying some taboos in your mind – inhibitions. What is sex? Just two persons meeting at the maximum point – not only holding hands, not only hugging each other's bodies, but penetrating into each other's energy realm. Why should you hate sex? Your mind must have been conditioned by the mahatmas, the so-called religious people who have poisoned the whole of humanity, who have poisoned your very source of growth.

Why should you hate it? If you love your man you would like to share your total being with him; there is no need to hate it. And if you hate sex, what are you saying? You are simply saying that you want the man to take care of you financially, to take care of the house, to buy you a car and a fur coat. You want to use the man. And you call it love? And you don't want to share anything with him.

When you love, you share all. When you love, you don't have any secrets. When you love, you have your heart utterly open, you are available. When you love, you are ready to go with him even to hell if he is going to hell.

But this happens. We are very expert with words; we don't want to say that we don't love, so we make it look as if we love and we hate sex. Sex is not all love, that's true; love is more than sex, that's true – but sex is the very founda-tion of it. Yes, one day sex disappears, but to hate it is not the way to make it disappear. To hate it is the way to repress it, and whatsoever is repressed will come up one way or other.

Please don't try to become a monk or a nun.

Listen to this story...

The nuns ran an orphanage, and one day the Mother Superior summoned to her office three buxom girls who were leaving and said, "Now you are all going out into the big sinful world and I must warn you against certain men. There are men who will buy you drinks, take you to a room, undress you and do unspeakable things to you. Then they give you two or three pounds, and you're sent away, ruined!"

"Excuse me, Reverend Mother," said the boldest one, "did you say these wicked men do this to us and give us three pounds too?"

"Yes, dear child. Why do you ask?"

"Well, the priests only give us apples."

Remember, sex is natural. One can go beyond it, but not through repression. And if you repress it, sooner or later you will find some other way to express it, some perversion is bound to enter; you will have to find some substitute. And substitutes are of no help at all; they don't help, they can't help. Once a natural problem has been turned in such a way that you have forgotten about it, and it has bubbled up somewhere else as a substitute, you can go on fighting with the substitute, but it is not going to help.

I have heard...

A stranger got into a suburban railway carriage in which two men were already sitting. One of them had a peculiar mannerism: he scratched his elbow again and again and again. This elbow-scratching was nearly driving the stranger mad by the time the victim got out at his station.

"Gravely afflicted, your friend," he said to the other man.

"Yes indeed; he has got a terrible dose of piles."

"I'm not talking about piles, I'm talking about all that scratching just now."

"Yes, that is right, piles. You see, he is a very religious man and a civil servant too, and that scratching of the elbow is just a substitute."

But substitutes never help; they only create perversions, obsessions. Be natural if you want to go beyond nature someday. Be natural; that is the first requirement. I am not saying that there is nothing more than nature; there is a higher nature – that is the whole message of Tantra. But be very earthly if you really want to rise high in the sky.

Can't you see these trees? They are rooted in the earth, and the better they are rooted the higher they go. The higher they want to go, the deeper they will have to go into the earth. If a tree wants to touch the stars, the tree will have to go and touch the very hell – that's the only way.

Be rooted in your body if you want to become a soul. Be rooted in your sex if you really want to become a lover. Yes, as more energy is converted into love, less and less will be need of sex; but you will not hate it.

Hate is not a right relationship with anything. Hate simply shows that you are afraid, hate simply shows that there is great fear in you. Hate simply shows that deep down you are still attracted. If you hate sex, then your energy will start moving somewhere else. Energy has to move.

Man, if he suppresses sex, becomes more ambitious. If you really want to be ambitious, you have to suppress your sex; only then can ambition have energy. Otherwise you will not have any energy. A politician has to sup- press sex –only then can he rush towards New Delhi. Sex energy is needed, repressed sex energy is needed, and great anger is needed. Whenever you are suppressing sex, you are angry at the whole world; you can become a great revolutionary. All revolutionaries are bound to be sexually repressed.

When, in a better world, sex will be simple, natural, accepted without any taboo and without any inhibition, politics will disappear and there will be no revolutionaries. There will be no need. When a man represses sex, he becomes too attached to money; he has to put his sexual energy somewhere. Have you not seen people holding their hundred-rupee notes as if they were touching their beloved? Can't you see in their eyes the same lust? But this is ugly. To hold a woman with deep love is beautiful; to hold a hundred-rupee note with lust is just ugly. It is a substitute.

You cannot deceive animals…

A man took his son to the zoo because he wanted to show his son the monkeys. The son was very interested; he had never seen monkeys. They went there – but no monkeys. So he asked the zookeeper, "What has happened? Where are the monkeys?"

And the zookeeper said, "This is their love season, so they have gone into the hut."

The man was very frustrated. For months he had been trying to bring the boy, they had traveled far – and now this was love season! So he asked, "If we throw nuts, won't they come out?"

And the zookeeper said, "Would you?"

But I think man *can* come out if we throw nuts. Man *has* come out. The zoo- keeper is wrong. The monkeys will not come, that is certain. If you give them money they will not come, they will say, "Keep your money, the love season is on! Keep your money." And if you say, "We can make you president of India," they will say, "You keep your presidency, the love season is on!"

But man, if you make him a president, can kill his beloved. If that is the stake, he can do that. These are substitutes. You cannot befool animals.

I have heard...

The spinster had a parrot who kept repeating, "I want to poke! I want to poke!" She found this slightly irritating until a married friend explained what it meant. Then she became very alarmed. "I love that bird, but I'll have to get rid of him or the vicar will never call again," she said.

But her more experienced friend said, "Well, if you really love him, you'll get him what he longs for, which is a female; then he won't keep on about it all the time."

Off went the spinster to the bird shop, but the man said, "No, I can't do anything right now. No lady parrots coming in all season, Miss. But I can sell you a lady owl at a reasonable price."

Anything was better than nothing, so she popped the owl into the parrot's cage and waited with thrilled anticipation.

"I want to poke! I want to poke!" said the parrot.

"Ooo-Ooo!" said the lady owl.

"Not you, you goggle-eyed freak!" said the parrot. "I can't stand women who wear glasses!"

Substitutes won't do. Man is living with substitutes. Sex is natural, money is unnatural. Sex is natural; power, prestige, respectability are unnatural. If you really want to hate something, hate money, hate power, hate prestige. Why hate love?

Sex is one of the most beautiful phenomena in the world. Of course, the lowest – that is true; but the higher moves through the lower: the lotus comes out of the mud. Don't hate the mud, otherwise how will you help the mud to release the lotus? Help the mud, take care of the mud so that the lotus is released. Certainly, the lotus is so far away from the mud that you cannot even conceive of any relationship. If you see a lotus you cannot believe that it comes out of dirty mud – but it does; it is the expression of the dirty mud.

The soul is released from the body, love is released from sex. Sex is a body thing, love is a spiritual thing. Sex is like mud, love is like a lotus. But without the mud the lotus is not possible. So don't hate the mud.

The whole Tantra message is simple; it is very scientific and it is very natural. The message is that if you really want to go beyond the world, go into the world deeply, fully alert, aware.

And the last question:

Osho,
I have many questions, but each time a voice inside me says, "Don't ask – find out for yourself." But now it is too much because I don't know where this voice is coming from.

The question is from Dharma Chetana. Can't you recognize my voice? Enough for today.

breaking the four seals

As higher awareness, they teach what they experience within.
What fetters them they will call liberation.
A glass trinket colored green, to them is a priceless emerald.
Deluded, they know not a gem from what they think it should be.

They take copper to be gold. Bound by discursive thought
they think these thoughts to be ultimate reality.
They long for the pleasures experienced in dreams.
They call the perishable body-mind eternal bliss supreme.

By the symbol EVAM they think self-clearness is achieved.
By the different situations that demand four seals
they call what they have fancied spontaneity.
But this is looking at reflections in a mirror.

As under delusion's power a herd of deer will rush
for the water in a mirage which is not recognized,
so also the deluded quench not their thirst, are bound by chains
and find pleasure in them, saying that all is ultimately real.

Tantra is transcendence. It is neither indulgence nor repression. It is walking on a tightrope, it is one of the greatest of balances. It is not as easy as it appears: it needs very delicate awareness. It is a great harmony.

It is very easy for the mind to indulge. The opposite, to renounce, is also very easy. To move to the extreme is very easy for the mind. To remain in the middle, exactly in the middle, is the most difficult thing for the mind because it is a suicide for the mind. The mind dies in the middle and the no-mind arises. That's why Buddha has called his path *majjhim nikaya* – the middle path. Saraha is a disciple of Buddha, in the same lineage, with the same understanding, with the same awareness.

So this very fundamental thing has to be understood, otherwise you will misunderstand Tantra. What is this razor's edge? What is this being exactly in the middle? To indulge in the world, no awareness is needed. To repress worldly desires, again no awareness is needed. Your so-called worldly people and your so-called otherworldly people are not very different; they may be standing back-to-back, but they are not very different at all; they are of exactly the same type of mind. Somebody is hankering for money, and somebody is so against money that he cannot even look at currency notes – he becomes afraid and a trembling arises in him. These people are not different; for both of them money is of great importance. One is in greed, one is in fear, but the importance of the money is the same: both are obsessed with money.

One is continuously thinking of women, dreaming, fantasizing. Another has become so afraid that he has escaped to the Himalayas just to avoid women. But both are the same: for both, the woman is important, or the man – the other is important. One seeks the other, one avoids the other, but the other remains their focus.

Tantra says the other must not be the focus, neither this way nor that way. This can happen only through great understanding. The lust for a woman has to be understood – neither indulged in nor avoided, but understood. Tantra is very scientific.

The word *science* means understanding, the word *science* means knowing. Tantra says knowing liberates. If you know exactly what greed is, you are free of greed; there is no need to renounce it. The need to renounce arises only because you have not understood what greed is. The need to take a vow against sex is needed only because you have not understood what sex is. And the society does not allow you to understand it.

The society helps you *not* to understand. The society has been avoiding the very subjects of sex and death down through the centuries. These subjects are not to be thought about, not to be contemplated, not to be discussed, not to be written about, not to be researched. They are to be avoided. Through that avoidance a great ignorance exists about them and that ignorance is the root cause. Then there are two types of people who come out of that ignorance: one who indulges madly, and one who becomes very tired and escapes.

Tantra says that one who is indulging madly will never understand because he will simply be repeating a habit, and he will never look into the habit and the root cause of it. He will never look into the causality of it. And the more he indulges the more mechanical he becomes.

Have you not observed it? Your first love had something superb, the second was not so superb, the third was even more ordinary, the fourth just mundane. What happened? Why has the first love been so praised? Why have people always said that love happens only once? Why? – because the first time it was not mechanical, so you were a little alert about it. The next time you were expecting it, you were not so alert. The third time you thought you knew about it, so there was no exploration in it. The fourth time it was just mundane: you have settled into a mechanical habit.

Through indulgence sex becomes a habit. Yes, it gives a little release – just like a sneeze, but not more than that. It is a physical release of energy. When you become too burdened with energy, you have to throw out that energy. Just to gather it again through food, through exercise, through sunlight – again gather it and again throw it out – that's what the person who indulges goes on doing. He creates great energy and then throws it out, for no purpose, for no significance. Having it, he suffers the tension of it. Throwing it out, he suffers the weakness of it. He simply suffers.

Never think that the man who indulges is a happy man – never! He is the most miserable man in the world. How can he be happy? He hopes, he desires happiness, but he never achieves it.

But remember, in saying these things Tantra does not propose that you move to the other extreme. Tantra is not saying that you should escape from this world of indulgence. Escaping will again become a mechanical habit. Sitting in a cave, the woman will not be available, but that doesn't make much difference. If some time a woman does become available, the man who has renounced will be more prone to fall than the man who was indulging in the world. Whatsoever you repress becomes very powerful within you.

I have heard...

There was a fireman who was horridly mean both to his wife and his lodger. One night he brought home a splendid pork pie and ate half of it for his supper. His wife and the lodger had to make do with dry bread and cheese. He carefully put the rest of the pie away and they all went to their beds.

In the middle of the night the firebells rang and off the landlord had to run. The wife, stark naked, entered the lodger's room, shook him awake and said, "He has gone out. Quick! Now is your chance."

"Are you sure it's all right?" inquired the lodger.

"Of course! Hurry up, lose no time!"
So the lodger went downstairs and finished the pork pie.

Now that must have been his repression – the pork pie. He must have been dreaming about it, thinking about it, fantasizing about it. The stark naked woman had no attraction for him, but the pork pie...

Remember, whatsoever you repress will become your attraction, will have a magnetic pull on you. The repressed becomes powerful; it gains power out of all proportion.

Listen to this anecdote...

Deep in a beautiful woodland park stood two lovely bronze statues, a boy and a girl posed in attitudes of love and longing. They had stood thus for three hundred years, their arms held out yearningly to each other yet never touching. One day a magician passed by and with compassion said, "I have enough power to give them life for one hour, so I am going to do this. For one hour they will be able to kiss, to touch, to embrace, to make love to each other."

So the magician waved his magic wand, and immediately the statues leaped off their pedestals and hand in hand ran into the shrubbery.

There was a great commotion: loud thumps, shouts, squawkings and flutterings. With irresistible curiosity the magician tiptoed over and peered into the leaves. The boy was holding down a bird, over which the girl squatted. Suddenly he jumped up and exclaimed, "Now it is your turn to hold him down while I shit upon him!"

Three hundred years of birds shitting upon them. Then who bothers about lovemaking? That was their repression.

You can go and sit in a cave and become a statue, but that which you have repressed will hover around you, will be the only thing that you will ever think about.

Tantra says beware. Beware of indulgence and beware of renunciation. Beware of both; both are traps. And either way you are trapped in the mind.

Then where is the way? Tantra says awareness is the way. Indulgence is mechanical, repression is mechanical, both are mechanical things. The only way out of mechanical things is to become aware, alert. Don't go to the Himalayas; bring a Himalayan silence within you. Don't escape; become more awake. Look into things deeply, with no fear. Don't listen to what your so-called religious people go on teaching. They make you afraid: they don't allow you to look into sex, they don't allow you to look into death – they have exploited your fears tremendously.

The only way to exploit a person is first to make him afraid. Once you are afraid you are ready to be exploited. Fear is the basis, it has to be created first. You have been made afraid: sex is sin, so there is fear. Even while making love to your woman or man you never look directly into it, even while making love you are avoiding. You are making love *and* avoiding. You don't want to see the reality of it – what it is exactly, why it infatuates, why it has a magnetic pull over you? What is it exactly, how does it arise, how does it take possession of you, what does it give and where does it lead? What happens in it and what happens out of it? Where do you arrive again and again making love? Do you arrive anywhere? These things have to be encountered.

Tantra is an encounter with the reality of life. And sex is fundamental; so is death. They are the two most basic, fundamental chakras – the *muladhar* and the *svadhishthan*. Understanding them, the third chakra opens. Understanding the third, the fourth opens, and so on and so forth. When you have understood the six chakras, that very understanding hits the seventh chakra and it blooms into a one-thousand-petaled lotus. That day is of superb glory. That day godliness comes to you, that day you come face-to-face with existence; that day is the meeting day. That day is the day of cosmic orgasm. That day you embrace the divine and the divine embraces you. That day the river disappears into the ocean forever and forever; then there is no coming back.

But understanding has to be gained from each state of your mind. Wherever you are, don't be afraid. That is the Tantra message: wherever you are, don't be afraid. Drop only one thing: fear. Only one thing has to be feared and that is fear. Unafraid, with great courage, look into the reality, whatsoever the reality is. If you are a thief, then look into that. If you are an angry person, look into that. If you are greedy, look into that. Wherever you are, *look* into it. Don't escape: looking into it, go through it. Watching, go through it. If you can walk the path into greed, into sex, into anger, into jealousy, with eyes open – you will be freed of it.

This is the Tantra promise: truth liberates. Knowing frees. Knowing is freedom. Otherwise, whether you repress or you indulge, the end is the same.

It happened...

There was a man who had a most attractive wife. But he began to be suspicious of her. It is natural: the more beautiful wife you have, the more the suspicion.

Mulla Nasruddin has married one of the ugliest of women. I asked, "Why, Mulla? What went wrong? What took possession of you?"

He said, "Nothing, just understanding."

I said, "What type of understanding is this?"

He said, "Now I will never be jealous, and I will never suspect my wife, because I can't imagine any person being in love with her."

This man was very suspicious of his wife. At last he could stand it no longer. Being on nights, he asked the foreman for a pass out, and went home at two in the morning to find his best friend's car outside, just as he had feared. He let himself in, crept up the stairs and rushed into his wife's bedroom. There she lay on top of the bed – stark naked, but smoking a cigarette and reading a book.

He went wild and searched under the bed, in the wardrobe, even in the airing cupboard, but he could not find any man. He went berserk and wrecked the bedroom. Then he started on the living room – threw the TV out of the window, slashed the armchairs, overturned the table and sideboard. Then he turned his attention to the kitchen, where he smashed all the crockery and then threw the fridge out of the window. Then he shot himself.

When he got up to heaven's gates, who should he see also waiting for admission but his late best friend, who said, "What are you doing up here?"

So the wronged husband explained all about how he had lost his temper and all about it, and then added, "But how does it come about that you are up here too?"

"Ah, me? I was in the fridge."

Both end the same way – whether you are in a Himalayan cave or in the world does not make much difference. The life of indulgence and the life of repression both end in the same way because their mechanism is not different. Their appearance is different, but their inner quality is the same.

Awareness brings a different quality to your life. With awareness things start changing, changing tremendously. Not that you change them, no, not at all. A man of awareness does not change anything and a man of unawareness continuously tries to change everything. But the man of unawareness never succeeds in changing anything, and the man of awareness simply finds change happening – tremendous change happening.

It is awareness that brings change, not your effort. Why does it happen through awareness? – because the awareness changes you. And when you are different, the whole world is different. It is not a question of creating a different world, it is only a question of creating a different you. You are your world, so if *you* change, the world changes. If you don't change, you can go on changing the whole world – nothing changes. You will go on creating the same world again and again. You create your world. It is out of you that your world is projected.

Tantra says awareness is the key, the master key which opens all the doors of life. So remember – it is really delicate – if I talk about the foolishness of repression, you start thinking about indulging; if I talk about the foolishness of indulgence, you start thinking about repression. It happens every day – you move to the opposite immediately. And the whole point is not to be tempted by the opposite. To be tempted by the opposite is to be tempted by the devil. That is the devil in the Tantra system, to be tempted by the opposite. There is no other devil; the only devil is that the mind can play a trick upon you: it can propose the opposite.

You are against indulgence? The mind says, "So simple. Now repress. Don't indulge, escape. Drop this whole world. Forget all about it." But how can you forget all about it? Is it so simple to forget all about it? Then why are you escaping far away? Then why are you afraid? If you can forget all about it so simply, then be here and forget all about it. But you can't be here – you know the world will tempt you. And this momentary understanding, this false understanding that you think you have got, will not be of much use. When the temptation comes from desires you will be a victim; you know it. Before it happens you want to escape, you want to escape fast. You want to escape from the opportunity. Why? Why do you want to escape from the opportunity?

In India the so-called saints won't stay with householders. Why? What is the fear? In India the so-called saints won't touch a woman, won't even look. Why? What is the fear? From where does this fear come? Just avoiding the opportunity… But to avoid the opportunity is not a great achievement. And by avoiding the opportunity, if you attain to a certain celibacy that celibacy is just false.

I have heard…

A countryman went into a London pub with a dog. The man ordered a pint, the dog ordered a whisky. "What the hell?" said the barman.

"Yes," said the owner, "he is the most intelligent dog in the West Country. I brought him to see the sights of the town."

"If I give him five pence will he get me a paper?" asked the barman, "because I forgot to get one."

"Of course I will," piped the dog. Then, receiving the money, "Back soon – ta, ta."

The dog did not return, so after an hour the worried owner went in search. He finally found his dog in a back alley nicely on the job with a bitch.

"Well I'm damned!" said the owner. "You have never done that before."

"No," said the dog, "I have never had the money before."

Just avoiding the opportunity is not of much use – it is just a false facade; you can believe in it but you cannot deceive existence. In fact, you cannot even deceive yourself. That which you have left behind in a repressive way will be continuously popping up again and again in your dreams. It will drive you crazy. Your so-called saints are not even able to sleep well – they are afraid of sleep. Why? – because in sleep, the world that they have repressed asserts itself in dreams. The unconscious starts relating; the unconscious says, "What are you doing here? You are a fool." The unconscious spreads its net again.

While you are awake you can repress, but how can you repress when you are asleep? You lose all control. The conscious represses, but the conscious goes to sleep. That's why in all the old traditions saints have always been afraid of sleep. They cut down their sleep from eight hours to seven, from seven to six, from six to five – four, three, two. And foolish people think it a great achievement. They think, "This saint is a great saint, he sleeps only two hours." In fact he is simply showing one thing – that he is afraid of his unconscious. He does not allow the unconscious time to relate.

When you sleep for only two hours, the unconscious cannot relate because those two hours are needed for the body's rest. You dream better dreams, good dreams, beautiful dreams after your body's sleep is complete – that's why you dream better in the morning, in the early morning. First the body need has to be finished, the body needs rest. Once the body has rested, then the mind needs rest; that is a secondary thing.

One thing is that when the mind needs rest, then the unconscious, in a restful mood, releases its desires and dreams arise. The second thing is that if you only rest for two hours in the night, there may be dreams but you will not be able to remember them. That's why you remember only the late dreams that you dream early in the morning. You forget the other dreams of the whole night because you are so deeply asleep that you cannot remember. So the saint thinks he has not dreamed about sex, he has not dreamed about money, he has not dreamed about power, prestige, respectability. If he sleeps for two hours, the sleep is so deep, it is such a necessity for the body, that it is almost like a coma – so he cannot remember. You remember dreams only when you are half awake and half asleep. Then the dream can be remembered because it is close to the conscious; half asleep, half awake, something of the dream filters into your conscious, moves into the conscious. In the morning you can remember a little bit of it. That's why you will be surprised that if you go and ask a laborer who works hard the whole day, "Do you dream?" he will say, "No."

People say primitive people don't dream. It is not true that they don't dream – they can't remember, that's all. All dream, but they can't remember. Working hard the whole day chopping wood or digging a ditch or breaking stones is such hard work, for eight hours, that when you fall asleep you are almost in a coma. Dreams come but you cannot remember them, you cannot recapture them.

Your so-called saints have always been afraid of sleep...

Once a young man was brought to me. He was going crazy. He was a follower of Swami Sivananda of Rishikesh. I asked him, "What is the matter with you?"

He said, "Nothing is the matter. I am a spiritual man. People think I am going crazy."

I inquired of his parents – they were very worried; I went into the details. The details were this: he had gone to Swami Sivananda and Sivananda had said, "You sleep too much. This is not good for spiritual health, you should sleep less." So he cut his sleep to three hours – from eight hours to three.

Now he started feeling sleepy the whole day, naturally. So Sivananda said, "You are *tamasic*: you have very low, bad energy in you. Change your food. You must be eating food which makes you heavy and sleepy." So he started living just on milk. Now he started becoming weak. First sleep was cut, then food was cut; now he was in such a state that at any time he could topple over.

Without food it becomes more difficult for you to go into deep sleep, even for three hours; food is a must for a good sleep. When the stomach has nothing to digest, the whole energy moves into the head. That's why on a fasting day you cannot sleep well. The energy is not in the stomach; it is released into the head. When the energy is needed in the stomach, the head cannot get it because the head is secondary, the stomach is primary.

There is a certain hierarchy in the body: first things first. The stomach is basic. The stomach can exist without the head, but the head cannot exist without the stomach. So the stomach is basic, more fundamental; when the stomach needs energy it pulls energy from everywhere.

Now he could not even sleep for three hours. His eyes became dull, dead; his body lost all luster, aliveness, and there was a subtle trembling. Holding his hand, I could feel his whole body trembling; the body had not rested for months. And now he thought that he was becoming spiritual.

This type of nonsense has continued long enough to become respectable. When a thing continues for long enough it becomes respectable – just because it has been there for so long.

So listen to your body, your bodily needs. Listen to your mind, listen to your mind's needs. Don't avoid. Go into those needs, explore those needs with loving care. Befriend your body, befriend your mind, if you want to get beyond them one day. Befriending is very essential. That is the Tantra vision of life: befriend life energies. Don't become antagonistic.

Now the sutras. The sutras are of great significance. Says Saraha to the king:

> As higher awareness, they teach what they experience within.
> What fetters them they will call liberation.
> A glass trinket colored green to them is a priceless emerald.
> Deluded, they know not a gem from what they think it should be.

He is talking about the so-called mahatmas, the so-called yogis, in the same way that I talk again and again about the so-called saints. Saraha is saying: As higher awareness, they teach what they experience within.

Now this is a great statement. It has to be decoded. First: the ultimate experience of reality is not an experience at all, because when you experience something there is always duality – the experiencer and the experienced. So there cannot be any ultimate experience in the sense that you experience yourself – no. How can you experience yourself? Then you will be divided in two, then the subject-object duality will come in.

Tantra says that whatsoever you know, know that you are not that. This is a great statement, a very penetrating insight. If you see something, know well that you are not that thing because you are the seer. You can never be the seen. You cannot be reduced to an object. You are subjectivity, pure subjectivity, irreducible subjectivity; there is no way to turn yourself into an object, into a thing. You cannot put yourself in front of yourself, or can you? You cannot put yourself in front of yourself because whatsoever you put there will not be you. You will always be the one in front of whom the thing is put.

Saraha says truth is not an experience, cannot be. Truth is an experiencing, not an experience. It is a knowing, not knowledge. The difference is great. You experience a thing when it is separate from you. You cannot experience yourself in the same way. So Tantra has coined a different word: experiencing. In Sanskrit we have two words: anubhav, and anubhuti. Anubhav means experience, anubhuti means experiencing. There is nothing to experience. There is nothing in front of you, there is just emptiness – but you are there, fully there, with nothing to obstruct. There is no object: it is pure subjectivity – only the container, no content. The movie has stopped; only the screen, the pure white screen... But there is nobody to look at this white screen. You are the white screen. Hence a new word: anubhuti, experiencing.

In English there is no separate word, so I have to use experiencing to show the difference: experience becomes an object, experiencing is a process, not an object. Knowledge is an object; knowing is a process. Love is an object; loving is a process.

Tantra says that your innermost core consists of processes, not of things. Knowing is there, no knowledge. Loving is there, no love. Nouns exist not, only verbs. This is a profound insight into reality. Only verbs. When you say, "This is a tree," you are stating a very wrong thing: this is a tree-ing, not a tree because it is growing, it is not a static thing. When you say, "This is a river," just look at what you are saying – nonsense. It is a river-ing, it is moving, it is dynamic. Not for a single moment is it the same, so why do you call it "river"? Even a rock is not a rock; it is also a process.

Existence consists not of things but of events. Don't say to a woman, "I love you." Just say, "I am in that state of loving." Love is not a thing; you can only be in a state of loving, you cannot love.

There are Buddhist languages in which everything exists as a process. When for the first time the Bible was being translated in certain Buddhist countries – Burma, Thailand – the Christian missionaries were at a loss: they could not find a word for God. It is okay if you say a river is river-ing and a tree is tree-ing, and a man is man-ing and a woman is woman-ing – it is okay. But about God – he is! There is no becoming in God. But in Burmese all words are really verbs. Each verb shows becoming. But to call God "becoming," a process, was very hard for Christians, very difficult. God is always the same, eternally the same. Nothing ever happens to God.

Buddhists say if nothing ever happens to God, then he is dead. Then how can he be alive? Life is where things happen, life is happening. And about the ultimate experience... It is okay to say this about mundane reality. You can say, "This is a chair," and there is no need to bother much about it; it is simple. Now to say about everything, "This is a chair-ing and this is a tree-ing," will create difficulty in expression. But about the ultimate reality one should be very alert. At least there, one should be alert.

Saraha says: *As higher awareness, they teach what they experience...* Now if you have read Pundit Gopi Krishna's books, he says kundalini is the ultimate experience. It cannot be. Saraha would not agree, he would laugh at Pundit Gopi Krishna.

If you experience a certain energy rising in your spine, you are the one who is seeing it. The spine is separate, so too is that kundalini rising in it separate. How can you be it? I can see my hand: just by seeing my hand I have become separate from it. I cannot be the hand. I am using it, but I am separate from it. Maybe I am inside the hand, but I cannot be the hand.

Kundalini is not a spiritual experience. A spiritual experience simply means the moment when there is nothing to be experienced. All experiences dissolved, you sit alone in your purity. You cannot call it an experience.

So Saraha says that these so-called yogis and saints go on saying that they have attained to higher consciousness – but what have they attained? Somebody's kundalini has risen, somebody has seen a blue light inside, and things like that. Somebody has seen visions: somebody has seen Krishna and somebody has seen Mohammed and somebody has seen Mahavira and somebody has seen Mother Kali – but these are all imagination.

All experience is imagination.

The word *imagination* is beautiful – it comes out of *image*. All experience is nothing but images floating in your consciousness. When nothing floats in your consciousness – remember, not even nothing floats in your consciousness – when your consciousness is simply there without content, that contentless purity is what Tantra calls real experience. You cannot call it an experience – by its very nature, it is not. When you witness the witness, how can you call it witnessing? When you know the knower, how can you call it knowledge?

So the first thing he says is: *As higher awareness, they teach what they experience within.*

And the second thing to be remembered: the distinction between within and without is again false. It is good on a certain plane – you are living in the without, so you have to be told to go within. But without and within are two aspects of the same coin. One day you have to be told to drop both; as you have dropped the without, now drop the within too. Be transcendental – neither without nor within.

The within is as much without as the without: that is the Tantra insight. What is within? I am looking at you, you are without. Then I close my eyes and I see my kundalini – is it within? Whatsoever I can see is without, is "out" of me, it cannot be "in" me. Then I see a blue light; that is without. Of course I am seeing it with closed eyes; it is closer to me, but still without. I am seeing you with open eyes, you are without. In the night I see a dream, and you come in my dream – then are you within? You are also without, although my eyes are closed. But I am seeing you just as I am seeing you right now. Whatsoever is seen is without. The seer is neither without nor within.

So Saraha says that these people first go on talking about their experiences without, and then they start talking about their experiences within.

Just the other day we discussed this: you make love to a woman – this woman is without. Now, if the energy, the fire of your sexuality, rises high in you, comes to your throat, to the *vishuddha,* to the throat chakra, and there you start masturbating it with your tongue turned inward, do you call it within? It is without. It is as much without as it was while you were making love to a woman.

Tantra is such a great insight, such a profound insight, that it says one has to drop the without, and one has to drop the within too. One has to be in such a state that one can say, "I am neither out nor in, neither an extrovert nor an introvert, neither a man nor a woman, neither a body nor a mind." One has to come to a point where one can say I am neither in samsara, nor nirvana. This is the point, the door from all dualities, the exact middle of all dualities.

What fetters them they will call liberation. Now this will be a new fetter, maybe a little more beautiful than the outer fetters – maybe the outer fetters are made of iron and this fetter is made of gold – but a fetter is a fetter. Whether made of iron or of gold does not make any difference: you are fettered.

Now this new fetter will become your bondage. Kundalini rising, visions, spiritual visions, cosmic visions – now these will become your fetters. Now you will hanker for them, now you will desire them. First you desired money, now you will desire these spiritual experiences. First you desired power, now you will desire *siddhis,* spiritual powers – but the desire remains there, and the desire is the fetter. Only in non-desire is there liberation.

A glass trinket colored green to them is a priceless emerald. Deluded, they know not a gem from what they think it should be. If you don't know, if you are not alert and aware, you can be deceived. A *glass trinket colored green...* and you may think this is an emerald. Yes, the color is the same, the shape may be the same, even the weight may be the same, but still the value is different – and the value is the thing.

Yes, people have powers in the outside world. A president, a premier has some power, and then a yogi, a mahatma has some other powers – of the inner world, but nothing to be compared with the real emerald. The outer was a glass thing and this inner is also a glass trinket: colored, cut in the same shape, of the same weight as if it were a spiritual thing. It is not.

Spirituality is the pure sky where no cloud exists. So a really spiritual man cannot claim any spiritual experiences because all spiritual experiences are glass trinkets colored green; they are not emeralds.

That's why Buddha remained silent. When people would ask him, "Have you realized?" he would keep quiet. When people would say, "Do you know God?" he would not say anything, he would smile or laugh it away. Why? Why did he avoid it? – foolish people will think he avoided because he had not known, he avoided because he had not experienced. He avoided *because* he had experienced. He avoided because he knew that to talk about it would not be good; that would be a sacrilege.

Truth cannot be talked about. We can talk about the way but we cannot talk about the truth. We can talk about how to attain to it, but we cannot say what it is when we attain it. Saraha is saying all those who claim experiences are bogus: *Deluded, they know not a gem from what they think it should be.*

They take copper to be gold. Bound by discursive thought
they think these thoughts to be ultimate reality.
They long for the pleasures experienced in dreams.
They call the perishable body-mind eternal bliss supreme.

They take copper to be gold. The baser, the objective, they think is the subjective. The knower is not known yet. They have known something else and they have misunderstood; they think they have known the knower. They may have known the kundalini, they may have known some spiritual visions – great visions of poetry, great visions of splendor and grandeur – great visions, psychedelic, but: *They take copper to be gold. Bound by discursive thought, they think these thoughts to be ultimate reality.*

And these so-called saints and mahatmas are bound by logic: *Bound by discursive thought...* They go on arguing; they even go on trying to prove that God exists.

In Christianity, two thousand years have been wasted in proving that God exists. How can you prove that God exists? And if it can be proved then it can be disproved too. Logic is a double-edged sword, logic is a whore. If it can prove that God is, it can prove that God is not. And in fact the beauty of it is this: the same argument can prove that God is, and the same argument can prove that God is not.

Now the greatest argument that these so-called saints have been giving to the world is that the world needs a creator – because how can the world exist without a creator? Now it looks appealing, to childish minds at least; to imma-ture minds it looks appealing. Yes, such a vast existence – how can it be there without a creator? Somebody must be there who created it. And then just a small pinprick and the logic is gone and the balloon explodes. Somebody asks, "Then who created the creator?" It is the same logic. If you say the world needs a creator, then again your creator will need a creator, and so on and so forth, ad nauseam. You can go on and you can say number one created the world, and number two created number one, and number three created number two – you can go on and on. But the ultimate question will remain the same: Who created the first, the original?

If you accept that the original was not created, then what is all this fuss about? Then why not say that the world is uncreated? If God can be uncreated, then what is wrong in simply saying that the world is here without anybody having created it? That would seem more reasonable, rather than going into this foolish logic which leads nowhere.

Look at the arguments that have been given for God: they are all foolish and stupid. That's why you cannot convince a single atheist about your God.

Those who are already convinced – yes, they are convinced; that is not the point. You cannot convince a single skeptical mind – your arguments will not help. In fact, your own arguments will create difficulties for you.

What is Saraha saying? Saraha is saying that a man who has known his inner reality knows that there is no proof other than realizing it. He does not believe in discursive thoughts. He does not give any logic for it – it is illogical, it is beyond reason. It is so. You can experience it or you can leave it, but there is no way to prove it or disprove it. Theism and atheism are both meaningless. Religion has nothing to do with them; religion is an experiencing of that which is. Call it by whatsoever name you choose to call it: call it God, call it nirvana, call it *XYZ*, anything, that doesn't matter – but experience it. Tantra believes in experience; Tantra is not cerebral, it is existential.

They take copper to be gold. And this God proved by arguments they think is their God. Then they make images of the God, and then they worship; they are worshipping their own syllogism. What is in your churches and temples and mosques? – nothing but syllogism. The world needs a creator, so you believe in a creator. This is a belief, and all beliefs are false. Belief is a homemade thing. Yes, it consoles, it gives you a certain security, comfort. It is convenient to believe that somebody is looking after the world, otherwise one becomes afraid: nobody looking after it; at any moment anything could go wrong. It gives you confidence.

It is almost like when you are in an airplane and you know that the pilot is there and he is looking after things. And suddenly you go and look into the cockpit and there is nobody! Now what will happen? Just a moment before you were sipping tea and you were talking, and you were interested in the woman who was sitting by your side and you were trying to touch her body, and everything... Now everything is gone – the pilot is not there! Up to this moment everything was convenient. Now you will become very nervous, you will start trembling; you will lose all interest in men and women, and food and drink, and everything is finished. Your breathing will be disturbed, your blood pressure will be disturbed, your heart will start fluttering and you will start per-spiring in an air-conditioned plane.

It is convenient to believe that in the cockpit there is a pilot who knows and everything is going well – God takes care. You can remain the way you are. He is "the Father," he knows everybody. Not even a single leaf falls without his will, so everything is good. This is a convenience. Mind is very cunning. This God is part of the cunning mind.

Saraha says that belief is not truth, and truth is never a belief. Truth is an experiencing.

...they think these thoughts to be ultimate reality. They long for the pleasures

experienced in dreams. These *are* pleasures experienced in dreams. *They call the perishable body-mind eternal bliss supreme.* Sometimes you are deluded by the body, and if you somehow manage to go beyond the body, you are deluded by the mind, which is more of a deluder. The first three chakras belong to the body. The next three chakras belong to the mind. And the seventh chakra is beyond both.

Ordinarily the people who indulge remain in the first three, the lower chakras – they hang there. Those first three charkas, the *muladhar, svadhishthan* and *manipura*, are earthbound. They are earthly chakras, they are attracted by gravitation, they are pulled downward. The next three chakras, the *anahata, vishuddha* and *agya*, are skybound: gravitation does not affect them. They are under another law called levitation, they are pulled upward. These three consist of the mind. The body is pulled downward, mind is pulled upward. But you are neither; you are the seventh, which is neither body nor mind.

So the people who indulge live in the first three chakras, and the people who repress the first three chakras start living in the second three chakras, but they create a dream world. It is almost like this: one day you fast, and in the night you dream that you have been invited by the queen of England and a great feast is being given in your honor, and you are eating all sorts of things – all the things that you always wanted to eat but the doctor wouldn't allow. The fast creates this dream, but it cannot nourish you. In the morning you will be as hungry as before – more so. But this dream helps a little bit. How does it help? It helps you to continue sleeping. Otherwise your hunger would wake you again and again, you would keep waking up. This dream is a trick of the mind. The mind says, "There is no need to wake up; there is no need to go in the dark and search in the fridge. You can just sleep well. Look, the queen has invited you! There is so much food on the table, why don't you eat?" – and you start eating. This is a trick of the mind; it helps you to keep on sleeping.

It happens many times: your bladder is full and you start dreaming that you are in the bathroom. This helps – not that it unburdens the bladder but it keeps you deluded and the sleep can continue. Your beliefs, your imagination, your dreams, your temples, your churches, your *gurudwaras* help you to remain asleep. They are tranquilizers.

The perishable body-mind they call bliss supreme. Sometimes they think the bliss supreme is there in the body, and then they start thinking in the imagination of the mind that kundalini is rising – there is light, and a thousand and one visions and experiences. Beware of these visions.

A really spiritually oriented person is not interested in any content of consciousness. He is interested in consciousness itself.

By the symbol EVAM they think self-clearness is achieved.
By the different situations that demand four seals
they call what they have fancied spontaneity.
But this is looking at reflections in a mirror.

Through mantras, through sounds, one can achieve a certain mental tranquility. Yes, through Transcendental Meditation one can achieve a certain delusion. If you repeat a certain sound continuously it soothes you; it gives you a certain rhythm in the mind, it is rhythmic. If you repeat, "Om, om, om," or "Evam, Evam, Evam," or any mantra – "Coca-Cola" will do. If you repeat, "Coca-Cola, Coca-Cola, Coca-Cola," very lovingly and respectfully, it will help. You can also keep a Coca-Cola bottle in front of you and put some flowers and fruit before it; it will help. You have to create an atmosphere: you can burn some incense before the Coca-Cola bottle and repeat the mantra. If you do it long enough, there is every possibility that you will feel good. You have auto-hypnotized yourself, you have suggested something to yourself. You have suggested that tranquility is coming, silence is coming, happiness is coming. It is nothing but autosuggestion, very indirect autosuggestion.

Emile Coué proposes direct suggestions. Think: "I am getting better, I am getting healthy, I am getting happier" – direct suggestions. Emile Coué is a Western man – more honest, true and direct. Maharishi Mahesh Yogi suggests that you repeat "Om, om," "Ram, Ram" – this is indirect, more of the Eastern mind; not direct, but indirect. But all the suggestions are given: if you repeat this mantra twice every day for twenty minutes in the morning and twenty minutes in the evening you will become healthier, you will become more silent, you will become more blissful, this and that. All things are promised – even your salary will increase. You will be getting promotions and the whole world will cooperate with you in your ambitions.

This is given indirectly. And then you are not interested in the mantra, you are interested in these things – health, wealth, power, prestige, silence, joy; you are interested in these things. You repeat the mantra because of this interest. But each time you repeat "Om," you know that these things are going to happen. And these mantras work only to the extent that you believe in them. If you don't believe, they won't work. If you don't believe, Mahesh Yogi will say, "How can they work? You have to believe them, then they work."

Truth works without your belief, truth needs no belief on your part. Only untruth works through belief. Untruth needs belief on your part because only if you believe can you create a mind attitude, an autosuggestion, a climate in which it works.

By the symbol EVAM they think self-awareness is achieved. And Saraha is saying that this is nonsense. By repeating a certain sound no clarity is attained; you only become cloudier. It is not that you become more intelligent and aware, you become sleepier. Of course you will have better sleep – that is the good part of it. And it is not accidental that Mahesh Yogi's TM has become influential in America because America is a country which is suffering tremendously from insomnia. People cannot sleep, they need some trick to sleep; TM can help with getting a good sleep. And I am not against TM if you are just using it for good sleep – I am all for good sleep. But remember, it cannot lead you to any other realm, it cannot become your spiritual journey; it is a solace.

By the different situations that demand four seals... These four seals have to be understood. Tantra talks about four seals, four mudras. To attain to the ultimate, a person passes through four doors. He has to open four locks. Those four locks are called four seals, the four mudras. They are very important.

The first mudra is called the karma mudra. It is the outermost door, the very periphery of your being. It is the outermost, just like action; that's why it is called the karma mudra. *Karma* means action. Action is the outermost core of your being, it is your periphery; what you do is your periphery. You love somebody, you hate somebody, you kill somebody, you protect somebody – what you do is your periphery. Action is the outermost part of your being.

The first seal is opened through becoming total in your action – *total* in your action. Whatsoever you do, do totally, and there will arise great joy – not by repeating some mantra but by doing it totally. If you are angry, be totally angry; you will learn much out of total anger. If you are totally angry and fully aware of your anger, anger will disappear one day. There will be no point in being angry anymore: you have understood it, it can be dropped now.

Anything that is understood can be dropped easily. Only non-understood things go on hanging around you. So be total, whatsoever it is. Try to be total and alert: this is the first lock to be opened.

Remember always that Tantra is very scientific. It does not say to repeat a mantra. It says to become aware in your action.

The second seal is called the *gyana* mudra: a little deeper than the first, a little more inner than the first – like knowledge. Action is the outermost thing; knowledge is a little deeper. You can watch what I am doing, you cannot watch what I am knowing. Knowing is inner. Actions can be watched, knowings cannot be watched, they are inner. The second seal is that of knowing – the *gyana* mudra.

Now start knowing what you really know and stop believing things which you really don't know. Somebody asks you, "Is there a God?" and you say, "Yes, God is." Remember, do you really know? If you don't know, please don't say that you do. Say, "I don't know." If you are honest and you only say what you know, and you only believe what you know, the second lock will be broken. If you go on knowing things, believing things which you don't really know, the second lock will never be broken. False knowledge is the enemy of true knowledge. And all beliefs are false knowledge; you simply believe them. Your so-called saints go on telling you, "First believe, then you will know."

Tantra says to first *know,* then belief is there. But that is a totally different kind of belief; it is trust. You *believe* in God, you *know* the sun. The sun rises, you need not believe in it; it is simply there, you know it. God, you believe in. God is bogus; *your* God is bogus.

There is another God – the God which comes through knowing. But the first thing to be sorted out is to drop all that you don't know but believe that you know. You have always believed and you have always carried the load. Drop that load. Out of a hundred things you will be unburdened of almost ninety-eight things – unburdened. Only a few things will remain that you really know. You will feel a great freedom; your head will not be so heavy. And with that freedom and weightlessness you enter the second mudra. The second lock is broken.

The third mudra is called the *samaya* mudra. *Samaya* means time. The first, outermost layer is action, the second layer is knowing, the third layer is time. Knowledge has disappeared, you are only in the now; only the purest of time has remained. Watch, meditate over it. In the "now moment," there is no knowledge. Knowledge is always about the past. In the now moment there is no knowledge, it is completely free from knowledge. Just this moment, looking at me, what do you know? Nothing is known. If you start thinking that you know this and that, that will come from the past. That will not come from this moment, not from now. Knowledge is from the past, or a projection into the future. The now is pure of knowledge.

So the third is the *samaya* mudra – to be in this moment. Why does Saraha call it *samaya,* time? Ordinarily you think that past, present and future, are three divisions of time. That is not the understanding of Tantra. Tantra says only the present is time. The past is memory, the future is imagination. Only the present is time. The past is not, it has already gone. The future is not; it has not come yet. Only the present is.

To be in the present is to be really in time. Otherwise you are either in memory or you are in dreams, which are both false, delusions. So the third seal is broken by being in the now. First, be total in your action: the first seal is broken. Second, be honest in your knowing: the second seal is broken. Now, be just herenow: the third seal is broken.

And the fourth seal is called the *mahamudra,* the great gesture – innermost, like space. Now, purest space remains. Action, knowing, time, space

– these are the four seals. Space is your innermost core, the hub of the wheel, or the center of the cyclone. In your innermost emptiness is space, sky. These are the three layers: the first layer is of time, then the second is of knowing, then the third is of action. These are the four seals to be broken. It is not going to happen by reciting a mantra. Don't befool yourself. Great work is needed to go into your reality.

By the symbol EVAM they think self-clearness is achieved. By the different situations that demand four seals... Clearness is not achieved without your breaking these four seals. Clarity is attained only when you have entered your pure space.

...they call what they have fancied spontaneity. But this is looking at reflections in a mirror. Yes, you can create a mirror by chanting a mantra, and in the mirror you can see things. It is crystal gazing, it is not of much value. It is just looking into the lake and thinking that the moon is there. The moon is not there, it only reflects there. It is looking into the mirror and thinking that *you* are there; you are not there. Don't be childish – small children do that. Have you watched a small child brought for the first time before a mirror? He tries to enter into the mirror, he grabs the mirror and tries to find a way to go into it and meet the child who is there. When he finds it difficult, he tries to go through the back of the mirror: "Maybe there is a room and the child is sitting there?" This is what we go on doing.

Mind is a mirror. Yes, by repeating a TM mantra you can make this mirror very, very clear. But looking into the mirror you will not attain. In fact, the mirror has to be completely dropped, thrown away. You have to move inward. And this is very practical – first action, then knowing, then time, then space.

> *As under delusion's power a herd of deer will rush*
> *for the water in a mirage which is not recognized,*
> *so also the deluded quench not their thirst, are bound by chains*
> *and find pleasure in them, saying that all is ultimately real.*

This is the last sutra. Saraha says that looking into the mirror you are looking into a mirage. You are dreaming. You are helping an illusion to be created around yourself, you are cooperating in a dream. *As under delusion's power a herd of deer will rush for the water in a mirage which is not recognized, so also the deluded quench not their thirst, are bound by chains...* We are deluded by the reflections that are happening in our minds.

I have heard a beautiful story...

A man wishing to walk in the Welsh mountains made his headquarters at a pub in a country town. He found his evenings dull, for nothing happened, and pub conversation was mostly about sheep, mostly about Wales.

He asked the landlord how to set about finding the ladies of the town, and that worthy was shocked.

"Look man, this is Wales. We cannot have prostitutes – the chapel would never allow it."

The visitor looked sad and the landlord continued, "Of course we have human nature the same as anywhere, but the thing you mention is kept out of sight." He went on to explain that up the mountain, at the back, were caves, well-furnished and with all mod cons. What the stranger must do was go up to the mountain at dusk and shout, "Yoo-hoo!" and if the lady "Yoo-hooed" back, terms could be negotiated. If she was already engaged, there would be no answer.

That evening the Englishman yoo-hooed his way from cave to cave, but with no luck at all; he finally decided to go back and get drunk. But at the foot of the mountain he found a fresh cave. "Yoo-hoo!" he shouted. "Yoo-hoo! Yoo-hoo!" came back so clearly.

He rushed into the cave – and was killed by a train.

That is what a mirage is: you imagine, you fantasize, then you start seeing. And then any excuse will do. When a man is thirsty in a desert, lost, and the thirst burns like a flame inside and he thinks only of water – only of water and nothing else – there is every possibility that he will start seeing water somewhere. He will project it; his desire is so much that he will project it. He will start seeing illusory lakes, he will think a cool breeze has come. He will think he has seen a few birds flying, he will even think that he can see a few green trees – not only green trees, but their reflections in the water. He will rush.

That's how we have been rushing for millions of lives, yoo-hooing from one cave to another. And you don't see that each time you go you don't find any water, the thirst is not quenched. But you don't learn anything.

The greatest problem with man is that he does not learn. You loved a woman or a man, you were thinking that your thirst would be quenched – it is not quenched. But you don't learn anything; you start moving towards another cave. You have no money and you thought that if ten thousand rupees were there, everything would be okay. And then those ten thousand rupees also happen, but you have not learned anything. By that time you start thinking, "Unless there is one lakh of rupees, how can I be happy?" One lakh also happens, but you have not learned anything yet; now you think that unless ten lakhs are there, how can you be happy? And so on and so forth you go, from one cave to another, from one birth to another, from one death to another.

Man seems to be almost incapable of learning. Only those who learn know.

Start learning. Be a little more alert; let each experience give you knowing. You have asked so many times for so many things and nothing happened. Now stop asking. You desired so many things and each desire led you into frustration. Still you go on desiring? You did the same thing yesterday and the day before yesterday, and you will be doing the same thing today and tomorrow too – and nothing comes out of it. And you go on moving and doing the same thing again and again.

To learn is to become religious. The word *disciple* is beautiful; it means one who is capable of learning. It comes from a root which means "learning"; one who is capable of learning is a disciple.

Become disciples – disciples of your own life. Life is really your master. And if you cannot learn from life, where else can you learn? If even the great master – life – is defeated by you and cannot teach you anything, then who will be able to teach you anything?

This universe is a university. Each moment is a lesson, each frustration is a lesson. Each time you fail, learn something! By and by, the ray of knowing enters. Inch by inch, one becomes alert; inch by inch, one becomes capable of not repeating the old mistakes. The moment you start learning you are coming closer to God.

And don't trust small knowings, don't think that you have arrived. A small learning sometimes satisfies people so much that they stop. Then they stop moving. It is a great journey, it is an endless journey. The more you learn, the more you will be able to learn. The more you learn, the more you will become aware that much more is yet to be learned. The more you know, the more intense becomes the mystery. The more you know, the less you feel that you know. With knowing, new doors open. With knowing, new mysteries are revealed.

So don't be satisfied with a little knowledge. Unless God reveals himself to you, never be content. Let there be great spiritual discontent.

Only those who are fortunate enough to have this divine discontent in them – that nothing less than God will satisfy them – only they arrive. Nobody else.

Enough for today.

trust cannot be betrayed

The first question:

Osho,
Why am I always interested in married women?

There is nothing special about it – it is a very common disease which exists in almost epidemic proportions. But there are reasons for it. Millions of people, both men and women, are more interested in married persons. First, the person being unmarried shows that nobody has yet desired him or her; the married person shows that somebody has desired him. And you are so imitative that you cannot even love on your own. You are such a slave that when somebody else loves somebody, only then can you follow. But if the person is alone and nobody is in love with them, then you are suspicious. Maybe the person is not of worth, otherwise why should he or she wait for you? The married person has great attraction for the imitator.

Secondly, people love less; people, in fact, don't know what love is – they compete more. The married man... And you become interested; or the married woman... And you become interested because now there is a possibility to compete. The triangular fight is possible. The woman is not easily available, there is going to be struggle.

In fact, you are not interested in the woman, you are interested in the struggle. Now the woman is almost a commodity; you can fight for her and you can prove your mettle. You can displace the husband and you will feel very good – an ego trip; it is not a love trip. But remember, once you succeed in disposing of the husband you will not be interested in the woman anymore. You were interested in the married woman; how can you be interested in an *unmarried* woman now? – again you will start looking for some fight somewhere. You will always make it a triangle. This is not love.

In the name of love there is jealousy, there is competition, there is aggression, there is violence. You want to prove yourself. You want to prove yourself against another man: "Look, I have taken away your woman." Once you have taken away the woman, you will not be interested in her at all because she was not the desired thing; the desired thing was a sort of victory.

I have heard...

A certain prominent businessman lost his wife and the funeral became a public occasion. All the dignitaries of the town attended and almost all were known to the bereaved. There was, however, a stranger, and he seemed more upset than anyone. Before the funeral was over he broke down completely.

The bereaved husband asked, "Who was this weeping stranger?"

"Ah!" whispered someone, "Didn't you know? He was your late wife's lover."

The bereaved moved across to the sobbing man, patted him on the back and said, "Cheer up, old boy, cheer up. I shall probably marry again."

Beware. It is a disease to fall in love with a married woman or a married man. Look for reasons. It is not love; there is something else working behind your mind, in your unconscious.

Another thing: the married woman is not easily available. That too creates desire. Easy availability kills desire. The more unapproachable, the more inaccessible the woman is, the more the desire; you can dream about her. And in fact there is not much possibility that it will ever become an actuality. There is every opportunity to be romantic about a married woman; you can play with your fantasy. It is not easy to make her available to you. You are not interested in unmarried women because they will not leave much chance for romance. If you are interested, they are ready, there is no space left. There is not that long, long waiting.

Many people are interested not in love but in waiting; they say that waiting is far more beautiful than love. In a way it is so because while you are waiting you are simply projecting, you are dreaming. Of course, your dream is your dream and you can make it as beautiful as you want. The real woman is going to shatter all your dreams. People are afraid of the real woman. And a married woman becomes more unreal than real. The same is the case with a married man; he is far away. There is not much possibility that he will really enter into a love relationship with you.

I have heard...

A young man went to a very wise old man, and the young man said, "I am lovesick, sir. Can you help me?"

The wise man thought and he said, "There is only one cure for love, and that is marriage. And if marriage cannot cure it, nothing can cure it. If you get married you will be cured; never again will you think about love!"

Yes, marriage cures it so certainly, so absolutely, that if marriage cannot cure your love, then nothing can cure it – then you are incurable. It is good to fall in love with a married woman because then there is no possibility of a cure: you remain lovesick.

There are people who enjoy their lovesickness tremendously: weeping, crying, waiting, fantasizing, poeticizing, reading, writing poetry, painting, making music – all substitutes. The real woman is dangerous. The real woman only looks musical from far away. Come close and she is a *real* woman. She is not a fairy, not a fiction; her reality will have to be reckoned with. And when a woman comes close to you, not only is she real but she brings you down from your ivory towers to the earth.

In all the cultures of the world, woman is represented as the earth and man as the sky. The woman is very earthbound; she gravitates towards the earth. She is more earthly than man, more practical, more pragmatic than man. That's why you don't find great women poets, you don't find great women painters or great women composers, no. Women don't fly in the sky so much. They grip the earth, they penetrate the earth with their roots and stand there like strong trees. Man is more like a bird. When a man becomes married the woman brings him also to the earth, to the practical world. Poets don't like to be married. They want to remain always in love, they don't want to cure that sickness.

People fall in love with married women – this is a halfway house, it is a trick. They can believe that they are in love and they can avoid it also. Love creates great fear because love is a challenge, a great challenge. You will have to grow. You cannot remain juvenile and immature; you will have to grapple with the realities of life. Your so-called great poets are almost always very childish, immature people, still living in the fairyland of childhood. They don't know what reality is, they don't allow the reality to penetrate into their dreams.

A woman is a sure destroyer of fictions. She is not fictitious, she is a fact, a truth. So if you want to believe that you are in love and you still want to avoid love, it is good, safe, to fall in love with a married woman or a married man. This is very tricky; it is a deception, a self-deception. Women are also afraid to fall in love with a free man because with the free man or free woman there is involvement – a twenty-four-hour involvement.

With a married woman the involvement is not that big. You can have a few stolen kisses, you can meet her somewhere in a dark corner, always afraid that the husband may come, somebody may see. It is always halfhearted, it is always in a hurry, and you don't come to know the woman as she is in her twenty-four-hour life. You come to know only her painted face, you come to know only her performance – not her truth.

When a woman comes out of her house ready to go shopping, she is not the same woman. She is almost a different person: now she is a managed woman, now she is a performer. Women are great actresses. In the house they don't look so beautiful; out of the house they suddenly become tremendously beautiful, joyful, cheerful, delighted. They again become small, giggling girls in love with life. Their faces are different, radiant: their eyes are different, their makeup, their performance…

Seeing a woman on the beach or in the shopping center, you see a totally different kind of reality. To live with a woman twenty-four hours a day is very mundane, it has to be. But if you really love a woman you would like to know her reality, not her fiction, because love can exist only with reality. And love is capable enough of knowing the reality and of knowing all the defects of the woman and still loving her. Love is a tremendous strength.

When you are with a person twenty-four hours a day, man or woman, you come to know all the defects: all that is good and all that is bad too, all that is beautiful and all that is ugly too, all that is like light rays and all that is like dark night. You come to know the whole person. Love is strong enough to love the other knowing all the defects, limitations, frailties that a human being is prone to. But a fictitious love is not strong enough. It can only love a woman on a movie screen. It can only love a woman in a novel, it can only love a woman in poetry. It can only love the woman as a faraway, distant star. It can only love a woman who is not real.

Love is a totally different dimension: it is falling in love with reality. Yes, reality has defects, but those defects are challenges to growth. Each defect is a challenge to transcend it. And when two persons are really in love, they help each other to grow. They look into each other, they become mirrors to each other, they reflect each other. They help each other, they hold each other. In good times, in bad times, in moments of happiness, in moments of sadness, they are together, they are involved. That's what involvement is all about.

If I am only with you when you are happy and I am not with you when you are unhappy, this is not involvement; this is exploitation. If I am only with you when you are flowing and I am not with you when you are not flowing, then I am not with you at all. Then I don't love you, I love only myself and I love only my pleasure. When you are pleasurable, good; when you become painful I will throw you away. This is not love, this is not involvement, this is not commitment. This is not respect for the other person.

It is easy to love somebody else's wife because the husband has to suffer the reality and you enjoy the fiction; it is a very good division of labor. But this is inhuman. Human love is a great encounter. And love exists only if growth happens out of it – otherwise, what type of love is it?

Lovers are enhanced by each other, in every way. Lovers reach to higher peaks of happiness when they are together, and they also reach to deeper depths of sadness when they are together. Their range of happiness and sadness becomes vast: that's what love is. Alone, if you cry and weep your tears don't have much depth. Have you seen it? Alone, they are shallow. When you weep together with somebody then there is a depth, a new dimension to your tears.

Alone you can laugh, but your laughter will be shallow. In fact, it will be something insane – only mad people laugh alone. When you laugh with somebody there is a depth in it, there is sanity in it. You can laugh alone, but the laughter will not go very deep – cannot go. Together, it goes to the very core of your being. Two persons together, together in all the climates – day and night, summer and winter – in all the moods, grow.

The tree needs all the climates and all the seasons. Yes, it needs the burning hot summer and it needs the ice-cold winter. It needs the daylight, the sun showering on it, and it needs the silence of night so it can close into itself and go into deep sleep. It needs silent, cheerful, joyful days; it needs gloomy, cloudy days too. It grows through all these dialectics.

Love is a dialectic. Alone you cannot grow. Remember always that if you are in love, then don't avoid commitment, don't avoid involvement. Then go totally into it. Then don't just stand on the periphery ready to escape if things get too troublesome.

Love is a sacrifice too. You have to sacrifice much. You have to sacrifice your ego, you have to sacrifice your ambition, you have to sacrifice your privacy, you have to sacrifice your secrets; you have to sacrifice many things. So just to be in a romantic love needs no sacrifice. But when there is no sacrifice there is no growth.

Love changes you completely; it is a new birth. You are never the same person again as you were before you loved a woman or a man. You have passed through fire, you are purified. But courage is needed.

You ask: "Why am I always interested in married women?" Because you are not courageous. You want to avoid the involvement. You want it cheaply, you don't want to pay the price for it.

The second question:

Osho
It is not like making love any more – I feel I am in a temple with you all over.
At this moment I'm aware, which I never was before I met you. Everything is
different every time – for me and the other half. Thanking you is never adequate at
that moment. And yet we slip back. How can we take off? How can I take the help
of the woman outside to be united with the woman inside me?

The question is from Anand Kul Bhushan. The first thing: never think of the woman as "the other half"; she is not, neither are you. You are whole, she is whole. She is an individual and you are an individual. You are complete and she is complete. That old attitude that the woman is the other half has proved a great disaster. The moment you start possessing – it is a sort of possession – the moment you start destroying the individuality of the other, you are destroying something of great value. It is uncreative. Never think about the woman as the other half – she is not.

Two lovers are like two pillars in a temple: that's how Kahlil Gibran says it. They support the same roof, but they are aloof, they are not together. If the two pillars of the temple come very close, the temple will fall down, the roof will not be supported at all. Look at these pillars in the Chuang Tzu Auditorium: they stand aloof – they support the same roof. So should lovers be: aloof, individual, and yet supporting something in common.

The wife is not half of the husband, nor is the husband half of the wife. Neither is the husband surrendered to the wife, nor is the wife surrendered to the husband; they are both surrendered to the love god. Remember it; it has proved really paralyzing otherwise. The man has not suffered too much because it is man's idea about woman that she is the other half. He does not think that he himself is also the other half, no; it is man's idea that the woman is the other half. Man remains whole, the woman becomes the other half.

That's why after marriage the woman has to take the husband's name, not the husband. She disappears, she is destroyed; she is no longer a woman – she is a wife. The wife is an institution. The man still remains the man he was before. Something is added to the man, but something has been taken away from the woman. This is ugly.

The other day I was reading a beautiful poem:
"Tell me not about your love," a woman says to her lover...

> Tell me not about your love,
> I know it well.
> I've felt it in your glance,
> Felt it from the lash of the whip
> And worse,
> From out your tongue.
> Tell me not of your love;
> It is so fluid
> It has drowned me and mine
> In its burning intensity.
> I have but few places left unscarred –
> The heat of your love has all but consumed my brain,
> The security of your love has rendered me fatherless,
> The gift of your love branded me bastard.
> The testimony of your love has imprisoned me,
> Your song of love has made me voiceless.
> I shall sing no more.
> I am no more.
> You have loved me into oblivion.

Let me repeat: "You have loved me into oblivion." Then this love has not proved much of a love; it is a subtle way of domination. And when there is domination, love disappears. When there is possession, love disappears.

Please don't possess a woman and don't possess a man. Possession, possessiveness is not love. Remember, the woman has to remain intact as an individual. Her freedom must not be destroyed; her freedom has to be respected – whatsoever it takes. This is the Tantra vision: whatsoever it takes – unconditionally – the woman's freedom has to remain intact. If you really love her, you will love her freedom too – and she will love your freedom. If you love a person, how can you destroy his or her freedom? If you trust a person, you trust her or his freedom too.

One day it happened...

A man came to me who was really in a mess, very miserable. And he said, "I will commit suicide."

I said, "Why?"

He said, "I trusted my wife and she has betrayed me. I had trusted her absolutely, and she has been in love with some other man, and I never came to know about it until just now. I have got hold of a few letters... So then I inquired, and then I insisted, and now she has confessed that she has been in love all the time. I will commit suicide," he said.

I said, "You say you trusted her?"

He said, "Yes, I trusted her and she betrayed me."

"What do you mean by trust? Some wrong notion about trust... Your trust also seems to be political. You trusted her so that she would not betray you. Your trust was a trick; now you want to make her feel guilty. This is not trust."

He was very puzzled. He said, "What do you mean by trust then, if this is not trust? I trusted her unconditionally."

I said, "If I were in your place, trust would mean to me that I trust her freedom and I trust her intelligence and I trust her loving capacity. If she falls in love with somebody else, I trust that too. She is intelligent, she can choose. She is free; she can love. I trust her understanding.

"What do you mean by trust? When you trust her intelligence, her understanding, her awareness – you trust it. And if she finds that she would like to move into love with somebody, it is perfectly okay. Even if you feel pain, that is your problem, it is not her problem.

And if you feel pain, that is not because of love, that is because of jealousy. What kind of trust is this, that you say it has been betrayed? My understanding of trust is that it cannot be betrayed. By its very nature, by its very definition, trust cannot be betrayed. It is impossible to betray trust. If trust can be betrayed, then it is not trust."

Think over it. If I love a woman, I trust her intelligence infinitely, and if in some moments she wants to love to somebody else, it is perfectly good. I have always trusted her intelligence; she must be feeling like that. She is free; she is not my other half, she is independent. And when two persons are independent individuals, only then is there love. Love can flow only between two freedoms.

I understand Kul Bhushan's question. He has used these words *other half* unconsciously. I have seen his love for his wife, I have seen his wife's love for him. They are not each other's halves, not at all; it is just an unconscious habit of using words. But I wanted to make it clear.

The second thing: "It is not like making love any more..." When love grows deep, it becomes something else. When love does not grow, it becomes something else. Love is a very delicate thing. If it does not grow, it becomes bitter, it becomes poisoned; it becomes hatred. It can even fall below hatred – it can become indifference, which is the farthest from love.

Love is a hot energy. So is hate hot. But indifference is cold, frozen. You can think about love and hate and indifference on this scale. Exactly between hate and love there is a zero point – just as in a thermometer there is a zero point; below it is coldness, above it is warmth. Love is warmth. That zero point is hatred; below it you become even colder, you can become ice-cold – indifferent. If love does not grow, it starts falling downward. It has to move.

Love is energy; energy moves. If it moves, soon you will find it is no longer love; it has become meditation, it has become prayerful.

That's the whole approach of Tantra – that if love grows rightly, if love is tended carefully, it becomes prayerful. It becomes, finally, the ultimate experience of godliness.

Love is the temple of God.

So people who live in indifference cannot know the state of godliness. Indifference is the real atheism. People who live in a cold sort of way... Even the courts understand this. If somebody has been murdered in a hot way the courts don't take it so seriously; if somebody has been murdered out of passion, then the courts take a lenient view of it. Then the murderer must not be punished too severely. It was just an act of passion: it happened out of sudden rage.

But the courts are very hard when there is a murder of cold calculation. The cold murderer is the most dangerous man. He prepares everything in detail: he thinks, broods, contemplates about it, he calculates. He moves in a very, very mechanical and efficient way; he goes about his job very skillfully. He has no heart; he is just cold.

The cold heart is the dead heart. The cold heart is the dead, dried, fossil heart. If love does not go higher, it will go lower, remember; it cannot remain static – that is the point to be understood. Love cannot remain in a stasis: either it falls down or it goes up – but it goes. So if you really want to live a life of warmth, help love to grow.

Two persons fall in love. If their love does not immediately start becoming friendship, sooner or later there is going to be a divorce. Friendship should grow out of love; otherwise enmity will grow. Something is bound to happen. Love is an opening. Immediately start growing in friendship; otherwise enmity will grow. Something is bound to grow.

Love is fertile. If you are not sowing the seeds of beautiful flowers, then weeds will grow – but something is bound to grow. When love really moves deeper, it becomes prayerful. Then the whole quality is nonsexual, then the quality is nonsensuous. Then you have a certain feeling of reverence for the other – not sexual lust at all, but awe. In the very presence of the other you start feeling something divine, something sacred. Your beloved becomes your goddess or your god.

"It is not like making love any more – I feel I am in a temple with you all over." That's right, you are blessed. "At this moment I am aware, which I never was before I met you." The more love becomes prayer, the more awareness will happen, just like a shadow.

This is my insistence: if awareness happens, then comes love – love comes as the shadow. If love happens, then as the shadow comes awareness. Either you grow in love, or you grow in meditation, but the ultimate result is the same. Both come together: you try one and the other comes. It depends on you.

If you feel more in tune with love, then love is your path – the path of the devotee, *bhakta*. If you feel more in tune with awareness, then the path of meditation, *dhyana*. These are the only basic paths; all other paths are combinations of these two. If love grows, you will become more and more aware of it at every moment. The higher it goes, the higher will become your insight into things.

"Thanking you is never adequate at that moment." It cannot be, and there is no need. In fact, many times when we say thank you, we don't mean it. Somebody passes the salt at the table and you say thank you – do you mean it? You don't mean it, it is just a formality. Between a master and a disciple there should be no formality; there is no need, I am not passing the salt to you.

"Thank you" is a Western mannerism; in the East it is almost impossible. I have never thanked my father, I cannot. How can I thank my father? I have not thanked my mother. I have everything to thank her for, but I have not thanked her. How can I? To say thank you would be too inadequate, it would be too embarrassing. It would be too formal, it would lack love. It is better to keep silent about it. She understands.

Between a master and a disciple there is no formality possible; all formality will always be inadequate. There is no need. I understand, Kul Bhushan. I can see your heart full of gratitude. Only in silence can it be said. It can be said without saying it; if you try to say it, it will never look right.

"Thanking you is never adequate at that moment. And yet we slip back. How can we take off? How can I take the help of the woman outside to be united with the woman inside?" Slipping back is natural. The past is so big and the present moment is so small. The pull of the past is so great, and this awareness is just like a new leaf coming out of the tree – fresh, young, delicate, vulnerable. And the past is like a great Himalaya – rocks and rocks and rocks. This small leaf and this great Himalaya of rocks... This leaf had to fight this Himalaya of a past of thousands of lives lived mechanically, lived unconsciously. But still this small leaf will prove stronger than the whole Himalaya of rocks and rocks and rocks. Why? – because this leaf is alive, alive with love, aflame with love. This leaf is the leaf of awareness. It is going to win.

But many times you will feel that you have slipped – that's natural. Don't be worried about it, don't feel guilty about it. Whenever you remember, again start growing. Always keep the new leaf in your consciousness. Pour your whole consciousness into this new insight that is growing in you. In the beginning these moments are bound to be few and far between. But even if, once in a while, the moment comes when love is no longer love and has become prayerful, you are in a Tantra moment. Don't be worried about the dark nights; there is no need to worry. Move from day to day. Remember the day to day.

There will be nights – sometimes very long nights. Think about those nights just as tunnels of darkness. At one end is light, at the other end is light; between is a tunnel of darkness. And that too is good because it prepares your eyes to see the light more clearly. It gives rest, it relaxes. Don't think in terms of one night to another night and the day just in between, no. Even though moments are very few and far between – and very small moments – they are precious jewels, shining. Just think of those moments. One moment happened today, and another moment may happen after a year. Don't be worried about the year – that is irrelevant; from this moment to that moment let your eyes be focused. This whole year is just a tunnel from one day to another day, from one light to another light, from one love moment to another love moment, from one awareness to another awareness. Soon the slipping will be less, and soon the slipping will disappear. But there is no need to feel guilty, no need to feel repentant about it. It is natural; accept it.

"How can I take the help of the woman outside to be united with the woman inside?" Don't think of the "how." If love is there, it is going to happen. And love is not a how, love is not know-how. Just love for no reason at all. Just love with reverence, with awe. Just love: seeing in the other not the body but the soul, seeing in the other not the mind but the no-mind. If you can see the no-mind in your woman, you will be able to find your inner woman very easily. Then the outside woman is just a medium. Through the outer woman, via the outer woman, you will be thrown back to your inner woman. But if the other woman outside is just a body, then you are blocked. If the other woman is just a soul, an emptiness, just a zero, just a passage, then there is nothing to block you. Your energy will move back and will enter and will find your own inner woman.

Each woman and man can be helpful from the outside to find the inner woman and the inner man. But there is no how to it. Reverence is needed. Think in terms, meditate in terms, of the other's divinity. The other is divine; let that attitude prevail, let that climate surround you. And it is going to happen. It is already on the way.

The third question:

Osho,
Why are people missing you? Since I took sannyas I can see their stupidity very
clearly. Why can't they see it?

Don't be too hard on people. And it is none of your business. If they don't
want to see it, that is their decision and their freedom. Don't even call it stupidity because if you call it stupidity, a subtle ego will arise in you that you can
see and they cannot, that you are intelligent and they are stupid. No, this is
not good.

It happened once…

Mohammed went to the mosque to say his morning prayer and he took a
young man with him who had never gone to the mosque before. While coming
back – it was a summer morning and people were still asleep – while coming back, the young man said to Mohammed, "Hazrat, look at these sinners
still asleep. Is this a time to sleep? This is time to pray!" And this was the first
time that he himself had gone to pray.

Do you know what Mohammed said? Looking at the sky, he said, "Sorry."
The young man said, "To whom are you saying this?"
He said, "To God. I will have to go back to the mosque – and please don't
come this time. It was good that you had not gone to the mosque before; I
have done something wrong by taking you. It was good that you were also
asleep – at least you would not have gathered this ego. Now you are a saint
just because you have made one prayer, and these people are sinners. And
because I took you with me my own prayer is spoiled, so I am going back.
And please, never come again. At least I'm not going to take you with me."

And he went back to pray and to ask forgiveness from God. He was crying,
and tears were rolling down his face.

A few days ago you took sannyas – or a few weeks – and you think that
others are stupid? That is not right, that is not right at all. In fact, a sannyasin
is one who stops interfering in other people's lives. This attitude is an interfer-
ence. Why? If they don't want to see me, if they don't want to listen to me,
if they don't want to understand what is happening here, then that is their
freedom. They are not stupid, this is simply their freedom; they have to be
themselves.

If you gather such attitudes, that's how fanaticism is born; then one day
you can become a fanatic, then you can force them to come: "You will have to

come." Out of compassion you have to force them. That's what religions have been doing down the centuries: Mohammedans killing Hindus, Hindus killing Mohammedans, Christians killing Mohammedans, Mohammedans killing Christians. For what? – out of compassion. They say, "We will take you on the right path. You are going astray, we cannot allow you to go astray."

Freedom means *total* freedom. Freedom means to go astray too. If you don't allow a person to go astray, then what type of freedom is it? If you tell a child, "You are free only to do the right and I am deciding what is right. You are not free to do the wrong and I am deciding what is wrong" – what type of freedom is this? Who are you to decide what is right? Let everybody decide for himself.

It is very easy to gather such attitudes. That's why, down the ages, this foolishness has happened: millions of people have been killed in the name of love, in the name of God. How was it possible? Christians were thinking that they were doing a great duty because they thought, "Unless you come through Jesus, you will never come to God." If you look at their logic, it seems very, very compassionate. If it is really the case that you can come to God only through Jesus, then those people who were burning and killing and punishing people were really great saints.

But that is the problem. Mohammedans think that you can only come through Mohammed; Mohammed is the latest prophet, Jesus is out of date already. God has sent another message – more improved; a new edition has come. So why bother about Jesus when Mohammed has come? Certainly the latest one should be the best, so you have to come through Mohammed. Now there is only one God and there is only one prophet of God, and that is Mohammed. And if you don't listen they are ready to kill you – just out of love, for your own good.

And listen to the Hindus – they say that this is all nonsense, the first edition is the best, the Vedas. Why? – because God cannot commit any errors, so he cannot improve. The first is the best! He cannot commit any errors, so how can he improve? The first is the last, the alpha is the omega. God has given once and for all; then why these other editions? These are for stupid people who cannot understand the original. If you can understand the Vedas then there is no need to understand the Bible and the Koran; they are just meaningless. The first was the best. God trusted that man would understand. But then he found that man was very foolish, only a few wise people could understand. Then he had to lower himself a little. It is not improvement, it is just getting down to where man is, so he gave the Bible. But still it was not understood, so he gave the Koran. Still it was not understood, so he gave the Guru Grantha. That's how man has been falling.

In the Hindu concept perfection was in the past; since then man has been falling. This is the most stupid age: man has not been evolving, man has been falling. It is not evolution, Hindus say, it is involution. So the later the book, the more ordinary it has to be because it is meant for the ordinary people. The perfect people were in the days of the Vedas.

Now there are three hundred religions on the earth, and each one claiming, and each religion ready to kill the other. They are at each other's throats continuously. Something basic has gone wrong. This is what has gone wrong: you are asking me to allow you to become a fanatic. No, this is not going to happen with me at least – at least while I am here. Others are free to do whatsoever they like, to see as they like, to interpret as they like. You are not to take it for granted that they are stupid. They have their own minds – it is beautiful.

A Negro boy came home painted white and said, "The kids at school painted me white all over." So his mother beat him for getting messed up.

Father came home and said, "What is going on?" So Mother told him that the kids at school had painted our Sam white. So father gave him another thrashing for not standing up for himself.

Shortly afterwards a small voice was heard, "I have only been a white boy for two hours, but I already hate you black buggers!"

And you have been an orange man for just a few weeks. Please be patient, be intelligent and respectful of others' freedom, others' being, and their way, their style.

The fourth question:

Osho,
Why has sex been a taboo in all the societies down the ages?

It is a very complicated question, but very important too – worth going into. Sex is the most powerful instinct in man. The politician and the priest have understood from the very beginning that sex is the most driving energy in man. It has to be curtailed, it has to be cut; if man is allowed total freedom in sex, then there will be no possibility to dominate him: to make a slave out of him will be impossible.

Have you not seen it being done? When you want a bull to be yoked to a bullock-cart, what do you do? You castrate him, you destroy his sex energy. And have you seen the difference between a bull and an ox? What a difference! An ox is a poor phenomenon, a slave. A bull has a beauty; a bull is a glorious phenomenon, a great splendor. See a bull walking, how he walks like an emperor. And see an ox pulling a bullock cart. The same has been done to man: the sex instinct has been curtailed, cut, crippled. Man does not exist as a bull now, he exists like an ox. And each man is pulling a thousand and one bullock carts.

Look, and you will find behind you a thousand and one bullock carts, and you are yoked to them. Why can't you yoke a bull? The bull is too powerful. If he sees a cow passing by, he will throw off both you and the bullock-cart and he will move to the cow. He will not bother a bit about who you are and he will not listen. It will be impossible to control the bull.

Sex energy is life energy: it is uncontrollable. And the politician and the priest are not interested in you, they are interested in channeling your energy into certain directions. So there is a certain mechanism behind it; it has to be understood.

Sex repression, sexual taboo, is the very foundation of human slavery. And man cannot be free unless sex is free. Man cannot be *really* free unless his sex energy is allowed natural growth.

These are the five tricks through which man has been turned into a slave, into an ugly phenomenon, a cripple. The first is: keep man as weak as possible if you want to dominate him. If the priest wants to dominate you or the politician wants to dominate you, you have to be kept as weak as possible. Yes, in certain cases, exceptions are allowed – that is, when the services of fighting the enemy are needed; only then, otherwise not. The army is allowed many things which ordinary people are not allowed. The army is in the service of death, it is allowed to be powerful. It is allowed to remain as powerful as possible; it is needed to kill the enemy.

Other people are destroyed. They are forced to remain weak in a thousand and one ways. And the best way to keep a man weak is not to give love total freedom. Love is nourishment. Now the psychologists have discovered that if a child is not given love, he shrivels up into himself and becomes weak. You can give him milk, you can give him medicine, you can give him everything; just don't give love, don't hug him, don't kiss him, don't hold him close to the warmth of your body, and the child will start becoming weaker and weaker and weaker. And there are more chances of dying than surviving. What happens? Why? Just hugging, kissing, giving warmth, somehow the child feels nourished, accepted, loved, needed. The child starts feeling worthy, the child starts feeling a certain meaning in his life.

Now, from the very childhood, we starve people, we don't give as much love as is needed. Then we force the young men and young women not to fall in love unless they get married. By the age of fourteen they become sexually mature, but the education may take more time – ten years more, twenty-four, twenty-five years. Then they will be getting their MAs, or PhD's, or MDs, so we have to force them not to love.

Sexual energy comes to its climax nearabout the age of eighteen. Never again will a man be so potent, and never again will a woman be able to have a greater orgasm than she will be able to near the age of eighteen. But we force them not to make love. We force boys to have their separate dormitories – girls and boys are kept separate – and just between the two stands the whole mechanism of police, magistrates, vice-chancellors, principals, headmasters. They are all standing there, just in between, just holding the boys back from moving to the girls, holding the girls back from moving to the boys. Why? Why is so much care taken? They are trying to kill the bull and create an ox.

By the time you are eighteen you are at the peak of your sexual energy, your love energy. By the time you get married, twenty-five, twenty-six, twenty-seven – and the age has been going up and up... The more cultured a country, the more you wait because more has to be learned, the job has to be found – this and that. By the time you get married you are almost declining in your powers.

Then you love, but the love never becomes really hot; it never comes to the point where people evaporate, it remains lukewarm. And when you have not been able to love totally, you cannot love your children because you don't know how. When you have not been able to know the peaks of it, how can you teach your children? How can you help your children to have the peaks of it? So down the ages man has been denied love so that he should remain weak.

Second: keep man as ignorant and deluded as possible so that he can easily be deceived. And if you want to create a sort of idiocy – which is a must for the priest and the politician and their conspiracy – then the best thing is not to allow man to move into love freely. Without love a man's intelligence falls low. Have you not seen it? When you fall in love, suddenly all your capacities are at their peak, at their crescendo. Just a moment ago you were looking dull, then you meet your woman and suddenly a great joy has erupted in your being, you are aflame. While people are in love they perform at their maximum. When love disappears or when love is not there, they perform at their minimum.

The greatest, most intelligent people are the most sexual people. This has to be understood because love energy is basically intelligence. If you cannot love, you are somehow closed, cold; you cannot flow. While in love, one flows. While in love, one feels so confident that one can touch the stars. That's why a woman becomes a great inspiration, a man becomes a great inspiration. When a woman is loved she becomes more beautiful immediately, instantly! Just a moment ago she was just an ordinary woman; and then love has showered upon her and she is bathed in a totally new energy, a new aura arises around her. She walks more gracefully, a dance has come to her step. Her eyes have tremendous beauty now, her face glows, she is luminous. And the same happens to the man.

When people are in love, they perform at the optimum. Don't allow love and they will remain at the minimum. When they remain at the minimum they are stupid, they are ignorant, they don't bother to know. And when people are ignorant and stupid and deluded, they can be easily deceived. When people are sexually repressed, love-wise repressed, they start hankering for the other life; they think about heaven, paradise, but they don't think to create paradise herenow.

When you are in love, paradise is herenow. Then you don't bother; then who goes to the priest? Then who bothers that there should be a paradise? You are already there – you are no longer interested. But when your love energy is repressed, you start thinking, "Here is nothing. Now is empty. Then there must be somewhere, some goal…" You go to the priest and ask about heaven, and he paints beautiful pictures of heaven.

Sex has been repressed so that you can become interested in the other life. And when people are interested in the other life, naturally they are not interested in *this* life. And Tantra says this life is the only life. The other life is hidden in this life. It is not against it, it is not away from it; it is in it. Go into it – this is it!

Go into it and you will find the other too. Godliness is hidden in the world, that is the Tantra message. A great message, superb, incomparable.

Godliness is hidden in the world, godliness is hidden herenow. If you love, you will be able to feel it.

The third secret: keep man as frightened as possible. And the sure way is not to allow him love because love destroys fear. "Love casteth out fear." When you are in love, you are not afraid. When you are in love, you can fight against the whole world. When you are in love, you feel infinitely capable of anything. But when you are not in love, you are afraid of small things. When you are not in love, you become more interested in security, in safety. When you are in love, you are more interested in adventure, in exploration.

People have not been allowed to love because that is the only way to make them afraid. And when they are afraid and trembling they are always on their knees, bowing to the priest and bowing to the politician. It is a great conspiracy against humanity. It is a great conspiracy against *you*. Your politician and your priest are your enemies, but they pretend that they are public servants. They say, "We are here to serve you, to help you attain a better life. We are here to create a good life for you." And they are the destroyers of life itself.

The fourth: keep man as miserable as possible – because a miserable man is confused, a miserable man has no self-worth, a miserable man is self-condemnatory, a miserable man feels that he must have done something wrong. A miserable man has no grounding: you can push him from here to there, he can be turned into driftwood very easily. And a miserable man is always ready to be commanded, to be ordered, to be disciplined because he knows, "On my own I am simply miserable. Maybe somebody else can discipline my life?" He is a ready victim.

And the fifth: keep men as alienated from each other as possible, so that they cannot band together for some purpose of which the priest and the politician may not approve. Keep people separate from each other, don't allow them too much intimacy. When people are separate, lonely, alienated from each other, they cannot band together. And there are a thousand and one tricks to keep them away.

For example, if you are holding the hand of a man – you are a man and you are holding the hand of a man, and walking down the road singing – you will feel guilty because people will start looking at you: are you gay, homosexual, or something? Two men are not allowed to be happy together. They are not allowed to hold hands, they are not allowed to hug each other; they are condemned as homosexuals. Fear arises.

If your friend comes and takes your hand in his hand, you look around: is somebody looking or not? And you are just in a hurry to drop the hand. You shake hands in such a hurry. Have you seen it? You just touch each other's hand and shake and you are finished; you don't hold hands, you don't hug each other. You are afraid.

Do you remember whether your father ever hugged you? Do you remember your mother hugging you after you became sexually mature? Why not? Fear has been created. A young man and his mother hugging? Maybe some sex will arise between them, some idea, some fantasy. Fear has been created: the father and the son, the father and the daughter, no; the brother and the sister, no; the brother and the brother, no!

People are kept in separate boxes with great walls around them. Everybody is classified, and there a thousand and one barriers. Yes, one day, after twenty-five years of all this training, you are allowed to make love to your wife. But now the training has gone too deep in you, and suddenly you don't know what to do. How to love? You have not learned the language.

It is as if a person has not been allowed to speak for twenty-five years. Just listen: for twenty-five years he has not been allowed to speak a single word and then suddenly you put him on a stage and tell him, "Give us a great lecture." What will happen? He will fall there, then and there. He may faint, he may die.

Twenty-five years of silence and now suddenly he is expected to deliver a great lecture. It is not possible.

This is what is happening: twenty-five years of anti-love, of fear, and then suddenly you are legally allowed – a license is issued, and now you can love this woman. This is your wife, you are her husband, and you are allowed to love. But where are those twenty-five years of wrong training going to go? They will be there.

Yes, you will "love"; you will make an effort, a gesture. It is not going to be explosive, it is not going to be orgasmic: it will be very tiny. That's why you are frustrated after making love to a woman. Ninety-nine percent of people are frustrated after making love, more frustrated than they have ever been before. And they feel, "What? There is nothing! It is not true!"

Now, first the priest and the politician have managed that you should not be able to love, and then they come and they preach that there is nothing in love. And certainly their preaching looks right, their preaching looks exactly in tune with your experience. First they create the experience of futility, of frustration – then, their teaching. And both look logical together, of one piece.

This is a great trick, the greatest that has ever been played upon man. These five things can be managed through a single thing, and that is the love taboo. It is possible to accomplish all these objectives by somehow preventing people from loving each other. And the taboo has been managed in such a scientific way. This taboo is a great piece of art; great skill and great cunningness have gone into it, it is really a masterpiece. This taboo has to be understood.

First: it is indirect, it is hidden. It is not apparent because whenever a taboo is too obvious, it will not work. The taboo has to be very hidden, so you don't know how it works. The taboo has to be so hidden that you cannot even imagine that anything like it is possible. The taboo has to go into the unconscious, not into the conscious. How to make it so subtle and so indirect? The trick is: first go on teaching that love is great, so people never think that the priests and the politicians are against love. Go on teaching that love is great, that love is the right thing – and then don't allow any situation where love can happen, don't allow the opportunity. Don't give any opportunity, and go on teaching that food is great, that eating is a great joy – "Eat as well as you can" – but don't supply anything to eat. Keep people hungry and go on talking about love.

So, all the priests go on talking about love. Love is praised as highly as anything, just next to God, and denied every possibility of its happening. Directly encourage it; indirectly cut its roots. This is the masterpiece.

No priests talk about how *they* have done the harm. It is as if you go on saying to a tree, "Be green, bloom, enjoy," and you go on cutting the roots so that the tree cannot be green. And when the tree is not green you can jump upon the tree and say, "Listen! You don't listen, you don't follow us. We all go on saying 'Be green, bloom, enjoy, dance,'" and meanwhile you go on cutting the roots.

Love is denied so much – and love is the rarest thing in the world; it should not be denied. If a man can love five persons, he should love five. If a man can love fifty, he should love fifty. If a man can love five hundred, he should love five hundred. Love is so rare that the more you can spread it the better.

But there are great tricks. You are forced into a narrow, very narrow, cor-ner: you can love only your wife, you can love only your husband, you can love only this, you can love only that; the conditions are too much. It is as if there is a law that you can breathe only when you are with your wife, you can breathe only when you are with your husband. Then breathing will become impossible, then you will die. And you will not even be able to breathe while you are with your wife or with your husband. You have to breathe twenty-four hours a day. The more you breathe, the more you will be able to breathe while you are with your spouse.

Be loving.

Then there is another trick: they talk about "higher" love and they destroy the lower. And they say that the lower has to be denied: bodily love is bad, spiritual love is good. Have you ever seen any spirit without a body? Have you ever seen a house without a foundation? The lower is the foundation of the higher. The body is your abode, the spirit lives in the body, with the body. You are an embodied spirit and an ensouled body. You are together. The lower and the higher are not separate, they are one: rungs of the same ladder.

This is what Tantra wants to make clear: the lower has not to be denied, the lower has to be transformed into the higher. The lower is good. If you are stuck with the lower, the fault is with you, not with the lower. Nothing is wrong with the lower rung of a ladder. If you are stuck with it, *you* are stuck: it is something in you. Move.

Sex is not wrong, *you* are wrong if you are stuck there. Move higher. The higher is not against the lower; the lower makes it possible for the higher to exist.

And these tricks have created many other problems. Each time you are in love, somehow you feel guilty; guilt has arisen. When there is guilt, you cannot move totally into love; the guilt prevents you, it keeps you holding on. Even while making love to your wife or your husband there is guilt: you know this is sin, you know you are doing something wrong. Saints don't do it, you are a sinner. So you cannot move totally even when you are allowed – superficially – to love your wife. The priest is hidden behind you in your guilt feeling; he is pulling you from there, pulling your strings. When guilt arises you start feeling that you are wrong; you lose self-worth, you lose self-respect.

And another problem arises: when there is guilt you start pretending. Mothers and fathers don't allow their children to know that they make love; they pretend, they pretend that love exists not. Their pretension will be known by the children sooner or later. When the children come to know about the pretension they lose all trust, they feel betrayed, they feel cheated. And fathers and mothers say that their children don't respect them. You are the cause of it, how can they respect you? You have been deceiving them in every way, you have been dishonest, you have been mean. You were telling them not to fall in love – "Beware!" – and you were making love all the time. And the day will come, sooner or later, when they will realize that even their father, even their mother was not true with them. So how can they respect you?

First guilt creates pretension, then pretension creates alienation from people. Even the child, your own child, will not feel in tune with you. There is a barrier: your pretension. And when you know that everybody is pretending... One day, you will come to know that you are just pretending, and so are others. When everybody is pretending, how can you relate? When everybody is false, how can you relate? How can you be friendly when everywhere there is deception and deceit? You become very, very sore about reality, you become very bitter, you see it only as the Devil's workshop.

And everybody has a false face, nobody is authentic. Everybody is carrying masks, nobody shows his original face. You feel guilty, you feel that you are pretending, and you know that everybody is pretending, everybody is feeling guilty, and everybody has become just like an ugly wound. Now it is very easy to make these people slaves – to turn them into clerks, stationmasters, schoolmasters, collectors, deputy collectors, ministers, governors, presidents. Now it is very easy to distract them. You have distracted them from their roots. Sex is the root, hence the name *muladhar. Muladhar* means the very root energy.

I have heard...

It was her wedding night and the haughty Lady Jane was performing her marital duties for the first time.

"My Lord," she asked her bridegroom, "is this what the common people call lovemaking?"

"Yes, it is, my lady," replied Lord Reginald, proceeding as before.

After a while Lady Jane exclaimed indignantly, "It is too good for the common people!"

The common people have not really been allowed lovemaking: it is too good for them. But the problem is that when you poison the whole world, you are also poisoned. If you poison the air which the common people breathe, the air that the king breathes will also be poisoned. It cannot be separate, it is all one. When the priest poisons the common people, finally he also is poisoned. When the politician poisons the common people's air, finally he also breathes the same air; there is no other air.

A curate and a bishop were in opposite corners of a railway carriage on a long journey. As the bishop entered, the curate put away his copy of *Playboy* and started reading *The Church Times*. The bishop ignored him and went on doing *The Times* crossword. Silence prevailed.

After a while the curate tried to make conversation. And when the bishop began to do a lot of head scratching and "Tut-tut-tutting," he tried again. "Can I help you, sir?"

"Perhaps. I am only beaten by one word. What is it that has four letters, the last three are *u-n-t*, and the clue is 'essentially feminine'?"

"Why, sir," said the curate after a slight pause, "That would be 'aunt.'"

"Of course, of course!" said the bishop. "I say, young man, can you lend me an eraser?"

When you repress on the surface, everything goes deep inside the unconscious. It is there; sex has not been destroyed. Fortunately, it has not been destroyed; it has only been poisoned. It cannot be destroyed, it is life energy. It has become polluted and it can be purified. That is the whole process of Tantra: a great process of purification.

Your life problems can basically be reduced to your sex problem. You can go on solving your other problems, but you will never be able to solve them because they are not true problems. And if you solve your sex problem, all problems will disappear because you have solved the base.

But you are so afraid even to look into it. It is simple: if you can put aside your conditioning, it is very simple, it is as simple as this story...

A frustrated spinster was a pest to the police. She kept ringing up saying there was a man under her bed. She was finally sent to a mental hospital, but she still told the doctors there was a man under her bed. They gave her the latest drugs and she suddenly declared that she was cured.

"You mean, Miss Rustifan, you can't see a man under the bed now?"

"No, I can't. I can see two."

One doctor told the other that there was only really one sort of injection that would cure her complaint, which he called "malignant virginity" – why should they not set her up in her bedroom with Big Dan, the hospital carpenter?

Big Dan was fetched, told what her complaint was, and that he would be locked in with her for an hour. He said it would not take that long, and an anxious group gathered on the landing. They heard, "No, stop it, Dan. Mother would never forgive me!"

"Shut up yelling, it's got to be done at some time. It should have been done years ago!"

"Have your way by force then, you brute!"

"It's only what your husband would have done, had you had one."

Unable to wait, the medics burst in.

"I have cured her!" said the carpenter.

"He has cured me!" said Miss Rustifan.

He had sawn the legs off the bed.

Sometimes the cure is very simple, and you go on doing a thousand and one things. And the carpenter did well, just cutting the legs off the bed and it was finished! Now where could the man hide?

Sex is the root of almost all your problems; it has to be so because of thousands of years of poisoning. A great purification is needed. Tantra can purify your sex energy. Listen to the Tantra message, try to understand it. It is a great revolutionary message. It is against all priests and politicians, it is against all those poisoners who have killed all joy on the earth just so that man can be turned into – reduced to – a slave.

Reclaim your freedom. Reclaim your freedom to love. Reclaim your freedom to be, and then life is no longer a problem – it is a mystery, it is an ecstasy, it is a benediction.

Enough for today.

from nothing to nothing

Non-memory is convention's truth
and mind which has become no-mind is ultimate truth.
This is fulfillment, this is the highest good.
Friends, of this highest good become aware.

In non-memory is mind absorbed;
just this is emotionality perfect and pure.
It is unpolluted by the good or bad of worldliness
like a lotus unaffected by the mud from which it grows.

Yet with certainty must all things be viewed
as if they were a magic spell.
If without distinction you can accept or reject samsara or nirvana,
steadfast is your mind, free from the shroud of darkness.
In you will be self-being, beyond thought and self-originated.

This world of appearance has from its radiant beginning
never come to be; unpatterned, it has discarded patterning.
As such it is continuous and unique meditation;
it is non-mentation, stainless contemplation, and no-mind.

A n ancient scene – it must have been a morning like this…

The trees were dancing in the morning sun and the birds were singing, and the house of a great mystic of those days, Udallaka, was celebrating the return of his son, Swetketu, from the house of the master where he had been sent to study.

Swetketu comes. The father receives him at the door, but feels that something is missing; something is missing in Swetketu, and something is present which should not be present – a subtle arrogance, a subtle ego. That was the last thing the father was waiting for.

In those ancient days education was basically the education of the non-ego. A student was sent to the forest university to live with the master so that he could dissolve himself and have a taste of existence. Rumors had come that Swetketu had become a great scholar. There were rumors that he had won the greatest award. And now he had come, but Udallaka was not happy.

Yes, he had brought the greatest award that the university could have conferred. He had passed all the examinations, he had obtained the highest degree, and he had come loaded with much knowledge. But something was missing, and the father's eyes were full of tears. Swetketu could not understand it. He asked, "Is something wrong? Why are you unhappy?"

And the father asked, "One question: have you learned *that one*, by learning which everything is known, and by forgetting which all knowledge is futile, meaningless, just a burden – not a help, but a harm?"

Swetketu said, "I have learned all that was available there. I have learned history, I have learned philosophy, I have learned mathematics, I have learned the Vedas. I have learned language, I have learned art, I have learned this and that…" And he listed all the names of all the sciences of those days. But the unhappiness of his father remained the same.

He asked, "But have you learned that one, by learning which all is learned?"

The son was a little annoyed. He said, "Whatsoever my master could teach, I have learned. And whatsoever is written in the books, I have learned. What are you talking about? 'That one'…! Don't be mysterious, say it exactly. What do you mean?"

Naturally there was arrogance. He had come with the idea that now he knew all. Maybe he was thinking – as every student thinks – that now his father knew nothing. He must have come with the idea that now he had become a great knower. And there was his old father who was not happy, and he was talking about something mysterious: the one.

And the father said, "Do you see the tree yonder, over there? Go and bring a seed from that tree." It was a *nayagrod* tree. The son brought a seed from the tree, and the father asked, "Where does the tree arise from?"

And the son said, "From this small seed, of course."

"This big tree from this small seed? Break the seed and see where that tree arises from – that big tree." And the seed was broken, but there was nothing. In the seed there was emptiness. And the father asked, "Can you see that emptiness from which this big tree arises?"

And the son said, "I can infer it, but I cannot see it. How can you see nothingness?"

And the father said, "That is the one I am talking about. It is out of nothing that all comes, it is out of that creative void that all is born and one day dissolves back into. Go back and learn emptiness, go back and learn *shunya*. Go back – learn this void because this is the origin of all: the source. And the source is the goal too, the beginning is the end too. Go and learn this basic, fundamental thing. All else that you have learned is rubbish! Forget about it; it is all memory, it is all mind. Learn no-mind, learn no-memory. All that you have learned is knowledge. Learn knowing, learn awareness, learn understanding. What you have learned is objective, but you have not penetrated to your innermost core."

The world is thought to be a big tree.

These are the four steps in Tantra... The void is the first step – the void in the seed. The seed is nothing but a container of that creative void; it contains that creative void. When the seed breaks down into the earth, that void starts sprouting into a tree.

This nothingness – what physicists call no-matter – this nothingness, this *no-thingness* is the source. Out of this nothingness is born the tree. Then come flowers, fruits, and a thousand and one things. But each thing again becomes a seed and the seed falls to the earth and again becomes that voidness.

This is the circle of existence: from nothing to nothing, from nowhere to nowhere. In the middle of two nowheres is the dream, samsara. In the middle of the two nothings are all things. Hence these things are called dream-stuff; hence they are called maya; hence they are called nothing but thoughts, fantasies. This is the Tantra tree.

No-mind is the beginning of all and the end of all. Out of no-mind arises what Tantra calls "unorigination"; out of unorigination arises non-memory; out of non-memory arises memory. This is the Tantra tree.

No-mind, nothingness, means that all is potential, nothing is yet actual. All is possible, probable, but nothing has happened. Existence is fast asleep in the seed, resting – the state of rest, the state of unmanifest being. Remember it because only then will you be able to understand these sutras. These sutras are of great importance because by understanding them you can go into your own mind and search for the no-mind.

The first state: no-mind – everything is potential, nothing is actual. The second state: unorigination – still nothing has become actual, but things are getting ready to become actual. In a way it is the same as the first, but with a slight difference. In the first everything is absolutely at rest; the rest is absolute, nothing may happen for millions of years. In the second nothing has happened yet, but things are ready to happen at any moment; the potentiality is ready to explode into actuality. It is like a runner who is ready to run any moment the whistle is blown. He is on the verge, he is just standing on the line, absolutely ready; once the signal is given he will be running.

Unorigination means that nothing has originated yet, but it is ready to be born. Unorigination means the pregnant state. The child is in the womb, the child may come at any moment. Yes, it has not come yet, so in that way it is similar to the first state. But it is very, very ready; in that way it is not similar to the first state.

The third state is called non-memory. The child is born; the experience has become actual. The world has come in, but there is still no knowledge: non-memory.

Just think of the first day a child is born. He opens his eyes, he will see these green trees, but he will not be able to recognize that they are green. How can he recognize them as green? He has never known green before. He will not even be able to recognize that they are trees. He will see the trees, but he will not be able to recognize them because he has never known them before. His perception will be pure, uncontaminated by memory; hence this state is called non-memory.

This is the state Christians talk about when Adam lived in the Garden of Eden: no knowledge. He had not yet tasted the fruit of the tree of knowledge. This is the state in which every child lives early in life. For a few months the child sees, listens, touches, tastes, but no recognition arises, no memory is formed. That's why it is very difficult to remember the early days of your life. If you try to remember, you can easily go back to the fifth year. A little more effort – the fourth; a little more effort – and hard effort – and you can go back to the third. Then suddenly there is a blank, then you cannot remember. Why not? You were alive. In fact, you were so alive as you will never be so alive again. Those first three years were the most alive time of your life. Why is the memory of them not there? Why can't you penetrate into them? Because the recognition was not there. Impressions were there, but there was no recognition.

That's why Tantra calls this state non-memory. You see, but by seeing, knowledge is not created. You don't gather anything. You live moment
to moment; you slip from one moment into another without carrying the first
moment into the other. You don't have any past; each moment arises absolutely
fresh. That's why children are so alive and so fresh, and their life is so full of joy,
delight, wonder. Small things make them so happy, and small incidents make
them so tremendously excited, ecstatic. They are continuously surprised: just
a dog passing by and they are surprised. A cat comes in the room and they
are surprised. You bring a flower, and the color is tremendous. Children live in
a psychedelic world: everything is luminous. Their eyes are clear, no dust has
gathered yet; their mirror reflects perfectly. This is the state of non-memory,
the third state.

And then comes the fourth state: memory, the state of the mind. Adam
has eaten the fruit of knowledge; he has fallen, he has come into the world.
From no-mind to mind is the passage into the world. No-mind is nirvana; mind
is samsara. If you want to go back again to that original purity, that primal
innocence, that primordial purity of consciousness, then you will have to go
backwards. And these same steps will be the steps.

First, memory has to be dissolved into non-memory. Hence the insistence
of all meditations that the mind has to be dropped, thoughts have to be dropped.
Move from thought to no-thought, then from no-thought to unorigination, and
then from unorigination to no-mind – and the drop drops into the ocean. You
are again the ocean, you are again the infinite, you are again the eternal.

No-mind is eternity; mind is time.

The other day I talked about four mudras: the karma mudra, the action
gesture; the *gyana* mudra, the knowledge gesture; the *samaya* mudra, the
pure time gesture; and the *mahamudra,* the great gesture, the space gesture.
They are also connected with these four states.

The first, the karma mudra, is memory. Tantra says whatsoever you think
of as action is nothing but memory. In fact, action has never happened. It is a
dream that you have looked through, it is your projection. Action happens not,
action cannot happen in the very nature of things. Action is just a mind-dream:
you project it.

So the first, karma mudra, is exactly parallel to memory. The day you drop
memory, you go beyond action. Then, too, things happen through you, but
you are no longer the actor, you are no longer the doer of them; the ego disappears. Things flow through you, but you are not the doer of them. The trees
don't try to grow; growth happens, but they are not trying to grow. Flowers
bloom, but there is no effort involved. Rivers flow, but they are not tired. Stars
move, but they are not worried. Things are happening, but there is no doer.

The second state is the *gyana* mudra, the knowing gesture. You simply watch, you simply know, you don't do anything. Things happen, you are just a watcher; you don't become identified as a doer.

Then the third mudra is the *samaya* mudra. Then, by and by, even the knower is not needed; there is nothing to know. First action disappears, then knowledge also disappears. Then there is pure *now*-ness; time just flows in its purity. All *is*; nothing has to be done and nothing has to be known. You are a simple being; time goes on flowing by the side, you are undisturbed, unperturbed. All desire to do or to know has disappeared.

There are only two kinds of desires: the lower kind is to do something, the higher kind is to know something. The lower kind needs the body to do, the higher kind needs only the mind to know – but both are desires. Both have gone, now you sit alone. Things move, time flows, everything goes on happening, but you are neither a doer nor a knower.

And then the fourth gesture: the *mahamudra*, the great gesture. Even *you* are no more. Action dropped, knowledge dropped, even time dropped – and then you also disappear. Then there is silence. This is what silence is. What you call silence is not silence. Your silence is just a faraway reflection, a very poor silence. Sometimes you feel a little relaxed and the mind is not spinning as fast as it does ordinarily; the mind is a little relaxed, you feel silence. That's nothing.

Silence is when action has gone, knowledge has gone, time has disappeared – and you also. Finally you are gone. One day you suddenly find you are not: one day you suddenly find that everything has disappeared, nothing remains. In that nothingness – the great gesture – you are infinite.

With the first, the karma mudra, there are thoughts – and naturally, with thoughts, past and future, because thoughts are either of the past or they are of the future. With thoughts come anxiety, tension, anguish.

With the second, the *gyana* mudra, memory dissolves into non-memory: no past, no future – only now. Mind asleep, not dead yet, can wake up again. The *gyana* mudra happens so many times and is lost. That is the meaning of gaining meditation and losing it. In the second case mind is not destroyed, it simply goes to sleep. It has a little sleep, that's all; it goes into sleep. Then again it comes back, sometimes with a vengeance; comes back with tremendous energy – of course, it has rested! So after each deep meditation you will find that the mind is spinning more, has got more energy now; it has been at rest and has become more active. In the second, the *gyana* mudra, mind goes to sleep but has not disappeared yet – and you can have a little taste of no-mind for a moment. For a split second the ray enters – you are thrilled. And the taste creates trust; this is where trust arises.

Trust is not a belief; it is a taste. When you have seen this light, even for a single moment, then you can never be the same man again. You may lose it, but it will haunt you. You may not be able to get it again, but neither will you be able to forget it; it will always be there. And whenever you have time and energy, it will start knocking on your door.

This is the state that can happen very easily in the presence of a master; this is a contact-high. This second state, the *gyana* mudra, can happen in the presence of a man who has attained to the fourth stage, to no-mind.

Hence, down the ages seekers have been searching for a master. Where to get the taste from? You cannot get it through books; books will only supply belief. Where to get a living experience from? And you cannot have that living experience because you don't know what it is exactly, in what direction to move, what to do. And doubt is always there: whether it exists at all – maybe it is just the dream of a few mad people? And they *are* in a small minority – a Buddha, a Christ, a Saraha – they are a very small portion of humanity. The great majority of people live without such experiences. Who knows, these people may be mad. Who knows, these people may have a certain perversion. Who knows, these people may be cheats, frauds, they may be deceiving others. Or maybe they are not cheats: honest people, but they are themselves deceived. They may have autohypnotized themselves, they may have created a hallucination. Or maybe they have dreamed it, maybe they are dreamers – good dreamers.

There are good dreamers and bad dreamers. Bad dreamers are those whose dreams are always in black and white – flat, two-dimensional. Good dreamers are those whose dreams are in three dimensions, always colorful. These three-dimensional dreamers become poets. Do you remember ever having a dream in color? Very rarely does a person dream in color; otherwise dreams are in black and white. If you dream in color, then there is a possibility of your being a poet, a painter; otherwise not. Who knows, these mystics may be great dreamers and they dream in three dimensions, so their dream looks absolutely actual. And, naturally, they devote so much time to their dreams that it is possible they may become obsessed with the dream and the seeker doubts: "Nothing like this is really real."

This doubt persists, this doubt follows every seeker. It is natural, nothing to be worried about. How to drop this doubt? The scriptures simply say, "Drop it and believe." But *how* to drop it? You can believe, but deep down the doubt will continue.

Saint Augustine had a prayer which he used to pray every day to God: "God, I believe. I absolutely believe. But take care, have mercy on me, so the doubt does not arise again." But why? If the belief is absolute, then where does this fear arise from? Where does this prayer come from? "I believe," says Saint Augustine, "and you take care of my unbelief." But the unbelief is there. Maybe you have repressed it out of greed, out of lust for God; you may have repressed it out of lust and desire for the other world, but it is there, and it goes on gnawing at your heart. You cannot drop it unless some experience happens to you.

But how can the experience happen? The scriptures say that unless you believe the experience will not happen. Now this is a very complex phenomenon. They say that the experience will not happen unless you believe. But how can the experience happen? – because you cannot believe until the experience happens. Only experience can create belief – a belief without doubt, a doubtless trust.

This doubtless trust is possible only if you are in the presence of someone to whom it has happened. In the presence, someday, sitting silently, not knowing, not trying, not desiring, it happens. It happens like a flash of light, and your whole life is transformed. This is what is meant by conversion. You are converted, you are transformed, you have moved to a new plane.

The presence of somebody who lives higher than you has uplifted you. Unawares, in spite of yourself, you have been dragged. Once you have tasted, then there is trust. And when there is trust you can move into the third and the fourth. The presence of the master can lead you only to the second, the *gyana* mudra. Yes, he can give you a little knowing, a little taste of his being.

When Jesus was departing, he broke bread and said to his disciples, "Eat it, it is me," poured wine and said, "Drink it, this is my blood, this is me." This is very symbolic: it is a metaphor. This is the *gyana* mudra. Jesus was saying: You can have a little taste of me, you can drink me, you can eat me." Each disciple is a cannibal. He eats of the master, he absorbs the master; that's what eating means. What do you do when you eat something? You digest it, you absorb it – it becomes your blood, it becomes your bone, it becomes your marrow, it becomes your consciousness. That's what eating is.

What do you do with a master? You eat his presence, you eat his vibe, and you digest it. And, by and by, it becomes your consciousness. The day it becomes your consciousness you are a sannyasin, not before it. Before it, sannyas is formal. Before it, sannyas is just a beginning towards this phenomenon. Without being a sannyasin it will be difficult for this to happen, because with sannyas you become open and vulnerable. When you are open and vulnerable, someday, in some moment, things fall together. In some moment your energy is in such a state that the master's energy can pull it. In some moments you come very close. In some love moment, in some joy moment, in some celebration, you come close to the master, and you can be hooked. Just a glimpse, just a drop of that nectar goes down your throat, and you are converted.

Now you know. Now you know yourself, now there is no need to believe. Now, even if the whole world says that God does not exist, it does not matter: you will be able to fight against the whole world because you *know*. How can you deny your own knowledge? How can you deny your own experience?

That small drop is more powerful than the whole world.

That small drop is more potential than your whole past – millions of lives are nothing compared with that small drop.

But this can happen only when you are close. People come to me and they ask, "Why sannyas? Can't we be here without taking sannyas?" Yes, you can be here as long as you want, but you will not be close. You can sit just by my side, I can hold your hand, but that will not do. Vulnerability on your part, openness on your part...

Just a few days ago a young man was asking me, "What is the basic reason for the ochre robes, for the *mala*, for the locket? What is the rationale?"

"There is none," I told him. "It is just absurd."

He was puzzled. He said, "But if it is absurd, then why do you impose it?"

And I told him, "That's precisely why."

If I say something which is rational and you do it, that will not surrender you to me, that will not be the gesture. If something is rational and you are convinced of its rationality and then you follow it, then you are following your reason, not me. If something is rational and can be proved rationally, scientifically, and you follow it, you are not vulnerable to me, you are not available to me. That will not be of any use; you will still be following your reason. So each master down the ages has developed a few absurd things. They are simply symbolic. They simply show that yes, you are ready and you are not asking for the reason. You are ready to go with this man, and if he has some eccentric ideas, that too you allow. This loosens your head; it just makes you a little more open.

Enlightenment can happen in any color; orange is not a must, it can happen in any color. It can happen without any locket, it can happen without any *mala*. But then why? The "why" is its absurdity: the reason is that it is meaningless. It is just a gesture on your part that you are ready to go into something even if it is absurd. You are ready to go beyond your reason; that's the meaning of it.

This is a very small beginning, but small beginnings can end in big things. When the Ganges comes out of the Himalayas it is just a drip, drop: it is such a small phenomenon you can hold it in your hand. But by the time it reaches the ocean it is so vast and so huge and so enormous that it will drown you; you cannot hold it anymore.

This is a small gesture, wearing orange and the *mala* and the locket – a very absurd thing, a small gesture, the beginning of something. You love a man so much that you are ready to do something absurd for him, that's all. This makes you vulnerable to me, and you can get the measles more easily then.

Truth is infectious, and you have to be available to it. Doubt is a sort of inoculation: it protects. Reason protects. Protected, you will never move anywhere. Protected, you will only die. Protected, you are in your grave. Unprotected, you are available to existence.

To be in close proximity to a master, the phenomenon can happen one day; you are uplifted – suddenly you have wings, a little taste of the freedom and the sky. And then, afterwards, things can be done on your own.

Then the third becomes possible: the *samaya* mudra. Then you can start looking in the direction which has opened within you, and you can start moving. Now you know where to move, where to go; now you have a certain intuitive grasp of it, now you know a certain knack. Religion is not a science, religion is not an art, it is a knack. But the knack comes through taste, through experience.

The *samaya* mudra is unorigination, parallel to unorigination, *anutpanna*. Then mind is not just asleep, mind has dropped. But with the second, mind will come back; it is only asleep. With the third, mind will not come back easily, but it is still possible to bring it back. With the second it will come back, it will happen; with the *gyana* mudra it will come back on its own. With the third, the *samaya* mudra, if you want to bring it back you can bring it back, but otherwise it won't come on its own.

With the fourth, the *mahamudra*, even if you want to bring it back, it is impossible. You have gone beyond, you have transcended. This fourth stage, which is the beginning of existence, is the goal of Tantra.

Three things more, then we can enter into the sutra. From memory to non-memory you will need "awareness one." You will have to become more watchful about the thoughts, dreams, memories flicking by, moving around you. You will have to have more attention focused on thoughts. Thoughts are the objects and you will have to become aware of them. This is the first awareness: "awareness one."

Krishnamurti talks about this. He calls it "choiceless awareness." Don't choose. Whatsoever thought is passing by, don't judge; just watch it, just see that it is moving. If you go on watching, one day thoughts don't move so fast; their speed slows down. Then some day gaps start coming: one thought goes and another does not come for a long time. Then, after some time, thoughts simply disappear for hours and the road is just empty of traffic.

Ordinarily you are always in a rush hour. Thoughts are jamming in, one thought upon another, track behind track. It is not only one track, there are many tracks going on. And the man you call a thinker has more tracks than the ordinary man. If you know anything about chess, then you know that the chess-player needs a five-track mind. He has to think at least five moves ahead: if he is going to do this, then what will the other do? – Then what will he do? – Then what will the other do...? This way he has to go, at least five moves ahead. Unless he can hold these five moves in his mind he cannot be a great chess player.

The people you call thinkers have a multitrack mind, a very complex mind, and all the tracks are jammed. From every direction there is always a rush, and it is always rush hour, even in the night. When you are asleep the mind goes on and on, it goes on working. It is a twenty-four-hour worker, it does not ask for any holiday. Even God got tired after six days and had to rest on Sunday, but mind needs no Sunday. For seventy, eighty years, it goes on working and working and working. It is maddening: no rest.

You must have seen a photograph of Rodin's statue, The Thinker. In the East we laugh about the statue – so anxiety-ridden! Rodin's Thinker: you can see his head – even in the marble statue you can feel his anxiety. That is Rodin's art. You can think of how Aristotle was, or Bertrand Russell, or Friedrich Nietzsche – and there is no surprise if Nietzsche went mad. The way it is, this statue of Rodin is bound to go mad one day: thinking, thinking, thinking...

In the East we have not bothered much about thinkers; we have loved the non-thinkers. Buddha is a non-thinker, so is Mahavira, so is Saraha; these are non-thinkers. Even if they do think, they think only to move towards non-thinking. They use thinking as a jumping board for non-thinking.

The bridge from memory to non-memory is "awareness one"; it is awareness of the object. From non-memory to unorigination you will need a second awareness: that's what Gurdjieff calls "self-remembering." Krishnamurti's work is totally based on "awareness one"; Gurdjieff's work is totally based on "awareness two." With awareness one you look at the object, at the thought. You become attentive to the object. With "awareness two" you become doubly attentive – to both the object and the subject. Your arrow of consciousness is doubleheaded. On the one side you have to become aware of the thought, and on the other side you have to become aware of the thinker. Both the object and subjectivity have to be in the light of awareness. Gurdjieff's work goes deeper than Krishnamurti's. He calls it "self-remembering."

A thought is moving in your mind – for example a cloud of anger is moving. You can watch the cloud of anger without watching the watcher, then this is "awareness one." If you watch the cloud and at the same time you continuously remember who is watching – "I am watching" – then this is "awareness two," what Gurdjieff calls "self-remembering."

From memory to non-memory, awareness one will be helpful. But from non-memory you can very easily fall back again into memory because mind only goes to sleep. With the first awareness you simply tranquilize the mind, you drug the mind; the mind goes into sleep. It is a great rest and a good beginning, but not the end; necessary, but not enough.

With the second awareness, the mind falls into unorigination, *anutpanna.* Now it will be very difficult to bring it back. You *can* bring it back, but it will not come on its own. It is not impossible to bring it back, but it is not easy.

With Gurdjieff the work goes still deeper. But Tantra says that there is a third awareness: "awareness three." What is this "awareness three"? When you forget about the object and you forget about the subject and there is just pure awareness. You are not focused on anything, just a hovering pure awareness, not attentive about anything – just attentive, unfocused, unconcentrated. With the first you are concentrated on the object. With the second you are concentrated on the object and on the subject too. With the third you drop all concentration: you are simply alert. This third leads you to the state of no-mind.

Now the sutras:

> *Non-memory is convention's truth*
> *and mind which has become no-mind is ultimate truth.*

Tantra divides truth in two ways: the first it calls hypothetical truth, *vyavharika;* the second it calls ultimate truth, *parmarthika.* Hypothetical truth is called truth only for the name's sake, it is called truth because it looks like truth. It is so just in practice; it has a certain glimpse of the truth.

It is almost like this: if somebody shows you a picture of me and you say, "Yes, it is a true picture," what do you mean by a "true picture"? How can the picture be true? The statement that the picture is true simply means that it resembles the original. The picture in itself is untrue – all pictures are untrue, it is just paper. How can I be on the paper, how can I be the paper, how can I be the lines? Even a true photograph is just a photograph. But by saying, "It is a true photograph," we say that yes, it resembles the original.

I have heard one anecdote...

A very beautiful but talkative woman once came to see Pablo Picasso, and she was talking too much. Pablo Picasso was bored, but she was very rich so he could not throw her out either. She was a great customer of his paintings, so he had to listen. And she was going on and on and on.

Then finally she said, "Just the other day I saw your photograph in a friend's house. It was so alive and I loved it so much that I kissed it."

Picasso said, "Wait! Did it kiss back?"

The woman said, "What are you saying? Have you gone mad? How can a picture kiss back?"

Picasso said, "Then it was not me. It was certainly not me!"

A picture is true because it resembles. It is untrue because it is a picture. This is what Tantra calls *vyavharika* truth.

Non-memory is convention's truth... It is just so-so, it is just called truth conventionally. Memory you know; sometimes non-memory happens in the presence of a master, or while meditating or praying. But even non-memory is just a hypothetical truth; it is a photograph. Yes, it resembles the true no-mind, but only in resemblance. It is not yet the true no-mind.

To make you aware of it and to keep it in your mind, Tantra insists again and again that this has not to be taken as the goal; it is just the beginning. Many people become stuck when they attain to non-memory. When they can have a few glimpses of no-mind, they think they have arrived. It is tremendously beautiful, it is very alive; in comparison to memory it is ecstatic. But it is nothing in comparison to the real no-mind state because memory is still there, fast asleep, snoring; it can wake at any moment. Mind is still there waiting for its opportunity to come back. Yes, the traffic has stopped for a moment, but the traffic will start again.

It is good to have these glimpses because they will lead you further, but it is not good to get stuck. This is what happens through drugs: LSD, marijuana, mescaline. This is what happens, this second state, non-memory. For a moment, under the impact of the drug, memory disappears. It is a chemically enforced state: in chemical shock, memory disappears.

This is what happens through electroshock. We give electroshock to mad people whose memories have become such a burden to them that they cannot get out of it by themselves. We give them electroshock or insulin shock. Why? Because through the shock – electricity passing through their brainwaves, giving them such a shock – for a moment they become uprooted. They lose track, they forget what they were thinking, what was there. For a moment they are dazzled by the shock and when they come back they cannot recapture it. That's why electroshock helps. But electroshock or chemical shocks don't give you the real thing; they give you only a photograph.

Non-memory is convention's truth and mind which has become no-mind is the ultimate truth. So don't be contented unless you attain to no-mind, the fourth state.

This is fulfillment, says Saraha, this is the highest good.
Friends, of this highest good become aware.

This no-mind is fulfillment because you have arrived at the very source of life and existence. And, unless it happens, there is no contentment and no fulfillment. This is real flowering, this is the *sahasrar:* the one-thousand-petaled lotus has bloomed. Your life is released in fragrance and celebration and joy.

This is what godliness is. This is the highest good, the summum bonum. There is nothing higher than this. This is nirvana.

Friends, of this highest good become aware, Saraha says. Remember, there are three kinds of awareness: "awareness one" of the object, "awareness two" of the object and the subject, "awareness three," pure awareness. Go into these three stages of awareness so that you can attain the summum bonum.

And he says to the king and to the others who must have gathered to listen to this great discourse: "*Friends...*" He calls them friends; this has to be understood. From the side of the master the disciple is the friend, but not from the side of the disciple. Sometimes a few sannyasins write to me; just the other day there was a question... One sannyasin wrote, "Osho, I cannot think of you as my master, but I think of you as my friend. Is there something wrong in it?" Nothing from my side, it is perfectly okay. But something is missing from your side and you will be at a loss. Why is it so?

From the side of the master you are friends because he can see that it is only a question of time; otherwise you have already arrived. It is only a question of time and one day you will become awake. You are all buddhas. From the side of the master the whole existence is already enlightened. The rocks and the trees and the stars and the animals and the birds and men and women – the whole existence is enlightened from the side of the master. It is only a question of time, and time is irrelevant. You are all there. You don't know it, that is true, but the master knows.

The day I came to know my own self, I knew the very self of existence. Since then I have not looked at anybody as unenlightened; I cannot, it is impossible. Yes, you don't recognize the fact, but I cannot deny it. From my side you are friends; you are me. But from your side, if you think that you cannot accept me as your master and you can only think about me as a friend, then it is up to you. But know that you will miss.

What is the difference? When you accept a person as a friend, you mean that you accept him as your equal – a friend is equal to you. Yes, you are friends to me because I see that you are just equal to me, there is no difference. But if you see me as an equal to you, then your growth will stop.

When I see you as equal to me, I am raising you to my being. When you see me as equal to you, you are pulling me down to your level. Just see the difference. When I say that you are equal to me I am trying to pull you to me. When you say, "Osho, you are equal to us," you pull me to your level. Naturally you cannot pull anywhere else, you don't know any other level. And why is it difficult to accept somebody as your master? The ego: at most, the ego wants you to accept me as the friend.

It is up to you, it is your choice. If that is the way you want it to be, let it be that way – but then I am not responsible if nothing happens to you. Then it is your responsibility, utterly your responsibility, if nothing happens to you because you have created the barrier. I can flow towards you only when you look upward at me because the flow of energy is possible only downward.

I am not losing anything if you think of me as your friend. I am not losing anything even if you think of me as your enemy – that doesn't matter. You will be losing. The man who thinks that I am his enemy and the man who thinks that I am his friend both think of me in the same way. The man who thinks I am his enemy is making me equal to him, and the man who thinks I am his friend is doing the same. They are not different people. When you look upward you can be hooked by the upward energy, you can be pulled.

Saraha says: *Friends, of this highest good become aware.* From the master's side everybody is a friend. Those who think they are friends are friends; and those who think they are enemies are also friends.

> *In non-memory is mind absorbed;*
> *just this is emotionality perfect and pure.*
> *It is unpolluted by the good or bad of worldliness*
> *like a lotus unaffected by the mud from which it grows.*

In non-memory is mind absorbed... Memory watched is absorbed into non-memory. In non-memory, mind starts disappearing. And when the mind starts disappearing, there arises a new kind, a new quality of energy in you – heart energy. *...just this is emotionality perfect and pure.* Then the heart starts functioning. When the mind is dissolved, the energy that was involved in the mind becomes love. It has to become something – energy cannot be destroyed. No energy is ever destroyed, it is only transformed; it changes its form.

Mind takes almost eighty percent of your energy, giving you back nothing, returning nothing; it just goes on absorbing eighty percent of your energy. It is like a desert. The river goes on flowing and the desert goes on absorbing it, and nothing comes back. The desert does not even become green, does not even grow grass, does not even grow trees, does not even become a small pool of water – nothing! It remains dry and dead, and it goes on soaking up life energy. Mind is a great exploiter. That is where – in the desert of the mind, in the wasteland of the mind – you are lost.

Saraha says that when memory is dissolved and you attain to non-memory, suddenly your total quality changes. You become more loving; compassion arises in you. The same energy that was going into the desert moves into a fertile land. The heart is the land of fertility.

...just this is emotionality perfect and pure. It is unpolluted by the good or bad of worldliness... And in the heart there is no distinction between good and bad. The heart knows no distinctions; all distinctions belong to the mind. The heart simply loves without any distinctions. The heart simply flows without any categories, without any judgment. The heart is innocent: *It is unpolluted by the good or bad...like a lotus unaffected by the mud from which it grows.*

It grows from the same mind energy, from the same mud of thoughts, thinking, desire, lust – but it is a lotus. It grows out of the mud, but remains unpolluted by the mud.

> *Yet with certainty must all things be viewed*
> *as if they were a magic spell.*
> *If without distinction you can accept or reject samsara or nirvana,*
> *steadfast is your mind, free from the shroud of darkness.*
> *In you will be self-being, beyond thought and self-originated.*

So says Saraha to the king. He is giving him a great technique. Listen to it, meditate over it and try it.

You know well that you have dreamed millions of dreams, but in the dream, again and again, you forget that it is a dream; again it becomes reality. Tonight you are going to dream again. What kind of unconsciousness is this? Each night you dream and in the morning you find it was false. It was not there, it was just images, just imagination. Again you are a victim. Again you dream, and again you think that it is real. Why can't you see that it is unreal in the dream? What prevents you from seeing? So much experience of so many dreams and so many conclusions, and all without exception proving one thing: that dreams are not true. Again tonight you will be a victim: the dream will be there and you will think that it is true, you will live it as if it were true.

Tantra has developed a technique. The technique is: while you are awake, think of the world as a dream. For example, right now you are listening to me – think of it as a dream. It is easier to think it right now, rather than when in a dream. Many times you will listen to me in your dreams, but then it will be too difficult; you will be fast asleep. Right now it can be done more easily. Right now you can think that you are in a dream: Osho is in your dream, he is talking in your dream, these trees are dream trees, these *gulmohar* flowers are dream flowers, these birds are singing in your dream – all is just a magic spell. Think it while you are awake. Continue thinking it for at least two or three months and you will be surprised: one day, because you have practiced it, suddenly during a dream you will recognize it as a dream. And when the real trees also look like a dream through practice, what to say about unreal trees? They will look unreal.

And Tantra says that even these trees are basically just dream; they are not real stuff. What does Tantra mean by reality? Tantra means that which remains always and always. That which comes and goes is unreal. That which is born and dies is unreal. This is the definition of unreality in Tantra: that which is momentary is unreal; that which is eternal is real.

These trees were not here a few days ago and they will not be here after a few years. We were not here a few years ago and we will not be here after a few years. So this is a long dream. In the night the dream persists for only one, two, or six hours, and this dream persists for sixty years or seventy years. But just the duration of time cannot make much difference. Whether a dream is of one hour or one hundred years does not make much difference; the difference is only of duration. But both ultimately disappear.

How many people have lived on the earth, do you know? Where are they? If they had not existed, what difference would it have made? Whether they existed or not does not make much difference; they have all disappeared. That which appears and disappears is the dream.

Saraha says: *Yet with certainty must all things be viewed as if they were a magic spell.* He is giving a technique. View everything as if it were a magic spell, as if a magician has hypnotized you: all is false, and you are seeing it through hypnosis.

If without distinction you can accept or reject samsara or nirvana... If it is just a dream, then there is nothing to accept and reject. Then who bothers? You bother too much because you think it is real. Whether you are poor or rich does not make much difference. Whether you are beautiful or ugly does not make much difference. Whether you are respected or not does not make much difference. If it is just unreal, a dream world, maya, then what is there to choose? And what is there to reject? Then both acceptance and rejection drop. Then one lives purely, without entanglements, without disturbances, without in any way going off-center. Then one settles, then everything is okay.

If without distinction you can accept or reject samsara or nirvana, steadfast is your mind... Then whether you accept or reject does not make much difference. Then you can renounce the world or you can live in the world. If you know this much – that all is just a dream; if you remain in this climate that all is a dream...

Why is Saraha saying this to the king? Saraha is saying: "Sir, you live in the palace, I live in the cemetery; you live with beautiful people, I live with ordinary, ugly people; you live in richness, I live in poverty; you live in the capital, I live here at the cremation ground – but it is all the same. That palace is a dream and this cremation ground is a dream. Your beautiful queen is a dream and my arrowsmith woman is a dream. So what is the difference?"

If in the dream you become rich or you become poor, is there any difference in the morning? Do you feel very happy in the morning because you were very rich in the dream? Do you feel very unhappy in the morning because you were a beggar in the dream? It does not matter; when you are awake, it does not matter.

Saraha says, "Sir, I am awake. The third consciousness has happened; to me, all is dream – dream and all. To me, all is dream: dream within dream within dream. Now I don't make any distinction, I have gone beyond distinctions. No-mind has arisen. So whether people respect me or insult me, whether they think Saraha is a great brahmin, a great mystic, a great knower, or they think that he is a pervert, that he is mad, crazy, insane – it is perfectly okay."

This is true understanding. Then nobody's opinion can distract you. Then nothing can distract you – neither success nor failure, neither respect nor humiliation, neither life nor death. This is what the state of no-distraction is. One has come home.

Then, once mind is steadfast: ...*free from the shroud of darkness. In you will be self-being...* "I have come home," says Saraha. "My self-being has arisen, I have my center now. I have lost everything, except for one thing: my self-nature, my self-being. Now I know my origin, now I know my very source, now I know my reality ...*beyond thought and self-originated.* I have moved beyond thought. These things don't distract me, sir. Everything is okay as it is." This is the attitude of a real sannyasin: all is perfectly okay as it is.

The last sutra:

> *This world of appearance has from its radiant beginning*
> *never come to be; unpatterned, it has discarded patterning.*
> *As such it is continuous and unique meditation;*
> *it is non-mentation, stainless contemplation, and no-mind.*

This world of appearance has from its radiant beginning never come to be... Says Saraha: "This world that you are seeing has never been there; it only appears so. Just as a dream arises from nowhere and disappears back into nowhereness, so is this world."

This world of appearance has from its radiant beginning never come to be... From the very beginning nothing is – just a ripple on the silent lake, and then the ripple disappears. And you cannot catch hold of a ripple; it is just like a thought wave, just like a vibration.

...*unpatterned, it has discarded patterning.* And there is no pattern in it. It is not solid – how can it have any pattern? It is very liquid, it is very fluid; it has no pattern. Nobody knows what is good and what is bad. Nobody knows who is a saint and who is a sinner. Nobody knows what is virtue and what is sin. It is not patterned.

This is the Tantra understanding of the very core of reality: it is unpatterned. It is a creative chaos. Ultimately, finally, nothing has to be condemned and nothing has to be appreciated.

...*unpatterned, it has discarded patterning. As such, it is continuous and unique meditation...* This is a beautiful sutra. Saraha says to forget about its reality-unreality: *As such it is a continuous and unique meditation...* This existence all around, these trees, these birds, this cuckoo going mad, is continuous and unique meditation. If you can become aware of it, it can help you come home; ...*it is continuous and unique meditation...*

...*it is non-mentation...* Don't bring your mind in. Just listen to it, see it, touch it. Don't bring your mind in. ...*it is non-mentation, stainless contemplation...* Contemplate, but not through thoughts – just through transparency. Watch, look, be – not through analysis, not through logic. Relate through silence; that is "stainless contemplation." Relate through silence, relate through love. Relate: relate to this cuckoo, relate to the trees, to the sun, but don't think about them. Don't become a thinker: ...*and no-mind.*

So, first think of the world as a dream, and then think of the dreamer also as a dream. First the object is a dream, then the subject is a dream. When the subject and the object are both dropped, when the dream disappears and also the dreamer, then there is no-mind.

This no-mind is the very origin of all.

This is what Udallaka was saying to his son. He was asking, "Have you learned that one, by learning which all is learned and by forgetting which all is forgotten? Have you seen that one? Have you come to that one?"

And the son was disturbed and he said, "I have known all. But what are you talking about? My master never talked about this one."

So Udallaka said, "Then go back because all that you have brought is rubbish. Go back! In my family we have always been *real* brahmins." By real brahmin he meant: we have known Brahma, we have known the truth; we are not just brahmins by birth.

"Go back. Go back immediately!" The welcome was stopped, the music was stopped. With tears Udallaka sent his son back. He had come from the master's house after many years and was immediately sent back – not even one day's rest.

Very disturbed, the young man went back to the master. He said, "But why didn't you teach me that one my father asks about? Why? All these years wasted! And my father thinks that all of this is nonsense – I don't know *myself.* My father says, 'If you don't know yourself, of what value is all your knowing? What are we going to do with your knowing of the Vedas? You can recite the Vedas, but what are we going to do with it? And in my family,' my father says, 'We have always been *real* brahmins. Go back, and before I die become a real brahmin. Don't come back unless you have become a real brahmin.' So, sir, teach me that one."

The master laughed. He said, "That one cannot be taught. Yes, it can be caught, but it cannot be taught. That's why I had not taught it. But if you insist, then a situation can be created."

That's what all masters do: they just create a situation.

This commune is a situation. I cannot teach you truth, but I can create a situation in which you can start catching glimpses of it.

My being here is a situation, my talking to you continuously is a situation. Not that I can teach you truth by talking, but it is just a situation in which sometimes a tremor goes into you; in which sometimes you catch hold of a vibe, and it thrills you and takes you far away on a long journey inward.

So the master said, "I can create a situation. And this is the situation: gather all the cows of the ashram" – there were four hundred cows – "and take them to the deepest forest. Go away as far as you can, as far as possible, so that you are absolutely inaccessible to other human beings. Then come back only when your herd has grown to one thousand cows and bulls. It will take many years, but you go. And remember, don't see any human being. Cows will be your friends and your family; you can talk to them if you like." And Swetketu went into the deepest forest where no human being had ever entered and he lived with his cows for many years.

The story is of tremendous beauty. Naturally, what can you talk about with the cows? In the beginning he must have tried, and by and by thought that it was meaningless: the cows simply look at you, their eyes remain empty. There is no dialogue. Yes, in the beginning, just out of habit, he may have recited his Vedas, and the cows would have continued munching their grass. They would not be interested in the Vedas at all and they would not have praised him for being a great knower. He must have talked about astrology and the stars, but the cows were uninterested. What can you do with an audience of cows? By and by he stopped talking. By and by he started forgetting. By and by a great unlearning began.

Years passed. And the story says a moment came when the cows num-
bered one thousand. But by that time Swetketu had completely forgotten
about going back. He had really forgotten how to count – he had not been
counting for so many years.

The cows became very disturbed; the time had come. Then one cow dared
and she said, "Listen, now that we are one thousand, it is time. The master
must be waiting. We should go home, this is the time." So when the cows said
that it was time, Swetketu followed them.

When he came with those one thousand cows to the master's house, the
master came out to receive him and said to his other disciples, "Look at these
one thousand and one cows!"

But the disciples said, "There are only one thousand cows, and one is
Swetketu."

The master said, "He has disappeared, he is no longer there. He is a cow
– so innocent; look into his eyes."

This is the state of no-mind. And this has been the goal in the East – this
state where you are not, and in fact for the first time you are.

This state of death and this state of life, this state of the disappearance of
the ego and the false, and the appearance of the true and the authentic – this
is the state we call realization, God-realization, self-realization. This is the state
Saraha calls self-being, beyond thought, beyond mind.

Tantra means expansion. This is the state when you have expanded to
the uttermost. Your boundaries and the boundaries of existence are no longer
separate; they are the same. Less than that will not satisfy.

When you become universal, you come home.

When you become all, when you become one with all, when you are as
huge as this universe, when you contain all – when stars start moving within
you and earths are born in you and disappear – when you have this cosmic
expansion, then the work is finished.

You have come home. This is the goal of Tantra.

Enough for today.

CHAPTER 6

i am enough alone

The first question:

Osho,
What happens to my voice when you speak to me? What is the game?

When you are really in communion with me, you cannot speak. When you are really listening to me, you will lose your voice because in that moment I am your voice. The communion that happens between me and you is not between two persons. It is not a discussion, it is not a debate, it is not an argument, it is not even a dialogue. The communion happens only when you are lost, when you are not there. At the highest peak it is not even an "I-thou" relationship. It is not a relationship at all. I am not, and there comes a moment to you also when you are not. In that moment two zeros disappear into each other.

That's why, whenever you come to me, you lose your voice. And it is not happening only to you, it is happening to all those who are really coming closer to me. How can you come closer to me and still keep your voice? How can you be near me and still be yourself? Your voice is the voice of *you*. When the "you" starts disappearing, naturally the voice also starts disappearing.

Secondly, there is nothing to say. When you are in love with me, you know that if there is something to say, I will know. And if I don't know it, then it is not worth saying, then it is not needed; then it must be some irrelevant, vagrant thought. It has no need even to be uttered, it will be a sheer wastage of energy.

The mind goes on catching a thousand and one thoughts from everywhere, from all sources. Your thoughts are not yours: thoughts go on jumping from one head into another. Even without talking, even without being conveyed, thoughts are continuously jumping from one head to another head. You catch hold of them, and for a moment you are possessed by a thought and you think it is something essential. When you come to me, suddenly those thoughts that you have caught from others disappear.

It happens to many sannyasins. They come ready with many questions, and then, just sitting in front of me, they are at a loss; those questions have disappeared. It is significant, meaningful. It shows that those questions were not yours, they were not *truly* yours. When you are in front of me – really in front of me – when you are looking at me, only that which is essential will be left; the nonessential will go. Sometimes all your thoughts can disappear: not only do you lose your voice, you lose your mind too. And that is the only way to be around a master. Go on losing your mind. Hang loose, relaxed, untense. There is nothing to say. There is much to listen to but there is nothing to say.

And then, thirdly, everything is going so well with you. We only say things when things are not going well. I have heard...

A mother complained to several doctors of her five-year-old's failure to speak. Examinations yielded the fact that he was a remarkably healthy child and she was told not to worry. But worry she did. One day, in a hurry, she burned his oatmeal but served it anyway. He tasted it, spat it out, and said, "God, this stuff is awful. You must have burned it."

Delighted, she said, "You're talking! Why haven't you said anything before this?"

He looked at her with some disdain and said, "Well, everything has been alright up to now!"

And everything has been alright up to now you. There is nothing to say.

The second question:

Osho,
While in an art museum in Frankfurt recently, I entered a room with nothing but statues and carvings of Buddha. I put absolutely no faith in stone idols, but I was surprised to feel a very strong energy current in the room, similar to what I feel here listening to you. Was I imagining things? And if so, how can I trust what I feel here with you?

The first thing to be understood is that you will be surprised to know the Buddha statues have nothing to do with Gautam Buddha; they are all false. They don't resemble Buddha at all, but they have something to do with buddhahood – not with Gautam Buddha the person.

You can go into a Jaina temple and you will see twenty-four statues of twenty-four *tirthankaras,* the founders of Jainism, and you will be unable to make out any difference between them. They are all alike. To make a distinction, Jainas make small symbols on them to know who is who, because they are all alike. So if somebody's symbol is a lion figure, then just underneath the feet is a small lion figure; then they know whose statue it is. Somebody's symbol is a snake, then they know whose statue this is. If those symbols were hidden, not even a Jaina could make any demarcation: "Whose statue is this? Mahavira's? Parswanatha's? Adinatha's?" And you will also be surprised to know that they are exactly like Buddha – no difference.

When the West first became acquainted with Mahavira, they thought it was nothing but the same story as that of Buddha because the statue was the same, the philosophy was the same, the understanding was the same, the teaching was the same. So it had to be just the same thing: it was nothing different from Buddha. They thought Mahavira was another name for Buddha. And, of course, both were called Buddha because "buddha" means "the awakened one." So Buddha was called Buddha and Mahavira was also called Buddha. And both were called *jinas – jina* means the conqueror, one who has conquered himself. Buddha was called "the *jina*" and Mahavira was called "the *jina*," so they thought they were the same person. And the statues were a great proof: they look absolutely alike. They are not photographic, they don't represent a person; they represent a certain state. You will have to understand this, then the thing will be explained.

In India three words are very important: one is *tantra,* which we are talking about, another is *mantra,* and the third is *yantra. Tantra* means techniques for expanding your consciousness. *Mantra* means finding your inner sound, your inner rhythm, your inner vibration. Once you have found your mantra, it is of tremendous help: just one utterance of the mantra and you are in a totally different world. That becomes the key, the passage, because once uttering that mantra, you fall into your natural vibe. And the third is *yantra.* These statues are yantras. *Yantra* means a certain figure which can create a certain state in you. A certain figure, if you look at it, is bound to create a certain state in you.

Have you not seen? Looking at a Picasso painting you will start feeling a little uneasy. Concentrate on a Picasso painting for half an hour and you will feel very bizarre – something is going crazy. You cannot look at a Picasso painting for half an hour. If you keep Picasso paintings in your bedroom, you will have nightmares, you will have very dangerous dreams: being haunted by ghosts, tortured by Adolf Hitler and things like that; a war victim in a concentration camp – things like that.

When you look at something, it is not only that the figure is outside; when you look at something, the figure creates a certain situation in you. Gurdjieff used to call this "objective art." And you know it: listening to modern pop music, something happens in you; you become more sexually excited. There is nothing but sound outside, but the sound hits inside, creates something in you. Listening to classical music you become less sexual, less excited. In fact, with great classical music you almost forget sex; you are in a tranquility, a silence, a totally different dimension of your being. You exist on another plane.

Looking at a Buddha statue is looking at a yantra. The figure of the statue, the geometry of the statue, creates a figure inside you. And that inside figure creates a certain vibe. It was not just imagination that happened to you in the Frankfurt museum; those Buddha statues created a certain vibe in you.

Look at the statue of Buddha sitting so silently in a certain yoga posture: if you go on looking at the statue, you will find something like that is happening within you too. If you are in the company of ten persons who are sad and you are the eleventh person, how long can you remain happy? Those ten persons will function like a yantra, a yantra of sadness; you will fall into sadness sooner or later. If you are unhappy and you are in company with people are joking and laughing, how long can you remain sad? Those laughing people will create laughter in you. They will change your focus, they will change your gear; you will start moving in a different direction. This happens every day – knowingly, unknowingly.

When you see a full moon, what happens to you? Or when you listen to the birds and look at the green trees, what happens to you? When you go into a forest and look at the greenery, what happens to you? Something green inside starts happening. Green is the color of nature, green is the color of spontaneity, green is the color of life; something green starts happening in you. The outer color reflects something inside, vibrates with something inside, creates something inside. Looking at a green tree you become more alive – you become younger!

When you go to the Himalayas and you see the mountains, the snow-capped mountains – eternal snow which has never melted, the purest snow where no man has ever walked, uncontaminated by human society and human touch – when you look at a Himalayan peak, that uncorrupted, virgin snow creates something virgin in you. A subtle peace starts happening inside.

The outer is not just the outer and the inner is not just the inner, they are joined together. So beware what you look at, beware what you listen to, beware what you read, beware where you go – because all that creates you.

That's what happened in Frankfurt. The Buddha statues, the many statues all around you, created a subtle geometry. You will be surprised – that is the basic reason why the statues were created; they are not idols, as you think. The Christian and the Mohammedan and the Judaic idea has given a very wrong notion to the world. Statues are not idols; they are very scientific. They are not objects to be worshipped; they are geometries to be imbibed. It is a totally different thing.

In China there is one Buddha temple which has ten thousand Buddha statues – all Buddha statues; wherever you look, the same figure. The ceiling has the same figure, all the sides have the same figure, the walls have the same figure. Ten thousand Buddha statues! Just think, sitting cross-legged in a Buddha posture and you are also surrounded by ten thousand Buddhas! It creates a geometry. From everywhere Buddha impinges upon you. From every nook and corner he starts surrounding you. You are gone; your ordinary geometry is no longer there, your ordinary life is no longer there. For a few moments you are moving on higher planes, at higher altitudes.

That's what is happening here. While listening to me something is created by my presence, by my words, by your attitude, by so many people dressed in orange around you. It is a situation, it is a temple. A temple is a situation; it is not just that you are sitting in a lecture hall. So many people listening to me with such love, gratitude, with such silence, with such sympathy, with such rapport – this place becomes holy. This place becomes a *tirtha;* it is sacred. When you come into this place, you are riding on a wave; you need not make much effort. You can simply allow it to happen. You will be taken away, far away to the other shore.

A marriage broker arranged with a family to bring over a girl he thought would be a fine match for their son. After dinner the girl left and the family began to attack the marriage broker.

"What kind of a girl did you bring? A monster! One eye in the middle of her forehead, the left ear way up here, the right ear way down there and the chin way back!"

The marriage broker interrupted. "Look, either you like Picasso or you don't!"

Modern painting represents the ugly in existence. The ugly has become predominant for a certain reason. This century is one of the ugliest centuries: two world wars within fifty years, millions of people killed, destroyed: such cruelty, such aggression, such violence, such madness. This century is a nightmarish century. Man has lost track of his humanity. What man has been doing to man! Naturally this madness has erupted everywhere – in painting, in music, in sculpture, in architecture – everywhere the ugly human mind has created ugliness.

Ugliness has become an aesthetic value. Now the photographer goes and looks for something ugly. Not that beauty has stopped existing; it exists as much as before, but it is neglected. The cactus has replaced the rose. Not that the cactus is something new; it has existed always, but this century has come to know that thorns seem to be more real than a roseflower. A roseflower seems to be a dream; it does not fit with us, hence the roseflower has been expelled. The cactus has entered your drawing room. Just one hundred years ago nobody would have ever thought to bring a cactus home. Now if you are modern, your garden will be full of cactuses. The rose looks a little bourgeois; the rose looks a little out-of-date; the rose looks Tory, orthodox, traditional. The cactus looks revolutionary. Yes, the cactus is revolutionary – like Adolf Hitler and Josef Stalin and Mao Zedong and Fidel Castro. Yes, the cactus seems to be closer to this century.

The photographer looks for some ugly thing; he will go and photograph a beggar. Not that the beggar has not existed before – he *has* existed before; he is real, certainly real, but nobody has been making art out of him. We are feeling humble before the beggar, we are feeling apologetic before the beggar, we are feeling that something which should not be is still there; we want the beggar not to be there. But this century goes on searching for the ugly.

Still the sun penetrates the pines on a certain morning. The rays penetrating the pines create such a web of beauty – it still exists; but no photographer is interested, it no longer appeals. Ugliness appeals because we have become ugly. That which appeals to us shows something about us.

Buddha is a roseflower, the highest possibility. And remember, it is not exactly a Buddha figure; nobody knows what Buddha looked like. But that is not the point. We were not interested in those days – at least not in the East – we were not interested in the real at all, we were interested in the ultimately real. We were not interested in the factual, we were interested in truth itself.

Maybe Buddha had a little longer nose, but if the artist thought that a little smaller nose would be more in tune with meditation, then he dropped that long nose of Buddha, he made it a little smaller. Maybe Buddha had a big belly, who knows? Japanese Buddha statues have big bellies, but Indian Buddhas don't have big bellies – different attitudes.

In Japan they think that a meditator has to breathe from the belly, from the navel. And when you breathe from the belly, the belly of course becomes a little bigger. Then the chest is not as protruding as the belly, the chest is relaxed. So Japanese Buddhas have big bellies. That too is for a certain reason: to indicate to you that belly-breathing is the right breathing. It has nothing to do with Buddha; nobody knows whether he had a big belly or not.

Indian statues don't have big bellies because Indian Yoga does not insist on belly-breathing: the belly has to be in. That too has a certain different reason. If you want the sexual energy to move upward, then it is better not to belly-breathe. When the belly is pulled in, the energy is sucked upward more easily – different techniques.

Belly-breathing is also good for a certain meditator; it is very relaxing. But then the energy cannot move in the same way as it moves when the belly is pulled in. The Indian statues of Buddha have small bellies – almost no bellies. Nobody knows exactly how Buddha looked. The statues are very feminine, very round; they don't look masculine.

Have you ever seen any statue with a mustache and beard? – no. The people who painted Jesus were more realistic. The people who painted Buddha were not concerned with facticity, they were concerned with ultimate truth. They were not concerned how Buddha looked, they were concerned how buddhas should look. The emphasis was not on Buddha but on the people who would be looking at these statues – how the statue was going to help those people.

So Buddha is not painted as old. He must have become old, he became eighty-two – he was very old, certainly, very old and ill. A physician had to follow him continuously. But no statue has painted him as old, ill, because that is not the point. We are not interested in the physical body of Buddha, we are interested in his inner geometry; that inner quality of Buddha is always young, it is never old. And it is never ill, it is always in a state of wellbeing; by its very nature it cannot be ill. The body is young, the body is old, the body becomes crippled, the body dies. Buddha is not born, never dies; Buddha remains eternally young. Looking at a young statue, something of youth will happen in you and you will feel something fresh.

Now, Indians would never have preferred Jesus to be pictured, painted, sculptured on the cross. It is ugly, it is sad. Even if it is historical it is not worth remembering because whatsoever you think has happened, you tend to help it happen again. There is no obligation towards facts: we don't owe anything to the past, we need not remember the past as it was. It is in our hands to choose the past – to choose the past in such a way that a better future can be created.

Yes, Jesus was crucified, but if he had been crucified in India, we would not have painted that. Even on the cross we would have painted a totally different thing. The Western painting is of Jesus in anguish, in sadness – naturally, he is being killed. When you look at, when you concentrate, meditate, on Jesus, you will feel sad.

It is not accidental that Christians say that Jesus never laughed. And it is not accidental that you are not allowed to dance and laugh and be gay in a church. Church is a serious affair: you have to be very serious – long faces. In fact when Jesus is being crucified just there on the altar, how can you laugh and sing? In India you can sing and laugh and enjoy. Religion is a merriment, a celebration.

The whole point is that the Western mind is historical, the Eastern mind is existential. The West pays too much attention to mundane facts, the East never pays any attention to history. You will be surprised to know that until Western people came to India, India had not known anything like history. We have never written history, we have never bothered about it. That's why we don't know when exactly Buddha was born, when exactly he died. We have never paid much respect to facts. Facts are mundane: what does it matter whether he was born on Monday or Tuesday or Thursday? What does it matter, how does it matter? In fact it does not matter at all; any day will do and any year will do. That is not the point. The point is: *who* was born? Who was this man in his innermost core?

History thinks about the periphery, myth thinks about the innermost core. India has written mythology, but not history. We have puranas; puranas are mythology, they are not histories. They are poetic, mystic visions of how things should be, not how they are. They are the vision of the ultimate. And Buddha is the vision of ultimate *samadhi.*

Those Buddha statues you saw in the Frankfurt museum are the states of inner silence. When a person is absolutely silent, he will be in that state. When everything is still and quiet and calm inside – not a thought moves, not a small breeze blows; when everything has stopped, time has stopped – then you will also feel to sit like a buddha. Something of the same geometry will happen to you. It is objective art – less concerned with the reality of Buddha, more concerned with those people who will be coming and will be seeking buddhahood. The emphasis is different: it is on what will happen to those who will watch these statues and will kneel down before these statues and will meditate on these statues.

In India there are temples like Khajuraho where all sorts of sexual postures are sculptured. Many postures are so absurd that even a de Sade or a von Sacher-Masoch would not be able to imagine them. The most perverted person also could not imagine them. For example, a man and woman standing on their heads and making love – it does not seem that anybody is going to try or imagine it. Why did they paint these pictures? They are examples of objective art.

These temples of Khajuraho were no ordinary temples; they were a kind of therapy, they exist as a therapy. Whenever somebody was suffering from some sexual perversion he was sent to Khajuraho. He had to look at and meditate on all those abnormal, bizarre things. He had something perverted in his mind; that perversion was inside the unconscious. What does psychoanalysis do? It tries to bring things from the unconscious to the conscious, that's all. And psychoanalysis says that once something comes from the unconscious to the conscious it is released, you are free of it.

Now, this was a great psychoanalysis, this Khajuraho. An abnormally per-verted man is brought there. He has repressed his perversions – sometimes they erupt, but he goes on repressing. He knows that something is there like a wound, but he has never been able to see it face to face. He is brought to Khajuraho. He moves slowly, meditating on each statue, each bizarre posture. And one day, suddenly, one posture fits with his inner perversion. Suddenly, from the unconscious, the perversion surfaces to the conscious, and it is released without any Freud or Jung or Adler there – just the temple will do. He is left in the temple. For a few weeks he can be there. For each meditator who really wanted to go into deep meditation in those days, it was good to visit a temple like Khajuraho.

On the walls of the temple are all those statues – very abnormal, very crazy, very perverted. Inside the temple there is no sexual painting, no sexual statue at all, no sexuality at all. Inside is either Buddha's statue, Shiva's statue or Krishna's statue.

What is the meaning of it? Why sex on the wall just outside, and inside no sex? It is a technique. First you have to move on the periphery so that you can become free of sex. When a person feels that now those sexual statues don't attract him at all – now he goes on sitting before them and nothing hap-pens inside, he remains calm and quiet, no sexual arousal, no excitement; for weeks he waits, and no sexuality is felt – then he is capable of entering the temple.

It is symbolic. Now his sexuality can go beyond. Those temples were Tantra temples, one of the greatest experiments ever done. They are not obscene, they are not pornographic, they are spiritual – a great experiment in spiritual-ity, a great experiment in transforming human energy towards higher levels.

But first the energy has to be freed from the lower level. And to free it there is only one way: to make it absolutely conscious, to bring all the fantasies of the unconscious mind to the conscious. When the unconscious is completely unburdened, you are free. Then you don't have any blocks, then you can move inward. Then you can go inside the temple, then you can meditate on Buddha, on Shiva, or Krishna.

It was not imagination, it was objective art which you stumbled upon unknowingly.

The third question:

Osho,
What do you have that I haven't got? (And I'm not talking about the ashram and car and secretary and all that stuff.)

You must be talking about "all that stuff," otherwise why do you mention it at all? The very mentioning of it shows the mind. You must have been afraid, the idea must have crossed your mind. And as for myself, I don't have any ashram, and I don't have any car, and I don't have any secretary; in fact, I don't have anything. Having is not the thing, but being. I am just here; being is my wealth, not having. If the ashram is here, it is for you, not for me. If a secretary is there, it is for you, not for me. All that exists here is for you. It does not have anything to do with me.

I am enough alone.

But somewhere deep in your mind you must be too attached to things. When you formulate a question, remember, it shows much about you. A question is not only a question, it is very symbolic also.

Several men in the smoking room were arguing as to who was the greatest inventor. One contended for Stevenson, who invented the railroad, another for Edison, another for Marconi, still another for the Wright brothers. Finally one of them turned to a small man who had been listening but who had said nothing. "What do you think, Mr. Mandel?"

"Well," came the reply with a knowing smile, "the man who invented 'interest' was nobody's fool."

And the Jew is hidden in everybody; the Jew goes on thinking only of money, interest, things, having.

The first thing: change your focus from having to being. You can have the whole world and it is not going to help; you will remain a beggar. And I am not saying renounce the world, mind you. I am not saying renounce the world – don't jump to the opposite conclusion. I am saying you can have the whole world and you will not have anything, that's all I am saying. I am not saying renounce it because the minds of those who renounce also remain focused on having. You count money, they also count money. You say, "I have got this many thousand dollars"; they say, "I have renounced that many thousand dollars" – but the counting continues. You are a bookkeeper and they are also bookkeepers. And bookkeeping is the world.

To know who you are is to become an emperor. To *be* is to be an emperor. To *have* is to be poor.

There are two kinds of poor men in the world: those who have and those who have not. But both are poor because those who have, have nothing, and those who have not, of course, have not got anything. Both are poor. Those who have are puzzled: "What to do with it now?" They are stuck with it; they have wasted their whole life in having it, now it is there and they don't know what to do with it. It has not satisfied anything, it has not brought any fulfillment, it has not brought any flowering. They have not come to celebrate life yet. Godliness has not happened through it. It never happens through having.

You ask: "What do you have that I haven't got?" If you insist on speaking in terms of having, then you have got more than I have got. You have got infinitely more: greed, anger, lust, ambition, ego – and a thousand and one things.

What I have got? – just nothing. Exactly, just nothing. If you think from the viewpoint of having, then I am the poorest man because I have got just nothing. But if you think from the viewpoint of being, then I am the richest man – because once you drop ego you don't lose anything, you only lose a disease. When you drop greed you don't lose anything, you only lose a disease. When you drop anger you don't lose anything, you gain. Each time you drop things like this which you have, you become richer.

When greed disappears, sharing comes into existence. When anger disappears, compassion comes into existence. When hate, jealousy, possessiveness disappear, love comes into being.

I have got only myself. But that self expresses itself in many, many dimensions – in sharing, in love, in compassion. So I can say you have more, much more, and yet I will say *you* are not yet. I am, and you are not.

The fourth question:

Osho,
What do you mean when you say that man is a machine?

That man is a machine! Three scenes – the first...

"Hello, Bernie old pal!" greeted Charlie, somewhat potted. "Let's go into a bar and celebrate the cigar habit."

"What are you talking about?" asked Bernie.

"Listen," Charlie went on, "My wife wanted me to stop smoking. And her system is, when I feel like a cigar to get an *O Henry!* candy bar instead."

"Did you do that?" Bernie inquired.

"Yeah! And that's why I am celebrating. I'm back on cigars – that candy bar idea doesn't work. Believe me, I tried it. Every time I wanted a cigar I bought an *O Henry!* candy bar. But you want to know something? I couldn't keep it lit!"

When I say that man is a machine, I mean man functions through habits, not through awareness. When I say that man is a machine, I mean man functions through his past, not through his spontaneity.

The second scene...

A night worker had let his whiskers grow until his favorite baseball team won the pennant, much to the disgust of his young and pretty wife.

On the day his team clinched the pennant he laid off work, got himself a shave, went home early, and slipped into bed. In the darkness he took his wife's hand and placed it upon his smoothly shaven face.

She turned slightly while running her fingers over the now smooth chin, and said, "Make it snappy, kid! Old Whiskers will be home any minute now."

When I say that man is a machine, I mean man does not see what is the case, man does not look into the present moment, man is not responsive to reality. Man goes on living in old ideas, man lives through habits.

The third scene...

One day Mulla Nasruddin read a small poem in a magazine. He loved it. The poem was:

> *Sir, Why not buy a bunch or two*
> *Of springtime flowers fair?*
> *And take them home one cheerless day,*
> *But carry them with care.*
> *Just hand them to your wife and say,*
> *"I thought of you in town today."*

Mulla Nasruddin did exactly that. He bought some flowers, but instead of entering the house as usual, he knocked. And when his wife opened the door, he just handed them to her. To his great surprise she burst out crying. "Why, whatever is the matter?" he asked.

"Oh," she replied, "I've had an awful day. I broke the teapot, the baby has been crying, the cook has left, and now you come home drunk!"

That's what I mean when I say that man is a machine. And you don't become aware of it, because how can a machine become aware? You need somebody to hammer on your head continuously, in the hope that sometime the hammer will really hit you, shock you out of your habits, and for a moment you will be awake.

That's the whole purpose of a master: to go on hitting you from this side, from that side, from all the sides, and to go on changing techniques, situations, devices so that some day you are caught unawares.

If even for a single moment you become aware, you will know that your whole past has been a mechanical past. You will know only then – but not by my saying it – that man is a machine. You will know only then, when you have tasted one moment of awareness. Then your whole life will be simply known, seen, recognized as mechanical. Because even to know that it has been mechanical, you need something to compare it with. You don't have anything to compare it with; you live among machines. Your father is a machine, your mother is a machine, your wife is a machine, your friends, your boss – you live among machines. You are a machine. How to become aware?

Once Mulla Nasruddin's wife told me that she had not been aware that her husband was drinking until he came home sober one night. If a man is con-tinuously drinking it is very difficult to know that he is drinking; you become accustomed to seeing him in that way.

You are a machine. It hurts – that's the purpose of calling you a machine. Let it hurt. If it doesn't hurt, then you are incurable. If it hurts, then there is a possibility. If it hurts, it means that somehow, deep down in the unconscious, you also feel that yes, it is so.

Do you live in the present moment? Do you recognize things as they are right now? Or do you just go on seeing them through old eyes, old mind, memory? Don't you have clichés? You immediately put things into certain boxes, readymade boxes. For example, you are a Hindu and you meet a man and you were very interested in the man – the man looks beautiful and is very nice and you like his vibe. Then you ask him about himself and he says, "I am a Mohammedan." Finished. All that nice vibe is no longer there: you have shrunken back. You have a box, a fixed box, that Mohammedans are not good. You are a Hindu: Mohammedans are bad. You immediately categorize him, you pigeonhole him. Now you are no longer interested in the reality of the man. The reality was saying something else, but it was going against your pat categories and theories.

I have heard…

A young woman went to the big town nearby to work there. They were very poor and the mother was old, and as the young woman was the only child she had who had gone to work to earn some money. After a few months she came back with lots of money. The mother was very happy. She asked, "So now, tell me, what did you do there?"

The daughter was really honest and replied, "I have become a prostitute."

"What!" the mother screamed – and fainted. When she came to after half an hour the mother again asked, "Tell me again what you have become?"

And the daughter said, "I told you, mother, that I have become a prostitute."

The mother said, "Thank God! I thought you said you had become a Protestant!"

They were Catholics, of course.

Categorization goes on continuously in the mind. Watch: when you do something, do you respond to the fact herenow, or do you follow certain pat theories? When you do something, do you do it with attention, awareness, or do you just do it like a robot?

I talked the other day about three awarenesses: awareness one, awareness two, awareness three. This is the first awareness: to watch yourself, to watch your actions, to watch your reactions, to watch your responses. How are you behaving – as a man or as a machine? And out of one hundred, ninety-nine times you will find that you are behaving like a machine. But if you start becoming a little alert, then you are becoming something more than a machine; the plus point is arising in you. That awareness will help you to become man. Only when you are aware are you man. Fully aware, you are fully man. Fully unaware, you are a machine.

The fifth question:

Osho,
Since I have been here, everything I have wished for has happened for me. Now I have all I could possibly want and I feel like my heart is breaking. What is happening?

You have misunderstood. The heart is breaking out of joy, the heart is breaking out of delight, sheer delight. In a certain moment joy becomes unbearable. When joy is unbearable, then you are really joyful. Then joy is at the pinnacle, then joy is at the hundred-degree point. If you can bear this much joy, sooner or later you will start evaporating through this joy, you will start disappearing into the divine. Don't be afraid, nothing wrong is happening to you; you are blessed.

But it happens, our ideas... If you see somebody crying, you think that he is sad, he must be in misery. You start consoling. Have you heard the expression "tears of joy"? There are tears of joy too. So don't be in a hurry to console – maybe he is just being joyful. But we only know of people crying when they are unhappy; we don't know of people crying when they are happy because people are not happy at all. So tears of joy are only in poems, found in poems – not in the eyes.

But tears have nothing to do with sadness. It is an ugly state of humanity, a sad state of affairs, that men cry and weep only when they are sad, miserable. Tears have nothing to do with misery as such, tears come only when something is overflowing. It may be sadness, it may be joy, it may be love, it may be anger. You can watch women: when they become too angry they start crying. It is anger, not sadness. Watch a small child: if he laughs too much he starts crying. It is too much, unbearable; he starts overflowing into tears. Tears are just an indication that the cup is overfull – they start overflowing.

You say: "Since I have been here everything I have wished for has happened to me..." That's why the joy is becoming unbearable; you are coming closer to home. "Now I have all I could possibly want and I feel like my heart is breaking. What is happening?" Something tremendously beautiful is happening. Don't try to analyze it and don't try to think about it. Don't try to interpret it, otherwise the mind can destroy the whole thing. It is mind trying to interfere with the heart. This question is from the mind. The heart is overfull with joy, that's why it is breaking; it cannot contain it, the joy is too much. Let it break. That's what I am here for, that's why you have come to me.

Let it break, let it go into pieces. Out of joy, let it explode. Let it disappear into infinity.

The sixth question:

Osho,
Why am I always afraid of others' opinions?

Because you are not; because you are not yet. You are nothing but a piled-up phenomenon of others' opinions. Who are you? Somebody says you are beautiful so you are beautiful, and somebody says you are ugly so you are ugly, and somebody says you are wonderful so you are wonderful. And somebody says, "I have never seen such a nasty person," so you are a nasty person.

People go on saying, and you go on collecting all these things, and that is your image. That's why your image is very contradictory, ambiguous: one person says you are beautiful, another says you are ugly. You want to forget this person's idea that you are ugly, but you cannot forget it; it will be there. If you keep the opinion that you are beautiful you will have to keep the opinion that you are ugly too.

Your image is very ambiguous, you don't know exactly who you are. You are a hodgepodge, what we in India call a kedgeree, a mixture of so many things. You don't have a soul yet. You don't have any individuality, you don't have any integrated center, you are just a junkyard of others' opinions. That's why you are afraid, because if others' opinions change, you change; you are in the grip of *their* hands.

And this is the trick society has used to rule over you. Society has a technique: it makes you very ambitious for social respect. Through it, it manipulates you. If you follow the rules of society, it respects you; if you don't follow the rules of society, it insults you tremendously, it hurts you very badly. And to follow the rules of society is to become a slave. Yes, society pays you great respect for being a slave, but if you want to be a free man the society becomes angry, it does not want to have anything to do with you.

To really be a free man and to exist in any society is very difficult. And I say it to you from my own experience. It is almost impossible to exist because the society does not want any free man. The free man is a danger to the society's existence. The society likes zombies, machines, robots – always ready just to fall anywhere into a queue. Just call loudly to them, "Attention!" and they start falling in line just mechanically. They don't ask why, they are imitators.

And the society pays them well: it gives them respect, it gives them prizes, awards, honors – it has to, this is the trick. It never gives any award to those who are free; it never honors them. How can it honor them? – they are enemies. A free man is an enemy in an unfree society, a moral man is an enemy in an immoral society, a religious man is an enemy in an irreligious society. In a world of materialism a spiritual man is always in difficulty: he does not fit in anywhere.

To fit in with others the society gives you as much as you want; it gives you a good image, it buttresses you. But if you don't listen, then it starts changing its opinion. It can demolish you within seconds because your image is in social hands. So this is the first thing to be understood.

You ask: "Why am I always afraid of others' opinions?" Because you are not yet, you are nothing *but* others' opinions, hence the fear: they can take back their opinions. The priest has said that you are a very good man. Now, if you behave, you will remain a good man. If you don't behave according to him – and he may be himself a neurotic, but you have to behave according to him – if you don't behave, if you do something on your own, the priest will look at you and say, "Now you are going against morality, you are going against religion, you are going against tradition. You are falling into sin." He will change his opinion of you – and you were "good" because of his opinion.

Be yourself. Nobody can make you good and nobody can make you bad. Except yourself, nobody can make you good and nobody can make you bad. These false images are just living in dreams.

A man was told by his doctor, "You are going to make medical history, man. You are the only male ever recorded who has become pregnant!"

The man replied, "This is terrible! Whatever will the neighbors say? I am not even married."

Now, he is not interested in history and in setting a medical record, he is worried about what the neighbors will say because he is not even married.

We are continuously afraid. This fear will continue if you don't drop collecting opinions. Drop them – *all* opinions. Somebody believes that you are a saint? Drop it because he is dangerous; he will manipulate you through his idea. Once you listen to him and you believe him, he becomes the master and you become the slave.

Sometimes people come to me and say, "You are a great saint." I say, "Sorry, excuse me. Never utter such a word to me because I am not going to be manipulated by anybody. I am just myself – saint or sinner, that doesn't matter." The man is thinking that he is trying to praise me. Maybe he is not even aware of what he is doing. Whenever you praise a person you become powerful. Whenever you praise a person and he accepts your praise, he has fallen a victim. Now you will control him. Now whenever he wants to do something, any innocent thing…

Just think: you call a certain man a saint, a mahatma, a great sage. Now, one day he wants to smoke – what to do? He cannot smoke because what will happen to his sainthood? Now, it seems too much to pay with sainthood just for a smoke; he cannot smoke because so many people call him a saint. Or he will become a hypocrite. He may start smoking behind the door and he will not say that he smokes, and he will condemn smoking like anything when he is in public. Then he will have two faces, the public and the private. Then he will be split.

Never accept others' opinions, good or bad. Just tell them, "Sorry. Please keep your opinion to yourself. I am myself." If you can remain that alert, nobody will ever be able to manipulate you, you will remain free. And freedom is joy. Freedom is difficult, remember, because society consists of slaves.

Freedom is difficult, but freedom is the only joy there is. Freedom is the only dance there is, and freedom is the only door towards godliness. A slave never reaches to godliness, he cannot.

The seventh question:

Osho,
It has been said that the English make the best servants in the world. When you gave me my name you translated it as "in service of love." I know now that it can also be translated as "the servant of love." I have wondered about this. Sometimes it seems that I am most in service of love when I am most myself and not intending to serve. Otherwise it seems more like subservience and that I am suffering from the English cultural disease of politeness, servility and helpfulness. Will you please comment?

The question is from Prem Dasi. *Prem Dasi* actually means "the servant of love." But while giving sannyas to her, I had knowingly translated it as "in service of love." The exact translation is "the servant of love." I translated it as "in service of love" for a certain reason.

I would like you to become more and more serving, but I would not like you to become servants. Servants don't serve, only masters serve; servants do their duty. *Duty* is a four-letter, ugly word. They have to do it; there is no beauty in it, there is no joy in it. So be in service, but never be a servant; that is one thing.

The second thing: when you become a servant you learn habits, but service is an ongoing process. To become a servant is to attain to a character, a dead character. People know you are a public servant, people know that that man is a servant. A man in service is totally different, he is not predictable. He will choose to respond each moment. You cannot depend on him, on his past. That's why I translated it into "in service of love." Service is beautiful, but to be a servant is not good. Service is spontaneous.

For example, you are passing on a road, and you find a house is on fire and you rush into it, and you save a child who was going to die. But you don't *have* to do it; you were not in search of some public service. You were just going for a morning walk and the house was on fire. You were not thinking about it at all – it was just the situation and the response: you are in service. But a servant is dangerous because if he cannot find somebody to serve, he will force somebody to be served.

I have heard about a Christian missionary who was teaching his students, the Sunday school students, small boys and girls. He was telling them to do one good thing, one good work, at least once a week. Next Sunday he inquired whether they had done any good job, if they done any public service, if they been of some help to somebody. Three boys stood up, and he was very happy. Out of thirty, at least three – but that too is a great percentage, because who listens?

So he asked the first boy, "What did you do? Tell the whole class."

And the boy said "Sir, I helped an old woman to cross the road."

The missionary said, "Very good. Always take care of old women."

And then he asked another boy, and the boy replied, "I also helped an old woman to cross the street."

Then the priest was a little puzzled, but he saw nothing to be puzzled about as there are so many old women; maybe the second boy also found a woman.

So he asked the third, and the third said, "I also helped an old woman to cross the street."

Then the priest said, "But this seems too much – you all three got old women?"

They answered, "No, there were not three, there was one. Only one woman was there – we all three helped."

So the priest said, "But three were needed? You are saying three were needed?"

"Even with six it would have been difficult because she didn't want to go to the other side. It was very difficult, sir, but we did it, because something was to be done! She was very angry!"

Never be a servant, otherwise you will be in search... And if you cannot find some place to serve, you will be very angry. The public servants are there all over the world; they are the most mischievous people. They create much mischief because when people don't want to be served, then too they force their service. They have to force, they have an investment there. They cannot allow a beautiful world to exist because what will happen to them?

Just think: no lepers left, no ill people left, no hospitals needed. And all have become enlightened – no schools, no colleges and no universities needed. What will happen to the public servants? They will start committing suicide. Nobody to serve! They need, they will manage somehow to create a situation where they can be of service; their whole prestige depends on it. It is an ego trip.

That's why, knowing well... I remember exactly when I gave sannyas to Prem Dasi: I was just going to translate it as "the servant of love," then I thought it would be wrong. The word means that, but I changed it and I told her "in service of love."

Be in service, but don't make service your character. I love people who live characterlessly, who live moment to moment, who just respond to situations. Otherwise you will be in bondage.

And you are right, Prem Dasi. You say: "I am most in service of love when I am most myself and not intending to serve." Perfectly true. It's how it is. When you intend to serve, it is no longer beautiful, it is no longer love. When you are yourself – utterly yourself – out of that independence, out of that being, love arises and you serve people. And there is no feeling that you are a servant and they are masters. You simply serve because you have so much to give that you have to share. You flow in your sharing, in your love, in your compassion.

The last question:

Osho,
Can prayer be sometimes harmful?

Never heard of it, except in one case. This is the story...

Two girls married on the same day and took their new husbands to the same honeymoon hotel. The four of them sat in the lounge, thinking how obvious it would look if they all went to bed at the same early hour. But after a while it was decided that the girls should go out in the direction of the "Ladies" and then slip up to their rooms, and the men would have a last drink at the bar. After about ten or fifteen minutes the men would leave casually in the same manner and join the brides.

However, just as they were about to follow the girls, every light in the place failed – which was disconcerting in a strange building. Nevertheless, each was convinced he could find his room, and so they set off.

Harry groped upstairs and along the passages, counting doors in his careful way – for he was a very careful man – and found the room. Just to make sure, he struck a match and saw bits of confetti on the landing. Then quietly entering, he carefully took off his clothes, put on his pajamas, knelt down and said his prayers, climbed into bed and began to make love.

At that very moment all the lights came on and he saw that he was in the "right" room as it were, but on the wrong floor, and this was the other man's bride! He grabbed his clothes and hurried off to his own room – only to find that the other man was an atheist!

Enough for today.

CHAPTER 7

intelligence is meditation

Mind, intellect, and the formed contents of that mind are It,
so too are the world and all that seems from It to differ,
all things that can be sensed, and the perceiver,
also dullness, aversion, desire and enlightenment.

Like a lamp that shines in the darkness of spiritual unknowing,
it removes obscurations of a mind
as far as the fragmentations of intellect obtain.
Who can imagine the self-being of desirelessness?

There's nothing to be negated, nothing to be
affirmed or grasped; for It can never be conceived.
By the fragmentations of the intellect are the deluded fettered;
undivided and pure remains spontaneity.

If you question ultimacy with the postulates of the many and the one,
oneness is not given, for by transcending knowledge
are sentient beings freed.
The radiant is potency latent in the intellect, and this
is shown to be meditation; unswerving Mind is our true essence.

The Tantra vision is a direct approach towards God, towards reality, towards that which is. It has no mediators, no middlemen, it has no priests. Tantra says the moment the priest enters, religion is corrupted. It is not the Devil who corrupts religion, it is the priest. The priest is in the service of the Devil.

God can only be approached directly. There is no via media. You cannot go via somebody else because God is immediacy, God is herenow, already surrounding you. Within, without, only God is.

There is no need to find somebody to help you to find God. You are already in it, you have never been away from it. Even if you want to, you cannot be away from it. Even if you make all the efforts, it is impossible to go away. There is nowhere else to go, and there is nothing else to be.

Tantra is not a religion in the ordinary sense because it has no rituals, it has no priests, it has no scriptures. It is an individual approach towards reality. It is tremendously rebellious. Its trust is not in the organization, its trust is not in the community; its trust is in the individual. Tantra believes in *you*.

I have heard...

It happened in a Billy Graham revival meeting – a guy was collecting donations and then he started to split with the money. Two policemen caught him red-handed and brought him to Billy Graham. Naturally Billy Graham was very angry and said to the man, "This money belongs to God, and what were you trying to do? Trying to cheat God?"

The man said, "Sir, I took the money in an effort to get closer to God – by eliminating the middleman, of course."

The middleman is not needed at all. The real master never tries to become the middleman; he is not. He does not help you to reach to God; he helps you only to become aware of that which is already there. He is not a bridge between you and God, he is just a bridge between your unawareness and awareness. The moment you become aware, you are joined to God directly, immediately, without anybody standing between you and him.

This Tantra vision is one of the greatest visions ever dreamed by man: a religion without priests, a religion without temples, a religion without organizations; a religion which does not destroy the individual but respects individuality tremendously, a religion which trusts in the ordinary man and woman. And this trust goes very deep. Tantra trusts in your body – no other religion trusts in your body. And when religions don't trust in your body, they create a split between you and your body. They make you an enemy of your body, they start destroying the wisdom of the body.

Tantra trusts in your body. Tantra trusts in your senses. Tantra trusts in your energy. Tantra trusts in you – in toto. Tantra does not deny anything; it transforms everything.

How to attain to this Tantra vision? This is the map to turn you on, and to turn you in, and to turn you beyond.

The first thing is the body. The body is your base, it is your ground, it is where you are grounded. To make you antagonistic towards the body is to destroy you, is to make you schizophrenic, is to make you miserable, is to create hell. You *are* the body. Of course you are more than the body, but that "more" will follow later on. First, you are the body. The body is your basic truth, so never be against the body. Whenever you are against the body, you are going against God. Whenever you are disrespectful to your body you are losing contact with reality, because your body is your contact, your body is your bridge. Your body is your temple.

Tantra teaches reverence for the body, love, respect for the body, gratitude for the body. The body is marvelous; it is the greatest of mysteries.

But you have been taught to be against the body. So sometimes you may be mystified by the tree, by the green tree; sometimes mystified by the moon and the sun, sometimes mystified by a flower – but never mystified by your own body. And your body is the most complex phenomenon in existence. No flower, no tree has such a beautiful body as you have; no moon, no sun, no star has such an evolved mechanism as you have.

You have been taught to appreciate the flower, which is a simple thing. You have been taught to appreciate a tree, which is a simple thing. You have even been taught to appreciate stones, rocks, mountains, rivers, but you have never been taught to respect your own body, never to be mystified by it. Yes, it is very close, so it is very easy to forget about it. It is very obvious, so it is easy to neglect it. But it is the most beautiful phenomenon.

If you look at a flower, people will say, "How aesthetic!" And if you look at a woman's beautiful face or a man's beautiful face, people will say, "This is lust." If you go to a tree and stand there, or look in a dazed state at a flower – your eyes wide open, your senses wide open to allow the beauty of the flower to enter you – people will think you are a poet or a painter or a mystic. But if you go to a woman or a man and just stand there with great reverence and respect, and look at the woman with your eyes wide open and your senses drinking the beauty of the woman, the police will catch hold of you. Nobody will say that you are a mystic, a poet; nobody will appreciate what you are doing.

Something has gone wrong. If you go to a stranger on the street and say, "What beautiful eyes you have!" you will feel embarrassed, he will feel embarrassed. He will not be able to say thank you to you. In fact he will feel offended.

He will feel offended, because who are you to interfere in his private life? Who are you to dare? If you go and touch the tree, the tree will feel happy. But if you go and touch a man, he will feel offended. What has gone wrong? Something has been damaged tremendously and very deeply.

Tantra teaches you to reclaim respect for the body, love for the body. Tantra teaches you to look at the body as the greatest creation of God. Tantra is the religion of the body. Of course it goes higher, but it never leaves the body; it is grounded there. It is the only religion which is really grounded in the earth: it has roots. Other religions are uprooted trees – dead, dull, dying; the juice does not flow in them. Tantra is really juicy, very alive.

The first thing is to learn respect for the body – to unlearn all the nonsense that has been taught to you about the body. Otherwise, you will never turn on, and you will never turn in, and you will never turn beyond.

Start from the beginning. The body is your beginning. The body has to be purified of many repressions. A great catharsis is needed for the body, a great *rechan*. The body has become poisoned because you have been against it, you have repressed it in many ways. Your body exists at the minimum, that's why you are miserable.

Tantra says bliss is possible only when you exist at the optimum, never before it. Bliss is possible only when you live intensely. How can you live intensely if you are against the body? You are always lukewarm, the fire has cooled down. Down the centuries, the fire has been destroyed. The fire has to be rekindled.

Tantra says to first purify the body – purify it of all repressions. Allow the body energy to flow, remove the blocks. It is very difficult to come across a person who has no blocks; it is very difficult to come across a person whose body is not tight. Loosen this tightness; this tension is blocking your energy, the flow cannot be possible with this tension. Why is everybody so uptight? Why can't you relax? Have you seen a cat sleeping, dozing in the afternoon? How simply and how beautifully the cat relaxes. Can't you relax the same way? You toss and turn in your bed; you can't relax. And the beauty of the cat's relaxation is that it relaxes utterly and yet is perfectly alert. A slight movement in the room and it will open its eyes, it will jump and be ready. It is not that it is just asleep. The cat's sleep is something to be learned; man has forgotten.

Tantra says to learn from the cats – how they sleep, how they relax, how they live in a non-tense way. And the whole animal world lives in that non-tense way. Man has to learn this because he has been conditioned wrongly, man has been programmed wrongly.

From the very childhood you have been programmed to be tight. Out of fear you don't breathe. Out of fear of sexuality people don't breathe because when you breathe deeply, your breath goes exactly to the sex center and hits it, massages it from the inside, excites it. Because you have been taught that sex is dangerous, each child starts breathing in a shallow way, hung up just in the chest. He never goes beyond that because if he goes beyond it, suddenly there is excitement; sexuality is aroused and fear arises. The moment you breathe deeply, sex energy is released. Sex energy *has* to be released, it has to flow all over your being. Then your body will become orgasmic. But afraid to breathe, so afraid that almost half the lungs are full of carbon dioxide...

There are many, many thousands of holes in the lungs and ordinarily fifty percent are never cleaned, they always remain full of carbon dioxide. That's why you are dull, that's why you don't look alert, that's why awareness is difficult. It is not accidental that Yoga and Tantra both teach deep breathing, *pranayama,* to unload your lungs of the carbon dioxide. The carbon dioxide is not good for you; it has to be thrown out continuously. You have to breathe in new, fresh air; you have to breathe more oxygen. Oxygen will create your inner fire, oxygen will make you aflame. But oxygen will also inflame your sexuality. So only Tantra can allow you real deep breathing; even Yoga cannot allow you real deep breathing. Yoga allows you to go down to the navel – not beyond that, not to cross the *hara* center, not to cross the *svadhishthan* because once you cross the *svadhishthan* you jump into the *muladhar.*

Only Tantra allows you total being and total flow. Tantra gives you unconditional freedom. Whatsoever you are and whatsoever you can be, Tantra puts no boundaries on you. It does not define you; it simply gives you total freedom. The understanding is that when you are totally free, then much is possible.

It has been my observation that people who are sexually repressed become unintelligent. Only very, very sexually alive people are intelligent people. Now, the idea that sex is sin must have damaged intelligence, must have damaged it very badly. When you are really flowing and your sexuality has no fight and conflict with you, when you cooperate with it, your mind will function at its optimum. You will be intelligent, alert, alive.

The body has to be befriended, says Tantra.

Do you touch your own body sometimes? Do you ever feel your own body, or do you remain as if you are encased in a dead thing? That's what is happening: people are almost frozen; they are carrying the body like a casket. It is heavy, it obstructs, it does not help you to communicate with reality. If you allow the electricity of the body flow to move from the toe to the head, if you allow total freedom for its energy – the bioenergy – you will become a river and you will not feel the body at all. You will feel almost bodiless. Not fighting with the body, you become bodiless. Fighting with the body, the body becomes a burden, and carrying your body as a burden you can never arrive to godliness.

The body has to become weightless so that you almost start walking above the earth; that is the Tantra way to walk. You are so weightless that there is no gravitation – you can simply fly. But that comes out of great acceptance. It is going to be difficult to accept your body. You condemn it, you always find faults with it. You never appreciate, you never love it, and then you want a miracle – that somebody will come and love your body. If you yourself cannot love your body, then how are you going to find somebody else to love it? If you yourself cannot love your body, nobody is going to love it because your vibe will keep people repelled.

You fall in love with a person who loves himself, never otherwise. The first love has to be towards oneself; only from that center can other kinds of love arise. You don't love your body: you hide it in a thousand and one ways. You hide your body's smell, you hide your body in clothes, you hide your body in ornamentation. You try to create some beauty that you continuously feel you are missing, and in that very effort you become artificial.

Now, think of a woman with lipstick on her lips – it is sheer ugliness. Lips should be red out of aliveness, they should not be painted. They should be alive out of love, they should be alive because you are alive. Now, just painting the lips you think that you are beautifying yourself. Only people who are very conscious of their ugliness go to beauty parlors, otherwise there is no need.

Do you ever come across a bird which is ugly? Do you ever come across a deer which is ugly? It never happens. They don't go to any beauty parlor, and they don't consult an expert; they simply accept themselves and they are beautiful in their acceptance. In that very acceptance they shower beauty upon themselves.

The moment you accept yourself you become beautiful. When you are delighted with your own body, you will delight others also. Many people will fall in love with you because you yourself are in love with yourself. As you are now, you are angry with yourself; you know that you are ugly, you know that you are repulsive, horrible. This idea will repel people; this idea will not help them to fall in love with you, it will keep them away. Even if they were coming closer to you, the moment they feel your vibration they will move away. There is no need to chase anybody, the chasing arises only because we have not been in love with ourselves. Otherwise people come: it becomes almost impossible for them not to fall in love with you if you are in love with yourself.

Why did so many people come to Buddha, and why did so many people come to Saraha, and why did so many people come to Jesus? These people were in love with themselves. They were in such great love and they were so delighted with their being that it was natural for whosoever would pass to be pulled by them; they would pull like a magnet. They were so enchanted with their own being, how could you avoid that enchantment? Just being there was such a great bliss.

The first thing Tantra teaches is to be loving towards your body, befriend your body, revere your body, respect your body, take care of your body. It is a gift of existence; treat it well and it will reveal great mysteries to you. All growth depends on how you are related to your body.

And then the second thing Tantra speaks about is the senses. Again, the religions are against the senses; they try to dull the senses and sensitivity. And the senses are your doors of perception, the senses are the windows into reality. What are your eyes? What are your ears? What is your nose? – windows into reality, windows into God. If you see rightly, you will see godliness everywhere. So eyes must not be closed, eyes have to be opened rightly; eyes must not be destroyed. Ears must not be destroyed, because all sounds are divine.

These birds are chanting mantras. These trees are giving sermons in silence. All sounds are God, and all forms are God. So if you don't have sensitivity in you, how will you know God? And you have to go to a church, to a temple to find it, and it is all over the place. In a man-made temple, in a man-made church, you go to find God? Man seems to be so stupid. God is everywhere, alive and kicking everywhere. But for that you need clean senses, purified senses.

So, Tantra teaches that the senses are the doors of perception. They have been dulled – you have to drop that dullness, your senses have to be cleansed. Your senses are like a mirror which has become dull because so much dust has gathered upon it; the dust has to be cleansed.

Look at the Tantra approach about everything. Others say: "Dull your senses, kill your taste!" And Tantra says to taste God in every taste. Others say to kill your capacity to touch. And Tantra says to flow totally into your touch because whatsoever you touch is divine. It is a total reversal of the so-called religions; it is a radical revolution – from the very roots.

Touch, smell, taste, see, hear as totally as possible. You will have to learn the language because the society has befooled you, it has made you forget. Each child is born with beautiful senses. Watch a child – when he looks at something he is completely absorbed, when he is playing with his toys he is utterly absorbed. When he looks, he becomes just the eyes. Look at the eyes of a child. When he hears, he becomes just the ears. When he eats something, he is just there on the tongue, he becomes just the taste. See a child eating an apple – with what gusto! With what great energy! With what delight! See a child running after a butterfly in the garden – so absorbed that even if God were available he would not run that way. Such a tremendous, meditative state – and without any effort. See a child collecting seashells on the beach as if he were collecting diamonds. Everything is precious when the senses are alive, everything is clear when the senses are alive.

Later on in life the same child will look at reality as if hidden behind a darkened glass. Much smoke and dust have gathered on the glass and you are hidden behind it and you are looking. Because of this, everything looks dull and dead. You look at a tree and the tree looks dull because your eyes are dull. You hear a song, but there is no appeal in it because your ears are dull. You can hear a Saraha and you will not be able to appreciate him because your intelligence is dull.

Reclaim your forgotten language. Whenever you have time, be more in your senses. Eating, don't just eat; try to learn the forgotten language of taste again – try. Touch the bread, feel the texture of it; feel with open eyes, feel with closed eyes. While eating, chew it – you are chewing God. Remember it! It will be disrespectful not to chew well, not to taste well. Let it be prayerful, and you will start a new consciousness arising in you. You will learn the way of Tantra alchemy.

Touch people more. We have become very touchy about touch. If somebody is talking to you and comes too close, you start moving backwards. We protect our territory. We don't touch and we don't allow others to touch; we don't hold hands, we don't hug. We don't enjoy each other's being.

Go to the tree, touch the tree. Touch a rock. Go to the river, let the river flow through your hands. Feel it! Swim, and feel the water again as the fish feels it. Don't miss any opportunity to revive your senses. And there are a thousand and one opportunities the whole day. There is no need to have some separate time for it. The whole day is a training in sensitivity. Use all the opportunities. Sitting under your shower, use the opportunity – feel the touch of the water falling on you. Lie down on the ground, naked, feel the earth. Lie down on the beach, feel the sand. Listen to the sounds of the sand, listen to the sounds of the sea. Use every opportunity; only then will you be able to learn the language of the senses again. And Tantra can be understood only when your body is alive and your senses feel.

Free your senses from habits. Habits are one of the root causes of dullness; find out new ways of doing things. Invent new ways of loving. People are very much afraid.

I have heard...

The doctor told the working chap that he could not complete his examination without a sample of urine. The small boy who was sent with the specimen spilled most of it while messing about. Fearing a good hiding, he topped it up with the urine of a cow in the field.

The doctor hastily sent for the man, who returned home to his wife in a furious temper and said, "That's you and your fancy positions! You *would* be on top, wouldn't you? And now I am going to have a baby!"

People have fixed habits. Even while making love they always do it in the same position – the missionary posture. Find out new ways of feeling. Each experience has to be created with great sensitivity. When you make love to a woman or a man, make it a great celebration, and each time bring some new creativity into it. Sometimes have a dance before you make love, sometimes feel prayerful before you make love, sometimes go running into the forest, then make love. Sometimes go swimming and then make love. Then each love experience will create more and more sensitivity in you, and love will never become dull and boring.

Find out new ways to explore the other, don't get fixed in routines. All routines are anti-life: routines are in the service of death. And you can always invent – there is no limit to invention. Sometimes a small change and you will be tremendously benefited. You always eat at the table – sometimes just go on the lawn, sit on the lawn and eat there, and you will be tremendously surprised: it is a totally different experience. The smell of the freshly-cut grass, the birds hopping around and singing, and the fresh air and the sun rays, and the feel of the wet grass underneath – it cannot be the same experience as when you sit on a chair and eat at your table. It is a totally different experience: all the ingredients are different.

Sometimes try just eating naked, and you will be surprised. Just a small change – nothing much, you are sitting naked – but you will have a totally different experience because something new has been added to it. If you eat with a spoon and fork, eat sometimes with bare hands and you will have a different experience; your touch will bring some new warmth to the food. A spoon is a dead thing; when you eat with a spoon or a fork, you are far away. That same fear of touching anything – even food cannot be touched. You will miss the texture, the touch, the feel of it. The food has as much feel as it has taste.

Many experiments have been done in the West on the fact that when we are enjoying anything, there are many things we are not aware of which contribute to the experience. For example, just close your eyes and close your nose and then eat an onion. Tell somebody to give it to you when you don't know what he is giving, whether he is giving you an onion or an apple. And it will be difficult for you to make out the difference if the nose is completely closed and the eyes are closed, blindfolded. It will be impossible for you to decide whether it is an onion or an apple, because the taste is not only the taste; fifty percent of it comes from the nose, and much comes from the eyes. It is not just taste, all the senses contribute. When you eat with your hands, your touch is contributing. It will be tastier, it will be more human, more natural.

Find out new ways in everything. Let that be one of your *sadhanas*. Tantra says that if you can go on finding new ways every day, your life will remain a thrill, an adventure. You will never be bored. A bored person is an irreligious person. You will always be curious to know, you will always be on the verge of seeking the unknown and the unfamiliar. Your eyes will remain clear and your senses will remain clear, because when you are always on the verge of seeking, exploring, finding, searching, you cannot become dull, you cannot become stupid. No child is stupid; only later on do people become stupid.

Psychologists say that by the age of seven, stupidity starts. It starts nearabout the age of four but by the seventh year it is very, very apparent. Children start becoming stupid by the age of seven. In fact, the child learns fifty percent of all the learning of his whole life by the time he is seven. If he lives for seventy years, then in the remaining sixty-three years he will learn only fifty percent – fifty percent he has already learned. What happens? He becomes dull, he stops learning. If you think in terms of intelligence, by the age of seven a child starts becoming old. The moment the child thinks, "I know," he has started becoming old. Physically he will become old later on – from the age of thirty-five he will start declining – but mentally he is already on the decline.

You will be surprised to know that your mental age, the average mental age, is twelve years. People don't grow beyond that, they are stuck there. That's why you see so much childishness in the world. Just insult a person who is sixty years of age and within seconds he is just a twelve-year-old child. And he is behaving in such a way – you will not be able to believe that such a grown-up person could behave in such a childish way. People are always ready to fall back. Their age is just skin-deep, hidden behind – just scratch a little and their mental age comes out. Their physical age is not of much importance. People die childish; they never grow.

Tantra says to learn new ways of doing things and free yourself of habits as much as possible. And Tantra says don't be imitative, otherwise your senses will become dull. Don't imitate! Find out ways of doing things in your own way; have your signature on everything that you do.

Just the other night, a sannyasin who is going back home was saying that love between her and her husband has disappeared. Now they are hanging together just for the children. I told her to meditate, to be friendly to her husband. If love has disappeared, not everything has disappeared; friendship is still possible – be friendly. And she said, "It is difficult. When a cup is broken it is broken."

I told her that it seemed she had not heard that Zen people in Japan will purchase a cup from the supermarket, bring it home and break it first, then glue it together again to make it individual and special – otherwise it is just a market thing. And if a friend comes and you give him tea in an ordinary cup and saucer, it is not good; that is ugly, it is not respectful. So they will bring a fresh new cup and break it. Of course, then there is no other cup in the world exactly like it, there cannot be. Glued together, now it has some individuality, a signature. And when Zen people go to each other's house or each other's monastery, they will not just sip the tea. First they will appreciate the cup, they will look at it. The way it has been joined together is a piece of art – the way the pieces have been broken and put together again.

The woman understood, she started laughing. She said, "Then it is possible." Bring individuality into things, don't just be an imitator. To imitate is to miss life.

I have heard...

Mulla Nasruddin had a very horny parrot. The parrot was continuously saying foul things, particularly whenever there was a guest, and Mulla was very worried; it was getting terrible. Finally somebody suggested to him that he take it to the vet.

So he takes the parrot to a vet. The vet examines the parrot extensively and says, "Well, Nasruddin, you have a horny parrot. I have a sweet, young, female bird. For fifteen rupees your bird can go in the cage with my bird."

Mulla's parrot is in the cage listening. And Mulla says, "God, I don't know – fifteen rupees?"

The parrot says, "Come on, come on, Nasruddin. What the hell?"

Finally the Mulla says, "All right," and gives the vet the fifteen rupees. The vet takes the bird, puts him in the cage with the female bird and closes the curtain. The two men go and sit down. There is a moment of silence, and then suddenly, "Qua! Qua! Qua!" Feathers come flying over the top of the curtain.

The vet says, "Holy Gee!" runs over and opens the curtain. The male has got the female bird down on the bottom of the cage with one claw – with the other claw he is pulling out all her feathers and shouting in delight, "For fifteen rupees I want you naked, naked!" Then seeing the vet and his master, Mulla Nasruddin, he screams again in joy and says, "Hey Nasruddin, isn't this the way you also like your women?"

Even a parrot can learn human ways, can become imitative, can become neurotic. To be imitative is to be neurotic. The only way to be sane in the world is to be individual, authentically individual. Be your own being.

The third thing that Tantra says is... First, the body has to be purified of repressions. Second, the senses have to be made alive again. Third, the mind has to drop neurotic thinking, obsessive thinking, and has to learn ways of silence. Whenever it is possible, relax. Whenever it is possible, put the mind aside.

Now you will say, "It is easy to say, but how to put the mind aside? It goes on and on." There is a way. Tantra says watch these three awarenesses. Awareness one – watch. Let the mind go, let the mind be filled with thoughts; you simply watch, detached. There is no need to be worried about it, just watch. Just be the observer, and by and by you will see that silent gaps have started coming to you. Then, awareness two – when you have become aware that gaps have started coming, then become aware of the watcher. Now watch the watcher and then new gaps will start coming – the watcher will start disappearing, just like the thoughts. One day the thinker also starts disappearing; then real silence arises. With the third awareness, both object and subject are gone; you have entered into the beyond.

When these three things are attained – the body purified of repressions, the senses freed from dullness, the mind liberated from obsessive thinking – a vision arises in you free from all illusion. That is the Tantra vision.

Now the sutras:

> Mind, intellect, and the formed contents of that mind are It,
> so too are the world and all that seems from It to differ,
> all things that can be sensed, and the perceiver,
> also dullness, aversion, desire and enlightenment.

When you have come to a state of silence where both the observer and the observed have disappeared, then you will come to know what this sutra means.

Mind, intellect, and the formed contents of the mind are It... Existence is one, it is all a unity. There are not two things in existence – it is oneness, it is one ocean. All divisions are there because we are divided inside; our divisions inside are projected onto the outside, and things look divided. When the body is pure, the senses open and the mind is silent, inner divisions disappear; inside there is pure space. When there is pure space inside, you become capable of knowing that the outside is also the same pure space. It is the same sky outside and in. In fact, there is no "out" and no "in" anymore, it is all one.

Mind, intellect, and the formed contents of the mind are It... Now you will recognize that even thoughts were not enemies, even desires were not enemies. They were also forms of the same divinity, of the same one existence. Now you will recognize that nirvana and samsara are not two. Now you will have a very, very deep laugh, recognizing that there is no difference between bondage and enlightenment; that to know and to be ignorant are not different because division is not possible; that between a buddha and a man who is not yet enlightened there is no difference.

But this is only known by a buddha. For the unenlightened man there is a great difference. A buddha cannot think because through thinking there is always division; through non-thinking divisions disappear.

...*so too are the world and all that seems from It to differ, all things that can be sensed, and perceiver also, also dullness, aversion, desire and enlightenment.* All is it. This is it! This totality is what Tantra calls *It.*

Now Saraha is saying to the king: Don't be worried. Whether in the palace or on the cremation ground, whether I am known as a learned brahmin or known as a mad dog doesn't matter: it is It. I have come to that indivisible experience where the perceiver and the perceived are one, where the observer and the observed are one. I have arrived. Now I can see that those divisions of good and bad, of the sinner and the saint, were meaningless. There is no difference between sin and saintliness.

This is why I call Tantra the greatest rebellious attitude in the whole history of human consciousness.

Saraha is saying, "Sir, for you divisions exist. This is a cremation ground and where you live is a palace. For me there is no division. In this cremation ground there have been many palaces in the past which have disappeared, and your palace will sooner or later become a cremation ground. Don't be worried, it is only a question of time. And if you can see, then there is no difference. It is the same reality, somewhere becoming a saint and somewhere becoming a sinner; it is the same It."

> *Like a lamp that shines in the darkness of spiritual unknowing,*
> *it removes obscurations of a mind*
> *as far as the fragmentations of intellect obtain.*
> *Who can imagine the self-being of desirelessness?*

Like a lamp... Saraha says, "Now, the third awareness is born in me. It is like a lamp that shines in the darkness of spiritual unknowing. Now I can see for the first time that matter and mind are one, that out and in are one, that body and soul are one, that this world and the other world are one, that this contains that too. Since this light happened to me," Saraha says, "now there is no problem. Whatsoever is, is good."

Like a lamp that shines in the darkness of spiritual unknowing, it removes obscurations of a mind... "All my obscurities, all my hindrances – things that were obstructing my vision – are removed. I can see reality directly. Repressions are no longer there, my energies are in a flow. I am not against my body, I am not inimical to my body, I am one with my body. The division is dropped. My senses are all open and functioning at the optimum. My mind is silent, there is no obsessive thinking. When I need to, I think; when I don't need to, I don't think. I am the master of my house. A light was born in me, and with that light, all obscurities have disappeared. Now nothing obstructs me, my vision is total. The wall that was around me has disappeared."

That wall consists of three things: repressions in the body, dust in the senses, and thoughts in the mind. These are the three bricks that the Wall of China around you is made of. Remove these bricks and the wall disappears. And when the wall is gone, you come to know the one.

...as far as the fragmentations of intellect obtain. Who can imagine the self-being of desirelessness? "And, sir, you have come to ask me what my experience is? It is difficult for you even to imagine. It is difficult for me to say, it is difficult for you to understand. But I can show you the way for you to experience it also – that is the only way. When you have tasted, only then will you know."

> *There's nothing to be negated, nothing to be*
> *affirmed or grasped; for It can never be conceived.*
> *By the fragmentations of the intellect are the deluded fettered;*
> *undivided and pure remains spontaneity.*

Saraha says, "I cannot say it is not, I cannot say it is. I cannot negate it, I cannot posit it. I cannot use no, I cannot use yes, because both fall short." It is bigger than both – it contains both, and yet it is plus, it is transcendental to both. Those who say God is, degrade God – they drag him down. Those who say God is not certainly don't understand at all. They are both the same: one negates, one posits.

The positive and the negative belong to the same mind, the same thinking mind. Yes and no are both parts of language, of thought. Saraha says, "I cannot say God is, I cannot say God is not. I can only show you the way: where it is, what it is, how it is. You can experience it. You can open your own eyes and see it."

Once it happened that a blind man was brought to Buddha. And the blind man was no ordinary blind man, he was a great academician, he was a great scholar, very skilled in argumentation. He started arguing with Buddha. He said, "People say light exists and I say no. They say I am blind, I say they are deluded. If light exists, then, sir, make it available to me so that I can touch it.

If I can touch it, or at least if I can taste it or I can smell it, or if you beat the light like a drum so that I can hear it... These are my four senses, and the fifth sense which people talk about is just imagination. People are deluded, nobody has eyes."

It was very difficult to convince this man that light exists because light cannot be touched, cannot be tasted, cannot be smelled, cannot be heard. And this man was saying that others were deluded, "They don't have eyes." He was a blind man, but a great logician. He said, "Prove that they have got eyes. What proof have you got?"

Buddha said, "I will not say anything, but I know a physician and I will send you to the physician. I know he will be able to cure your eyes."

But the man insisted, "I have come to argue about it!"

And Buddha said, "This is *my* argument: go to the physician."

The man was sent to the physician; his eyes were cured, within six months he was able to see. He could not believe it; he was ecstatically happy, he came dancing to Buddha. He was mad. He fell at Buddha's feet and said, "Your argument worked."

Buddha said, "Listen, it was no argument. If I had argued, I would have failed because there are things which cannot be argued about but can only be experienced."

God is not an argument, is not a syllogism. Nirvana is not an argument, it is not a conclusion; it is an experience. Unless you experience it, there is no way to even understand what it is. If you don't experience it, it is just absurd, meaningless.

There's nothing to be negated, nothing to be affirmed and nothing to be grasped; for It can never be conceived. In fact, there is nothing to grasp and nobody to grasp it; nothing to conceive and nobody to conceive it. Object and subject both disappear in it. The knower and the known both disappear in it. Then is the experience of the total, of the one, of the *It.*

By the fragmentations of the intellect are the deluded fettered; undivided and pure remains spontaneity. Says Saraha to the king, "Sir, people are prejudiced about reality. They have ideas about reality, and reality is not an idea. God is not an idea. God is not the word *God*; it is not a theory, it is not a hypothesis. It is a taste of reality, it is an orgasmic experience with the total."

People are fettered because of their minds. They have certain ideas, attitudes, fixed philosophies; they look through those philosophies. That's why they say Saraha has gone mad. They have a certain idea of what sanity should be, how sanity has to be. That's why they think Saraha has gone mad: they are looking through certain prejudices.

...undivided and pure remains spontaneity. But spontaneity is undivided and pure; it is primal innocence. "Look at me," says Saraha. "Look at my spontaneity. Don't think about what people say, don't think through certain prejudices of good and bad, virtue and sin, right and wrong. Just *look* at me! I am here, It is here. I am available; have a deep experience of my presence."

If you can feel spontaneity, innocence, purity, only that will help you to go withinward on the journey of Tantra.

> *If you question ultimacy with the postulates of the many and the one,*
> *oneness is not given, for by transcending knowledge*
> *are sentient beings freed.*
> *The radiant is potency latent in the intellect, and this*
> *is shown to be meditation; unswerving Mind is our true essence.*

If you question ultimacy with the postulates of the many and the one, oneness is not given... If you question, you miss; reality cannot be turned into a question. Yes, it can be turned into a *quest,* but not into a question.

And nobody can answer, only you can experience. That's why I say it can be a quest, but it can never be turned into a question. A question is that which can be answered. A quest is that which can only be experienced. Only when *you* arrive, do you arrive, there is no other way. There is no borrowed way. All knowledge is borrowed.

Hence, Saraha says *...for by transcending knowledge are sentient beings freed.* One has to be liberated from knowledge.

Knowledge does not liberate you; it is your deepest, subtlest bondage. Through knowledge you are not available to reality. Drop all knowledge. Dropping all knowledge, knowing becomes pure, then you are no longer clouded. Not knowing anything borrowed, your purity is intact; then, your mirror has no dust on it. Then, you start reflecting. Then, reality is reflected as it is. Never move with knowledge, otherwise you move not. Never trust borrowed experiences.

Something happened to Buddha, but that is not your experience. Something happened to Christ, but that is not your experience. Something has happened to me, but that is not your experience. What I say is that if you hoard it, it will become knowledge. What I say is that if it leads you on a quest, it will become knowing. Don't hoard it in your memory. Hoarding knowledge in the memory only burdens you; it is not liberation.

...for by transcending knowledge are sentient beings freed. The radiant is potency latent in the intellect... And you *have* that potency which can flower into nirvana, which can become enlightenment. Each intellect is nothing but

the intelligence hidden behind it. If you trust your intellect too much you will miss your intelligence. Now these two words have to be understood; they come out of the same root but their meaning is different. It is not necessary that an intellectual has to be intelligent. It is not necessary that an intelligent person has to be an intellectual. You can find nonintellectuals who are tremendously intelligent.

Christ is not an intellectual, Kabir is not an intellectual, Meera is not an intellectual, but they are tremendously intelligent people. Intellect is a false substitute for intelligence. Intellect is borrowed, intelligence is yours. Intelligence is your pure capacity to see, intelligence is your innocent capacity to understand. Intellect is borrowed knowledge; intellect is a pseudo coin, a counterfeit.

You collect information from everywhere, you collect much knowledge, and you become knowledgeable. But your intelligence has not grown, your intelligence has not really exploded. In fact, because of this intellectual effort, your intelligence will remain burdened; knowledge will gather like dust on a mirror. Intellect is the dust. Intelligence is the pure quality of the mirror to reflect.

Says Saraha: *The radiant is potency latent in the intellect...* In each intellect there is potential intelligence; don't overburden it with borrowed knowledge ... *and this is shown to be meditation...* If you don't burden it with knowledge, your intelligence becomes your meditation. A great definition of meditation: intelligence is meditation. To live intelligently is to live meditatively. This definition is of tremendous significance; it is really pregnant with great meaning. And to live intelligently is what meditation is. Meditation cannot be "done" in that way. You have to bring intelligence to your life.

You were angry yesterday, you were angry the day before yesterday. Now again the situation has come and you are going to be angry – what are you going to do? Are you going to repeat it in an unintelligent way, a mechanical way, or will you bring intelligence to it? You have been angry a thousand and one times – can't you learn anything from it? Can't you behave intelligently now? Can't you see the futility of it? Can't you see that every time you were frustrated by it? Each time anger has dissipated energy, distracted your energy, created problems for you and not solved anything.

If you see it, in that very seeing is intelligence. Then somebody insults you and there is no anger. In fact, rather than anger there is compassion for the man. He is angry, he is hurt, he is suffering. Compassion will arise. Now this intelligence is meditation: to look into one's life, to learn out of experience, to learn out of existential experience, to go on learning, not borrowing.

Buddha says anger is bad. Now look at the difference: if you are a Buddhist you will believe him. Buddha says anger is bad, so anger must be bad; how can Buddha be wrong? Now whenever anger arises you will repress it because Buddha says that anger is wrong. This is functioning through knowledge, functioning through intellect. But what foolishness! You have been angry so many times – is there any need to ask Buddha whether anger is wrong? Can't you yourself see into your own experiences?

If you see into your own experiences, then you know what anger is. And seeing into that, you are freed from anger. This is intelligence. Out of your intelligence you will become a witness to Buddha; you will say, "Yes, Buddha is right. My experience proves it." Not otherwise. Not: "Buddha is right so I have to experience it" – that is stupidity. But rather, if out of my experience I become a witness to Buddha, then I can say, "Yes, he is right because this is my experience too. But he is secondary; my experience comes first, it is primary. I am a witness to him, not a follower."

You who are my sannyasins here, please become my witnesses, not my followers. Let what I am saying be proved through your experience. Then you have been with me, then you have loved me. Then you have lived with me. If you simply accumulate what I am saying and you become great theorizers about it, you learn to philosophize about it, then you have missed. Then you will become intellectuals. And to become intellectual is to commit suicide as far as intelligence is concerned.

Don't become intellectuals. The real coin is available; why go on hankering for the counterfeit? Life is as available to you as it was to Buddha, as it is to me; why not learn through it?

To become intelligent is to be meditative. Yes, this is one of the greatest definitions of meditation I have come across. And I am a witness to it. That is the way one evolves spiritually.

The radiant is potency latent in the intellect, and this is shown to be meditation; unswerving Mind is our true essence. And the more intelligent you become, the more you will find your mind is no longer the old mind.

Tantra uses *mind* with two meanings: *mind* with a small *m* – that is your mind. And *Mind* with a big, capital *M* – that is the essential Mind, the Buddha Mind.

The little, tiny mind enclosed in knowledge, in boundaries, in prejudices – the mind that we call Hindu, the mind that we call Moslem, the mind that we call Jew, Christian; that mind, small, tiny mind, the mind that has been cultivated by the colleges and the universities; that mind, small mind, the mind that has been programmed by the society – that mind Tantra calls the small mind.

When these barriers are broken, when these obscurities are removed, then you attain to the great Mind, the Buddha Mind – *Mind* with a capital *M*. It is as big as the universe itself. It is universal: ...*Unswerving Mind is our true essence.* And that is the mind which is our true essence. Call it God, call it nirvana, or whatever you like, but this is our essence: to come to a state of absolute rest – unswerving, unwavering. To come to a state of eternity where time has disappeared, where all divisions have disappeared, where subject and object are no more, where the knower and the known are no more, where there is only pure awareness – awareness three.

These sutras are not just to be crammed, otherwise you will be betraying Saraha, you will be betraying me. These sutras have just to be meditated upon and forgotten. Then, whatsoever intelligence arises in you out of meditating on these sutras, use it in life. Moment to moment let that intelligence be sharpened again and again, against so many experiences.

And that intelligence will become the door to the divine. That intelligence is the door.

Enough for today.

CHAPTER 8

love makes no shadow

The first question:

Osho,
Yesterday, when you spoke of intelligence becoming meditation, there was
such a rush inside. It felt as if my heart would explode. It was as if you had said
something I'd been waiting to hear. Can you elaborate?

Intelligence is intrinsic to life. Intelligence is a natural quality of life. Just as
fire is hot, and air is invisible, and water flows downward, so is life intelligent.

Intelligence is not an achievement; you are born intelligent. Trees are intelligent in their own way, they have enough intelligence for their own life. Birds
are intelligent, so are animals. In fact, what religions mean by God is only this:
the universe is intelligent. There is intelligence hidden everywhere, and if you
have eyes to see, you can see it everywhere.

Life is intelligence. Only man has become unintelligent. Man has damaged the natural flow of life. Except in man, there is no unintelligence. Have
you ever seen a bird you can call stupid? Have you ever seen an animal you
can call idiotic? No, such things happen only to man. Something has gone
wrong. Man's intelligence has been damaged, corrupted, has been crippled.
And meditation is nothing but the undoing of that damage.

Meditation will not be needed at all if man is left alone. If the priest and the politician do not interfere with man's intelligence, there will be no need for any meditation. Meditation is medicinal. First you have to create the disease, then meditation is needed. If the disease is not there, meditation is not needed. And it is not accidental that the words *medicine* and *meditation* come from the same root. It is medicinal.

Each child is born intelligent. And the moment the child is born we pounce upon him and start destroying his intelligence, because intelligence is dangerous to the political structure, to the social structure, to the religious structure. It is dangerous to the pope, it is dangerous to the Shankaracharya of Puri, it is dangerous to the priest. It is dangerous to the leader, it is dangerous to the status quo, the establishment.

Intelligence is naturally rebellious. Intelligence cannot be forced into servitude. Intelligence is very assertive, individual. Intelligence cannot be converted into a mechanical imitation.

People have to be converted into carbon copies; their originality has to be destroyed, otherwise all the nonsense that has existed on the earth will be impossible. You need a leader because first you have to be made unintelligent; otherwise there would be no need for any leader. Why should you follow anybody? You will follow your intelligence. If somebody wants to become a leader, then one thing has to be done: your intelligence has to be destroyed somehow. You have to be shaken from your very roots, you have to be made afraid. You have to be made unconfident in yourself, that is a must. Only then can the leader come in.

If you are intelligent, you will solve your problems yourself. Intelligence is enough to solve all the problems. In fact, whatsoever problems are created in life, you have more intelligence than those problems. It is a provision, it is a gift of God.

But there are ambitious people who want to rule, dominate; there are ambitious madmen – they create fear in you. Fear is like rust: it destroys all intelligence. If you want to destroy somebody's intelligence, the first necessary thing is to create fear, create hell and make people afraid. When people are afraid of hell they will go to the priest and bow down to him. They will listen to the priest. If they don't listen to him – then hellfire. Naturally they are afraid. They have to protect themselves from hellfire, and the priest is needed, the priest becomes a must.

I have heard about two men who were partners in a business. Their business was unique and they used to travel around the country. One partner would come to the town. In the night he would go around and throw coal tar on people's windows, and then disappear by morning. After two or three days, the other would come. He used to clean off the coal tar; he would clean the people's windows and people would pay, of course – they had to pay. They were partners in the same business. One would damage, the other would come to undo it.

Fear has to be created, and greed has to be created. Intelligence is not greedy. You will be surprised to know that an intelligent man is never greedy. Greed is part of unintelligence. You hoard for tomorrow because you are not confident that tomorrow you will be able to tackle your life; otherwise, why hoard? You hoard, you become misers, you become greedy, because you don't know whether tomorrow your intelligence will be capable of coping with life or not. Who knows? You are not confident about your intelligence so you hoard, you become greedy. An intelligent person is not afraid, is not greedy. Greed and fear go together. That's why heaven and hell go together. Hell is fear, heaven is greed.

Create fear in people and create greed in people – make them as greedy as possible. Make them so greedy that life cannot satisfy them; then they will go to the priest and to the leader. Then they will start fantasizing about some future life where their foolish desires, stupid fantasies, will be fulfilled. Watch it. To demand the impossible is to be unintelligent.

An intelligent person is perfectly satisfied with the possible. He works for the probable, he never works for the impossible and the improbable, no. He looks at life and its limitations, he is not a perfectionist. A perfectionist is neurotic. If you are a perfectionist, you will go neurotic.

For example, if you love a woman and you ask for absolute fidelity, you will go mad and she will go mad. This is not possible: absolute fidelity means she will not even think, she will not even dream of another man. This is not possible. Who are you? Why has she fallen in love with you? – because you are a man. If she can fall in love with you, why can't she think of others? That possibility remains open. And how is she going to manage if she sees some beautiful person walking by and if a desire arises in her? Even to say, "This man is beautiful," is to desire – the desire has entered. You only say that something is beautiful when it feels worthy of being possessed, of being enjoyed. You are not indifferent.

Now, if you ask absolute fidelity, as people have asked, then there is bound to be conflict and you will remain suspicious. You will remain suspicious because you know your mind too: you also think of other women, so how can you trust that your woman is not thinking of other men? You know you are thinking, so you know she is also thinking. Now – distrust, conflict, agony. The love that was possible has become impossible because of an impossible desire.

People ask that which cannot be done. You want security for the future, which is not possible. You want absolute security for tomorrow. It cannot be guaranteed, it is not in the nature of life. An intelligent person knows that it is not in the nature of life – the future remains open. The bank can go bankrupt, the wife can escape with somebody else, the husband can die, the children may prove unworthy. Who knows about tomorrow? You may fall ill, you may become crippled… Who knows about tomorrow?

To ask security for tomorrow means to remain constantly in fear; it is not possible, so fear cannot be destroyed. Fear will be there, you will be trembling; and meanwhile the present moment is being missed. With the desire of security in the future you are destroying the present, which is the only life available. And you will become more and more shaken, afraid, greedy.

A child is born. A child is a very, very open phenomenon, utterly intelligent, but we jump upon him, we start destroying his intelligence. We start creating fear in him. You call it teaching, you call it making the child capable of coping with life. He is unafraid; you create fear in him. And your schools, colleges, universities all make him more and more unintelligent. They demand foolish things; they demand foolish things to be crammed, in which the child and his natural intelligence cannot see any point – for what? That child cannot see the point: why cram these things? But the university says, the college says, the home, the family, the well-wishers say, "Cram! You don't know now, but later on you will know why it is needed."

Cram history – all the nonsense that man has been doing to other men, all the madness – cram it! And the child cannot see the point: what does it matter when a certain king ruled England, from what date to what date? He has to cram those stupid things. Naturally his intelligence becomes more and more burdened, crippled; more and more dust collects on his intelligence. By the time a man comes back from the university he is unintelligent; the university has done its job.

It is very rare that a man can come from the university and yet be intelligent, still remain intelligent. Very few people have been able to escape the university, avoid the university, pass through the university and yet save their intelligence – very rarely. It is such a great mechanism to destroy you. The moment you become educated, you have become unintelligent. Can't you see this? The educated person behaves very unintelligently. Go to the primitive people who have never been educated and you will find a pure intelligence functioning.

I have heard…

A woman was trying to open a tin and she could not find the way to open it. So she went to look in the cookbook. By the time she looked into the book, the cook had opened it. She came back, and she was surprised. She asked the cook, "How did you do it?"

He said, "Lady, when you don't know how to read, you have to use your intelligence!"

Yes, it is right. When you don't know how to read you have to use your intelligence, what else can you do? The moment you start reading... Those three dangerous R's, when you have become capable of them you need not be intelligent; the books will take care.

Have you seen it? When a person starts typing, his handwriting is lost, then his handwriting is no longer beautiful. There is no need, the typewriter takes care. If you carry a calculator in your pocket you will forget all mathematics, there is no need. Sooner or later there will be small computers and everybody will be carrying them. They will have all the information of an *Encyclopaedia Britannica,* and then there will be no need for you to be intelligent at all; the computer will take care.

Go to the primitive people, the uneducated people, the villagers, and you will find a subtle intelligence. Yes, they are not more informed, that is true; they are not knowledgeable, that is true – but they are tremendously intelligent. Their intelligence is like a flame with no smoke around it.

The society has done something wrong to man – for certain reasons. It wants you to be slaves, it wants you to be always afraid, it wants you to be always greedy, it wants you to be always ambitious, it wants you to be always competitive. It wants you to be unloving, it wants you to be full of anger and hatred, it wants you to remain weak, imitative – carbon copies. It does not want you to become original Buddhas, original Krishnas or Christs – no. That's why your intelligence has been destroyed. Meditation is needed only to undo what the society has done. Meditation is negative: it simply negates the damage, it destroys the illness. And once the illness has gone, your well-being asserts itself of its own accord.

And in this century this has gone too far; universal education has been a calamity. Remember, I am not against education, I am against *this* education. There is a possibility of a different kind of education, which will be helpful in sharpening your intelligence, not destroying it; which will not burden it with unnecessary facts, which will not burden it with useless rubbish – knowledge; which will not burden it at all, but rather will help it to become more radiant, fresh, young.

This education only makes you capable of memorizing; that education will make you capable of more clarity. This education destroys your inventiveness; that education will help you to become more inventive.

For example, the education that I would like in the world will not require a child to answer in an old, stereotyped way. It will not encourage the answer that is written in the books, it will not encourage repetition, parroting. It will encourage inventiveness; even if the invented answer is not as right as the copied answer can be, still it will appreciate the boy who has brought a new answer to an old problem. Certainly his answer cannot be as right as Socrates' answer. Naturally, a small boy... His answer cannot be as exact as that of Albert Einstein, naturally. But to ask that his answer should be as right as that of Albert Einstein is foolish. If he is inventive he is in the right direction: one day he will become an Albert Einstein. If he is trying to create something new, naturally he has his limitations. But just his effort in trying to create something new should be appreciated, should be praised.

Education should not be competitive; people should not be judged against each other. Competitiveness is very violent and very destructive. Somebody is not good at mathematics and you call him mediocre. He may be good at carpentry, but nobody looks at that. Somebody is not good at literature and you call him stupid – and he will be good at music, at dance.

A real education will help people to find *their* life, where they can be fully alive. If a man is born to be a carpenter then that is the right thing for him to do, there is nobody to force anything else. This world can become such a great, intelligent world if a man is allowed to be himself, helped to be himself, supported in every way to be himself, and nobody comes in and interferes – in fact, nobody manipulates the child. If he wants to become a dancer, then that is good; dancers are needed, much dance is needed in the world. If he wants to become a poet, good; much poetry is needed, there is never enough. If he wants to become a carpenter or a fisherman, perfectly good. If he wants to become a woodcutter, perfectly good. There is no need for him to become a president or a prime minister; in fact if fewer people become interested in those targets it will be a blessing.

Right now everything is topsy-turvy. One who wanted to become a carpenter has become a doctor, one who wanted to become a doctor has become a carpenter: everybody is in somebody else's place. Hence so much unintelligence – everybody is doing somebody else's job. Once you start seeing it, you will feel why people are behaving unintelligently.

In India we have been meditating deeply and we have found a word – *swadharma, self-nature* – that carries the greatest implication for a future world. Krishna has said: "*Swadharme nidhanam shreyah* – it is good to die in your own self-nature, following your self-nature. *Para dharmo bhayavah baha* – somebody else's nature is very dangerous." Don't become imitators. Just be yourself.

I have heard...

Bill always wanted to go moose hunting, so he saved up enough money and went to the north woods. There, he was fitted out with necessary equipment and the storekeeper advised him to hire Pierre, the greatest moose-caller in the land.

"It's true," said the storekeeper, "that Pierre is expensive, but he has a sexy quality in his call that no moose can resist."

"How does that work?" asked Bill.

"Well," said the other, "Pierre will spot a moose at three hundred yards, then cup his hands and make his first call. When the moose hears that, he will become excited with anticipatory desire and approach to two hundred yards. Pierre will then call again, putting a bit more oomph into it, and the moose will skip with eager glee to a distance of a hundred yards. This time Pierre really gives his call a sexy delivery, prolonging it a bit, which impels the moose, agitated with carnal intent, to come to a point only twenty-five yards away from you. And that is the time, my friend, for you to aim and shoot."

"Suppose I miss?" wondered Bill.

"Oh, that would be terrible!" said the other.

"But why?" asked Bill.

"Because then poor Pierre gets mated."

That has happened to man – imitating, imitating. Man has completely lost the vision of his own reality. The Zen people say: "Seek out your original face."

So says Tantra. Tantra says to find out what your authenticity is. Who are you? If you don't know who you are, you will always be in some accident – always. Your life will be a long series of accidents, and whatsoever happens will never be satisfying. Discontent will be the only taste of your life.

You can watch it around you. Why do so many people look so dull, bored, just somehow passing the days, passing tremendously valuable time which they will not be able to recover – and passing with such dullness, as if only waiting for death. What has happened to so many people? Why don't they have the same freshness as the trees? Why doesn't man have the same song as the birds? What has happened to man?

One thing has happened: man has been imitating, man has been trying to become somebody else. Nobody is in his own home, everybody is knocking at somebody else's door; hence discontent, dullness, boredom, anguish...

When Saraha says that intelligence is the very quality of meditativeness, he means that an intelligent person will try just to be himself, whatsoever the cost. An intelligent person will never copy, will never imitate, he will never parrot. An intelligent person will listen to his own intrinsic call. He will feel his own being and move accordingly, whatsoever the risk. There is risk! When you copy others there is less risk. When you don't copy anybody you are alone, there is risk.

But life happens only to those who live dangerously. Life happens only to those who are adventurous, who are courageous, almost daredevils – only to them does life happen. Life does not happen to lukewarm people.

An intelligent person trusts himself, his trust is absolute about himself. How can you trust anybody else if you cannot even trust yourself?

People come to me and say, "We want to trust you." I ask them, "Do you trust yourself? If you trust yourself, then there is a possibility to trust me too, otherwise there is no possibility." How can you trust me if you don't trust yourself? You are the closest to yourself. You can trust me too if you trust yourself. If you trust yourself, then you will trust your trust in me; otherwise there is no possibility.

Intelligence is trust in your own being. Intelligence is adventure, thrill, joy. Intelligence is to live in this moment, not to hanker for the future.

Intelligence is not to think of the past and not to bother about the future. Past is no more, future is not yet. Intelligence is to make the uttermost use of the present moment that is available. The future will come out of it. If this moment has been lived in delight and joy, the next moment is going to be born out of it. It will bring more joy naturally, but there is no need to bother about it. If my today has been golden, my tomorrow will be even more golden. From where will it come? It will grow out of today. If this life has been a benediction, my next life will be a higher benediction. From where can it come? It will grow out of me, out of my *lived* experience. So an intelligent person is not concerned about heaven and hell, is not concerned about afterlife, is not concerned even about God, is not concerned even about the soul. An intelligent person simply lives intelligently, and God and soul and heaven and nirvana all follow naturally.

You live in belief; belief is unintelligent. Live through knowing; knowing is intelligence. And Saraha is absolutely right: intelligence is meditation. Unintelligent people also meditate, but certainly they meditate in an unintelligent way. They think that you have to go to the church every Sunday for one hour; that is given to religion. This is an unintelligent way to be related to religion. What has the church to do with it? Your real life is in the six days, Sunday is not your real day. You will live non-religiously for six days, and then you go to the church just for one or two hours – whom are you trying to deceive? Trying to deceive God that you are a church-goer?

Or, if you try a little harder, then every day twenty minutes in the morning, twenty in the evening you do Transcendental Meditation. You sit with closed eyes and you repeat a mantra in a very stupid way – om, om, om – which dulls the mind even more. To repeat a mantra mechanically takes your intelligence away; it does not give you intelligence. It is like a lullaby.

Down the centuries, mothers have known this. Whenever a child is restless and does not want to go to sleep, the mother comes and sings a lullaby. The child feels bored; and the child cannot escape – where to go? The mother is holding him on the bed. The only way to escape is in sleep, so he goes to sleep; he simply surrenders. He says, "It is foolish to be awake now because she is doing such a boring thing. She goes on repeating just a single line!"

There are stories that mothers and grandmothers tell to children when they don't go to sleep. If you look into these stories, you will find a certain pattern of constant repetition. Just the other day I was reading a story told by a grandmother to a small child, who does not want go to sleep because he does not feel like sleeping right now. His intelligence says that he is perfectly awake, but the grandmother is forcing him. She has other things to do, the child is not important.

Children are very puzzled – things look very absurd. When they want to sleep in the morning, everybody wants to wake them up. When they don't want to go to sleep, everybody is forcing them to. They become very puzzled: what is the matter with these people? When sleep comes, good – that is intelligence. When it is not coming, it is perfectly good to be awake.

So, this old grandmother is telling a story. At first the child remains interested, but by and by... Any intelligent child will feel bored; only a stupid child will not feel bored.

The story is that a man goes to sleep and dreams that he is standing before a great palace, and in the palace there are one thousand and one rooms. So he goes from one room to another – one thousand rooms – then he reaches the last room. And there is a beautiful bed, so he falls on the bed, falls asleep and dreams that he is standing at the door of a big palace which has one thousand and one rooms. So he goes into one thousand rooms, then he reaches the one thousand and first room... Again there is a beautiful bed, so he goes to sleep and dreams that he is standing before a palace...

This is the way it goes! Now how long can the child remain alert? Just out of sheer boredom the child falls asleep. He is saying, "Now be finished!"

A mantra does the same. You repeat "Ram, Ram," "Om, om," "Allah, Allah" – or anything. You go on repeating, you go on repeating. Now you are doing two jobs, both the grandmother's and the child's. Your intelligence is like the child, and your learning of the mantra is like the grandmother. The child tries to stop you, gets interested in other things, thinks of beautiful things – beautiful women, beautiful scenes – but you catch hold of him red-handed and bring him again to "Om, om, om." By and by your inner child feels that it is futile to struggle; the inner child goes to sleep.

Yes, the mantra can give you a certain sleep, it is an autohypnotic sleep. There is nothing wrong in it if sleep is difficult for you – if you suffer from insomnia it is good. But it has nothing to do with spirituality, it is a very unintelligent way to meditate. Then what is the intelligent way to meditate?

The intelligent way is to bring intelligence into everything that you do. Walking, walk intelligently, with awareness; eating, eat intelligently, with awareness. Do you remember ever eating intelligently, ever thinking about what you are eating? Is it nutritious, has it any nourishment value? Or are you just stuffing without any nourishment?

Have you ever watched what you do? You go on smoking... Then intelligence is needed: what are you doing? Just taking in smoke and throwing it out – and meanwhile destroying your lungs? And what are you really doing? Wasting money, wasting health. Bring intelligence in while you are smoking, while you are eating. Bring intelligence in when you go and make love to your woman, or to your man. What are you doing, have you really any love? Sometimes you make love out of habit – then it is ugly, then it is immoral.

Love has to be very conscious, only then does it become prayer. While making love to your woman, what exactly are you doing? Using the woman's body just to throw some energy that has become too much for you? Or are you paying respect – are you loving to the woman, do you have some reverence for the woman? I don't see it. Husbands don't respect their wives, they use them; wives use their husbands, they don't respect them. If reverence does not arise out of love, then intelligence is missing somewhere. Otherwise you will feel tremendously grateful to the other, and your lovemaking will become a great meditation.

Whatsoever you are doing, bring the quality of intelligence into it. Do it intelligently – that's what meditation is. And Saraha's statement is of tremendous significance: intelligence *is* meditation.

Intelligence has to spread all over your life, it is not a Sunday thing. And you cannot do it for twenty minutes and then forget about it – intelligence has to be just like breathing. Whatsoever you are doing – small, big, whatsoever... Cleaning the floor can be done intelligently or unintelligently. And you know that when you do it unintelligently there is no joy; you are doing a duty, somehow carrying it.

I have heard an illustration of how love can be reduced to duty and destroyed...

It happened in a church school class of ninth-grade girls. The class was studying Christian love and what it might mean to them and their lives. They finally decided that Christian love meant "doing something lovable for someone you didn't like." Children are very intelligent. Their conclusion is perfectly right. Listen to it again. They finally decided that Christian love meant "doing something lovable for someone you didn't like."

The teacher suggested that during the week they might test out their concept. When they returned the following week, the teacher asked for reports. One girl raised her hand and said, "I've done something!"

The teacher said, "Marvelous! What did you do?"

"Well," the girl replied, "in my math class at school there is this glunky kid..."

The teacher said, "Glunky...?"

And the girl replied, "Yes, you know...glunky. She's got four eyes, and she's all thumbs, and she's got three left feet, and when she comes down the hall in school everyone says, 'Here comes that glunky kid again.' She doesn't have any friends and nobody asks her to parties, and... You know, she's just glunky."

The teacher said, "I think I know just what you mean. What did you do?"

"Well, this glunky kid's in my math class and she's having a tough time. I'm pretty good in math so I offered to help her with homework."

"Wonderful!" said the teacher. "So what happened?"

"Well, I did help her, and it was fun, and she just couldn't thank me enough, but now I can't get rid of her!"

If you are doing something just as a duty – you don't love, you don't love it and you are doing it just as a duty – sooner or later you will be caught in it and you will be in difficulty over how to get rid of it. Just watch in your twenty-four hour day: how many things are you doing that you don't derive any pleasure from, that you don't grow from? In fact, you want to get rid of them. If you are doing too many things in your life which you really want to get rid of, you are living unintelligently.

An intelligent person will make his life in such a way that it will have a poetry of spontaneity, of love, of joy. It is *your* life and if you are not kind enough to yourself, who is going to be kind enough to you? If you are wasting it, it is nobody else's responsibility. I teach you to be responsible towards yourself. That is your first responsibility; everything else comes next – everything else! Even God comes next because he can come only when you *are*. You are the very center of your world, of your existence.

So be intelligent, bring in the quality of intelligence. And the more intelligent you become, the more capable you will become of bringing more intelligence into your life. Each single moment can become so luminous with intelligence. Then there is no need for any religion, no need to meditate, no need to go to the church, no need to go to any temple, no need for anything extra. Life in its intrinsicness is intelligent.

Just live totally, harmoniously, in awareness, and everything follows beautifully. A life of celebration follows the luminousness of intelligence.

The next question – it is related:

Osho,
Is it not good to serve people out of a sense of duty?

No, not at all; it is ugly. When you do something only out of duty, without love, you are harming yourself and you are harming the other too, because if you are not doing it out of love you will feel that the other has to be grateful, you will feel that you have obliged the other. You will wait for a return – in fact you will make a demand, gross or subtle: "Now, you do something for me, I have done so much for you."

When you do something out of love you do it without any idea of any return. It is not a bargain, you do it because you are happy doing it; the other is not obliged. Not that love is not returned; love is returned a thousandfold – but only love is returned, never duty. In fact, if you are doing a duty toward somebody, he will never be able to forgive you. You can see it in children: they are never able to forgive their parents. Their parents must have been doing a great duty. It is difficult to forgive those people who have been doing duty.

Respect arises for those people who have loved you – not out of any sense of duty, but just out of sheer joy. See the difference. A mother loves you just because she feels love for you; whether you return it or not is irrelevant. There is no bargain in it; it is not a contract, it is not business. If you don't return it, she will never mention it, she will never think about it. In fact, she has attained to so much joy while loving you, what more can she expect?

A mother always feels that she could not do as much as she wanted to do. But if the mother is doing it out of duty, then she feels she has done too much and you have betrayed her, you are not returning her love. And she will constantly hammer the fact into your head that she has done this and that, and that she has carried you for nine months in her womb, and she will relate the whole story again and again. That does not help to create love, it simply helps divorce. The children become very, very angry.

I know of a young boy...

I was staying with a family, and the father and mother brought the boy to me. They wanted me to teach the boy something because he was very ungrateful. I knew the family very well; I knew the father and the mother, so I knew why he was ungrateful. They had done all that they could do, but always only out of a sense of duty.

I told them, "You are responsible. You have never loved the boy, he feels hurt. You have never allowed him to feel worthy. Your love is not love, it is just like a hard rock on the heart of the boy. Now he is growing up and is capable of rebelling against you – that's why he's rebelling."

The boy looked at me with such gratitude. He started crying. He said, "Whosoever comes to the family, any guest, any friend, I'm always brought into the court – everybody has to teach me. You are the first man... This is exactly the case. These people have been torturing me and my mother goes on saying, 'For nine months I carried you in my womb.' And I say to her, 'But I had not asked you to. That had nothing to do with me, it was your business, you decided. Why didn't you get an abortion? I would not have interfered. Why did you get pregnant in the first place? I had not applied for it!'" And I knew he was angry, but he was right.

Now you ask, "Is it not good to serve people out of a sense of duty?" No, in fact, if you serve people out of a sense of duty, you will become their torturers, you will become very dominant over them. It is a way to dominate; it is political.

Start by massaging their feet and soon you will be at their necks, soon you will kill them. And naturally, when you start massaging their feet they put out their feet and say "Perfectly okay." But they don't know what is going to happen.

All public servants sooner or later become politicians. That is the right way to start your political life: become a public servant. Serve people out of sense of duty, and then sooner or later you can jump on their heads, then you can exploit them. Then you can crush them, and they cannot even utter a cry because you are a public servant. To become masters of people, the beginning is in public service.

My whole approach here is to make you alert to these traps. These are trips, ego trips. In the name of humbleness, humility, service, you are going on an ego trip. Do, but only do out of love; otherwise, don't do. Please don't do. It is better if you don't do anything.

You will be able to do because nobody can remain undoing continuously. Energy is created, and you have to give it – but give it out of love. When you give out of love, you feel grateful to the other because he has accepted your love, he has accepted your energy, he has shared with you, he has unburdened you.

Do only when you can feel grateful to the person you have done something for, not otherwise.

The third question:

Osho,
Why does jealousy always follow love as a shadow?

Jealousy has nothing to do with love. In fact, your so-called love also has nothing to do with love. These are beautiful words which you use without knowing what they mean, without experiencing what they mean. You go on using the word *love*: you use it so much that you forget the fact that you have not experienced it yet. That is one of the dangers of using such beautiful words: *God, love, nirvana, prayer* – beautiful words. You go on using them, you go on repeating them, and by and by the very repetition makes you feel as if you know.

What do you know about love? If you know anything about love, you cannot ask this question because jealousy is never present in love. And wherever jealousy is present, love is not present. Jealousy is not part of love; jealousy is part of possessiveness. Possessiveness has nothing to do with love. You want to possess; through possession you feel strong, your territory is bigger. And if somebody else tries to trespass on your territory, you are angry. Or if somebody has a bigger house than your house, you are jealous. Or if somebody tries to dispossess you of your property, you are jealous and angry. If you love, jealousy is impossible, it is not possible at all.

I have heard…

Up in the frozen Yukon, two trappers stopped at the last outpost to get supplies for the long dark winter. After they had loaded their sleds with flour, canned foods, kerosene, matches and ammunition, they were ready to mush off for six months in the wilds.

"Wait a minute, boys," the storekeeper called to them. "How about taking one of these?" And he showed them a large board curved like an hourglass.

"What is it?" asked one of the trappers.

The storekeeper winked. "It's called a love board. You can hug it when you get lonely."

"We'll take two!" exclaimed the men.

Six months later one of the trappers, bearded and haggard, returned.

"Where's your buddy?" asked the storekeeper.

"Had to shoot him," muttered the trapper. "Caught him messin' around with my love board!"

Jealousy has nothing to do with love. If you love your woman, how can you be jealous? If you love your man, how can you be jealous? If your woman is laughing with somebody else, how can you be jealous? You will be happy: it is your woman who is happy. Her happiness is your happiness – how can you think against her happiness?

But look, watch. You laughed at this story but it is happening everywhere, in every family. The wife even becomes jealous of the newspaper if the husband goes on reading it too much. She comes and snatches it away, she becomes jealous. The newspaper is substituting for her. While she is present, how dare you read your newspaper? That is an insult! When she is there you have to be possessed by her totally; not even a newspaper... The newspaper becomes a competitor, so what to say about human beings? If the wife is present and the husband starts talking to another woman and looks a little happy, which is natural – people get tired of each other; anything new, and one feels a little thrilled – now the wife is angry. You can know well that if a couple is going by and the man looks sad, then he is the husband married to that woman. If he looks happy, he is not married to the woman, she is not *his* wife.

Once I was traveling in a train and there was a woman in the same compartment. At each station a man would come in – sometimes he would bring bananas, sometimes he would bring tea and ice cream and this and that.

I asked her, "Who is this man?"

She said, "He's my husband."

I said, "I can't trust that, I can't believe it. How long have you been married?"

She became a little disturbed, she said, "Now that you insist, we are not married. But how did you come to know?"

I said, "I have never seen any husband coming in at every station. Once the husband gets rid of the wife, he will come in at the last station hoping that she has dropped out somewhere in the middle. Each station bringing things, this and that, and rushing again and again from his compartment..."

She said, "You are right, he's not my husband. He's my husband's friend."

"That's right – then there is no problem!"

You are not really in love with your woman, or with your man, or with your friend. If you are in love, then his or her happiness is your happiness. If you are in love, then you will not create any possessiveness.

Love is capable of giving total freedom. *Only* love is capable of giving total freedom. And if freedom is not given, then it is something else, not love. It is a certain type of egoistic trip. You have a beautiful woman; you want to show everybody all around the town that you have a beautiful woman – just like a possession. Just as when you have a car, and when you are in your car, you want everybody to know that nobody has such a beautiful car, the same is the case with your woman. You bring diamonds for her – but not out of love. She is a decoration for your ego. You carry her from one club to another, but she has to remain clinging to you and go on showing that she belongs to you. Any infringement of your right and you are angry, you can kill the woman whom you think you love.

There is great ego working everywhere. We want people to be like things. We possess them like things, we reduce persons to things. The same is the attitude about things also.

I have heard…

A rabbi and a priest were neighbors and there was a certain amount of rivalry between them. If the Cohens had their drive done up, Father O'Flynn had his re-laid – and so it went on. One day the priest had a new Jaguar, so the rabbi bought a Bentley. When the rabbi looked out of his window, it was to see the priest pouring water over the top of the car bonnet. He opened the window and shouted, "That's not the way to fill the radiator, you know."

"Aha!" said the priest, "I'm christening it with holy water – that's more than you can do to yours."

A little while later the priest was taken aback to see the rabbi lying in the road, hacksaw in hand, sawing the last inch off his car's exhaust pipe.

That is the mind – continuously in competition. Now he is doing circumcision. He has to do something. That is the way we are living, the way of the ego. The ego knows no love, the ego knows no friendship, the ego knows no compassion. The ego is aggression, violence.

And you ask: "Why does jealousy always follow love as a shadow?" Never. Love makes no shadow at all. Love is so transparent that it makes no shadow. Love is not a solid thing; it is transparency. No shadow is created out of love. Love is the only phenomenon on the earth which creates no shadow.

The fourth question:

Osho,
What is repression?

Repression is living a life that you were not meant to live, repression is doing things which you never wanted to do; repression is being the fellow that you are not. Repression is a way to destroy yourself, repression is suicide – very slow of course, but very certain, a slow poisoning. Expression is life; repression is suicide.

This is the Tantra message: don't live a repressed life, otherwise you live not at all. Live a life of expression, creativity, joy. Live the way God wanted you to live; live the natural way. And don't be afraid of the priests. Listen to your instincts, listen to your body, listen to your heart, listen to your intelligence. Depend on yourself; go wherever your spontaneity takes you and you will never be at a loss. And going spontaneously with your natural life, one day you are bound to arrive at the doors of the divine.

Your nature is God within you. The pull of that nature is God's pull within you. Don't listen to the poisoners, listen to the pull of nature. Yes, nature is not enough: there is a higher nature too – but the higher comes through the lower, the lotus grows out of the mud. Through the body grows the soul. Through sex grows *samadhi*.

Remember, through food grows consciousness. In the East we have said: *Annam Brahma* – food is God. What type of assertion is this, that food is God? God grows out of food: the lowest is linked with the highest, the shallowest is linked with the deepest.

Now, the priests have been teaching you to repress the lower. And they are very logical. Only they have forgotten one thing – that existence is illogical. They are very logical and it appeals to you, that's why you have listened down the ages and followed them. It appeals to reason that if you want to attain to the higher, don't listen to the lower. It looks logical: if you want to go high then you cannot go low. Then don't go low, go high – it is very rational. The only trouble is that existence *is not* rational.

Just the other day Dhruva was talking to me. In his Sahaj group sometimes he comes to some moments when the whole group falls silent – out of nowhere, out of the blue. And those few moments of silence are of tremendous beauty. And he was saying, "They are so mysterious, those moments. We are not managing them, we don't think about them, they simply come sometimes. But when they come, the whole group immediately feels the presence of something divine, of something higher, something greater than everybody else. And everybody immediately becomes aware that something is present, something mysterious. And everybody falls silent in those moments."

Now his logical mind thought, "It will be good if I can do the whole group in silence." He must have started thinking, "If those few moments – few and far between – are so beautiful, then why not do the whole group in silence?" I said, "There you go – logical, and existence is not logical. If you remain silent, those moments will never come again."

There is a polarity in life. The whole day you work hard, you chop wood, then in the night you go into your deepest sleep. Now, the logical thing is – you can think logically, it is mathematical – next morning you can think, "The whole day I worked so much and was tired, still I could come to such a deep sleep. If I practice rest the whole day, I will go into an even deeper sleep." So the next day you simply lie down in your armchair, you practice rest. Do you think you are going to have a good sleep? You will lose even ordinary sleep. That's how rich people suffer from insomnia.

Existence is not logical. Existence gives sleep to the beggars who have been working the whole day, moving from one place to another in the hot summer, begging. Existence gives good sleep to laborers, to stonecutters, to woodcutters. The whole day they have been tired and out of that tiredness they fall into deep sleep.

This is the polarity. The more you are exhausted energy-wise, the more is your need for sleep, because you can only get more energy from deep sleep. If you exhaust your energy, you create a situation in which you will fall into deep sleep; existence has to give you deep sleep. If you don't work at all, then there is no need. You have not used even the energy that was given you, so what is the point of giving you any more? Energy is given to those who use it.

Now, Dhruva is logical. He thinks, "If we do the whole group in silence…" But even those few moments will be missed, and the whole group will become very, very chattering inside. Of course, from the outside they will remain silent, but their minds will go crazy inside. Right now they are working hard, they are expressing their emotions, catharting, bringing everything up, throwing everything out; they become exhausted. There come a few moments when they are so exhausted that there is nothing else to throw out. In that moment, suddenly, there is a contact; a silence descends.

Out of work is rest, out of expression is silence. This is how existence works. Its ways are very irrational. Now, if you really want to be secure, you will have to live a life of insecurity. If you really want to be alive, you will have to be ready to die at any moment. This is existence's illogic! If you really want to be authentically true, then you will have to risk. Repression is a way to avoid the risk.

For example, you have been taught never to be angry and you think that a person who is never angry is bound to be very loving. You are wrong. A person who is never angry will not be able to love either. They go together, they come in the same package. A man who really loves will sometimes be really angry. But his anger is beautiful, it is out of love. His energy is hot, and you will not feel hurt by his anger. In fact, you will feel grateful that he was angry.

Have you seen it? If you love somebody and you do something and the person is *really* angry, frankly angry, you feel grateful because he loved you so much that he can afford anger. Otherwise why…? When you don't want to risk anger, you remain polite. When you don't want to say anything, you don't want to take any risks, you go on smiling; it doesn't matter. If your child is going to jump into the abyss, will you remain unangry? Will you not shout, will you not be a boiling energy? Will you go on smiling? It is not possible.

There is a story...

Once it happened in Solomon's court that two women came that were fighting for one child. Both were claiming that the child belonged to them. It was very difficult – how to decide? The child was so small that he could not say anything.

Solomon looked and he said, "One thing I will do: I will cut the child in two and divide the child. That is the only way possible. I have to be just and fair; there is no proof either way that the child belongs to A or to B. So I, as the king, have decided; cut the child in two and give half to each.

The woman who was holding the child continued to smile, she was happy. But the other woman became simply mad, as if she would kill the king! She said, "What are you saying? Have you gone mad?" She was in a rage. She was no longer an ordinary woman, she was anger incarnate, she was fire! And the woman said, "If this is justice, then I leave aside my claim; let the child remain with the other woman. The child belongs to her, he is not my child!" Angry, yet tears flowing down her face.

And the king said, "The child belongs to you. You take it. The other woman is just bogus, false." The other woman could not say anything – and the child was being killed! In fact she continued to smile, it did not matter to her.

When you love you can be angry. When you love you can afford it. If you love yourself – and that is a must in life, otherwise you will miss your life – you will never be repressive, you will be expressive of whatsoever life gives. You will be expressing it – its joys, its sadness, its peaks, its lows, its days, its nights.

But you have been brought up to become bogus, you have been brought up in such a way as to become hypocrites. When you feel angry, you go on smiling a painted smile. When you are in a rage you repress the rage. When you feel sexuality you repress that and you go on chanting your mantra. You are never true to what is within you.

It happened...

Joe and his little daughter Midge took a trip to an amusement park. En route they stopped for a huge meal. At the park they came to a hotdog stand and Midge exclaimed, "Daddy, I want..." Joe stopped her and bought her a hotdog with all the trimmings. At the popcorn stand Midge yelled, "Daddy, I want..." Joe cut her short and stuffed her with popcorn.

When they came to the ice cream vendor, little Midge once more shouted, "Daddy, I want…" Joe stopped her again, but this time said, "You want, you want! I know what you want – ice cream!"

"No, Daddy," she pleaded, "I want to vomit."

That's what she was wanting from the very beginning – but who listens? Repression is not listening to your nature. Repression is a trick to destroy you.

Twelve skinheads, punks, walk into a pub with their Levi jackets on and all their equipment. They walk up to the barkeeper and say, "Thirteen pints of bitter, please."

"But there are only twelve of you."

"Look, we want thirteen pints of bitter."

So he gives them the beer and they all sit down. There's a little old fellow sitting in a corner and the skinhead leader walks over to him and says, "Here you are, dad, here's a pint of beer for you."

The little fellow says, "Thank you, thank you – you are generous, son."

"It's all right, we don't mind helping cripples."

"But I'm not a cripple."

"You will be if you don't buy the next round."

That's what repression is – it is a trick to cripple you. It is a trick to destroy you, it is a trick to weaken you. It is a trick to put you against yourself. It is a way of creating conflict within you, and whenever a man is in conflict with himself, of course he is very weak.

The society has played a great game: it has put everybody against himself – so you are continuously fighting within yourself, you don't have any energy to do anything else. Can't you observe it happening in you? Continuously fighting… The society has divided you into a split person, it has made you schizophrenic and it has confused you. You have become driftwood: you don't know who you are, you don't know where you are going. You don't know what you are doing here, you don't know why you are here in the first place. It has really confused you. And out of this confusion are born great leaders: Adolf Hitler, Mao Zedong, Joseph Stalin. And out of this confusion arises the Vatican pope, and out of this confusion a thousand and one things arise. But *you* are destroyed.

Tantra says be expressive – but remember, expression does not mean irresponsibility. Tantra says to be expressive intelligently and no harm will happen to anybody from you. A man who cannot harm himself will never harm anybody. And a man who harms himself is a dangerous man in a way.

If he is not even in love with himself, he is dangerous: he can harm anybody. In fact he *will* harm.

When you are sad, when you are depressed, you will create other people around you who are sad and depressed. When you are happy, you would like to create a happy society because happiness can exist only in a happy world. If you are living joyfully, you would like everybody to be joyful. That is true religion: out of your own joy, you bless the whole existence.

But repression makes you false. It is not by repression that anger, sex, greed are destroyed, no. They are there – just the labels are changed. They go into the unconscious, they start working from there; they go underground. And, of course, when they are underground they are more powerful. The whole psychoanalytic movement tries to bring what is underground to the surface. Once it becomes conscious, you can be freed of it.

A Frenchman was staying in England and a friend asked him how he was getting on. He said he was doing very well, except for one thing. "When I go to a party, the hostess, she does not tell me where the 'pissoir' is."

"Ah, Georges, you mean she does not tell you where the toilet is? That's just our English prudery. Actually she will say, 'Do you want to wash your hands?' and that means the same thing."

The Frenchman made a mental note of this, and the next time he went to a party the guests standing around heard the hostess remark, "Good evening, Monsieur Du Pont, do you want to wash your hands?"

"No thank you, Madame, I have just washed them up against the tree in the front garden."

That's what happens: just the names change. You become confused, you don't know what is what. Everything is there – just the labels change, and that creates a sort of insane humanity. Your parents, your society, have destroyed you; you are destroying your children. Now, this is a vicious circle. Somebody has to come out of the vicious circle.

If you understand me rightly, then my sannyas is an effort to bring you out of the vicious circle.

Don't be angry at your parents – they could not do better than they have done. But now become more conscious, and don't do the same thing to your children. Make them more expressive, teach them more expression. Help them so that they become more authentic, so that they can bring out whatsoever is inside them. And they will be tremendously grateful forever because there will be no conflict within them. They will be in one piece, they will not be in fragments. And they will never be confused; they will always know what they want.

When you know exactly what you want, you can work for it. When you don't know what you really want, how can you work for it? Then anybody takes hold of you, anybody gives you any ideas, and you start following him. Any leader comes, anybody who can convince you argumentatively, and you start following him. You have followed many people, and they have all destroyed you.

Follow your nature.

Each generation destroys the other. Unless somebody becomes very alert, aware, the destruction is bound to happen.

The last question:

Osho,
Why did I get married to a woman who hates me? I hate her too.

How am I supposed to know why you got married to a woman you hate and who hates you? Maybe – this is just a guess – you got married *because* you hate each other.

There are two types of marriages: love marriages and hate marriages. Love marriages are very rare; in fact they don't happen. The so-called marriages are hate marriages. At least about women it is very true. If they want to torture you, they will marry you because there is no surer way to torture you. That is the best way.

I have heard...

Mulla Nasruddin had gotten himself in a very awkward situation. He had been carrying on with no less than three women at the same time, promising each one that he would marry her. Lately they'd been pressing him to make good his vow. At his wits' end, he consulted his lawyer.

"I suggest," said the lawyer, "that you let me notify all the newspapers that you have committed suicide. After that we'll hold a mock funeral; that should take care of your troubles."

They went into action immediately. While the lawyer phoned the newspapers, Mulla made the necessary arrangements with the undertaker. It was a very impressive funeral. At the proper time everyone filed solemnly around the coffin to bid a last farewell to the deceased. And then his three girlfriends entered.

"Poor Nasruddin," sighed the first girl as she gazed down at the body, "he was a louse, but I'll sure miss him."

"Good-bye, Nasruddin," wept the second girl, "too bad things didn't work out better."

But the third girl was enraged. "You dirty rat! – dying on me after you promised we'd be married. For that I'm gonna shoot you myself, even though you are dead! At least I'll have that satisfaction!" She then pulled a revolver out of her purse and leveled it at the prone figure.

"Hold it! Don't get so excited!" cried the corpse, sitting up. "You, I'll marry!"

I don't know why you got married to a woman who hates you and whom you hate. But watch out: you must be in a very deep mess. But everybody is, so don't feel worried. This is the natural, usual condition of humanity. Everybody is in a mess. Nobody knows why one is going to do a certain thing. Sometimes you get married to a woman because her face is appealing. But what has marriage to do with the face? After two or three days the honeymoon will be over and you will never look at the face again. And you never married the real woman, you only married a face, a certain figure, and the figure has nothing to do with it. Or maybe you liked the voice of the woman, the singsong voice, and you got married – people get married for foolish reasons. Now the singsong voice has nothing to do with it; the singsong voice will not prepare your food, it will not make your bed. After a few days, you will forget the voice.

The reality you will have to live with has nothing to do with these things. A certain woman has a certain figure, a certain curve – but what has a curve to do with life? A certain woman has a certain way of walking and it appeals to you. But can you waste your life, your married life, on such flimsy things? It is not possible.

Life needs more realistic approaches, more realistic foundations. But you go on doing superficial things like this. The reason is that you are not aware. It is not only a question of marriage, it is a question of your whole life. That's what you go on doing – you go on doing things on the spur of the moment, not seeing deeply that life needs more awareness, more responsibility, more understanding, more intelligence.

Start being more intelligent, and you will be less and less in trouble. Be more watchful. Become a witness.

Enough for today.

CHAPTER 9

no-mind is the door

Once in the realm that's full of joy,
the seeing mind becomes enriched
and thereby for this and that most useful;
even when it runs after objects it is not alienated from itself.

The buds of joy and pleasure
and the leaves of glory grow.
If nothing flows out anywhere
the bliss unspeakable will fruit.

What has been done and where and what in itself it will become
is nothing: yet thereby it has been useful for this and that.
Whether passionate or not
the pattern is nothingness.

If I am like a pig that covets worldly mire,
you must tell me what fault lies in a stainless mind.
By what does not affect one,
how can one now be fettered?

There are two ways to approach reality: the way of the intellect and the way of intelligence. The way of the intellect is to theorize about it, is to think about it, is to speculate about it. All speculation is meaningless because how can you speculate about that which you don't know? How can you even think about that which you don't know?

The unknown cannot be thought, there is no way to think about the unknown; all that you go on thinking is the known that goes on repeating in your mind. Yes, you can create new combinations of old thoughts, but just by making new combinations you are not going to discover the real. You will be deceiving.

Intellect is the greatest deceiver in the world. Through intellect man has deceived himself down the ages. Through intellect you explain away reality, you don't explain it. Through intellect you create such a dust around yourself that you cannot see the reality at all; you are cut off from the existential, and you are closed in your words, in your thoughts, in your arguments. You are lost in your scriptures – no man has ever been lost anywhere else. It is in the jungle of the scriptures where men get lost.

Tantra is the way of intelligence, not of intellect. It does not answer any questions; it does not explain anything at all, it is non-explanatory. It is not a questioning, it is a quest. It is not inquiry *about* the truth, it is an inquiry *into* the truth. It penetrates reality. It tries to destroy all the clouds that surround you so that you can see reality as it is.

Tantra is to go beyond thinking. That's why love has been so much praised by the Tantrikas. That's why the love orgasm has become a symbol for the ultimate reality: the reason is, it is only in the love orgasm that you lose your mind for a few moments. That is the only state of no-mind which is available to the ordinary man, that is the only possibility for you to have a glimpse of reality.

Hence, sexual orgasm has become tremendously important on the path of Tantra. Not that it gives you ultimate reality, but at least it gives you a chance to peek beyond the mind. It gives you a small window, very momentary; it does not stay long, but still that is the only possibility for you to have some contact with reality. Otherwise you are always surrounded by your thoughts and the thoughts explain nothing. All explanations are simply nonsense.

Now I would like to tell you a joke. You know I don't tell many of them…

The joke has to do with this fella standing on the corner – a colored fella. And he's standing on the corner and he looks up and he says, "Lord!" – he is on a personal basis – he says, "Lord, why did you make me so dark?"

And the Lord thinks, and the Lord broods, and the Lord tries to philosophize – some answer is needed – and the Lord says, "My boy, the reason I made you so dark is so that when you're running through the jungle, the sun won't give you sunstroke."

The colored fella says, "Yeah, yeah, I go for that. But Lord, why did you make my hair so coarse?"

The Lord replies, "Well, the reason I did that, my boy, is so that when you're running through the jungle in quest of the wildebeest and the water buffalo and the lion, your hair won't get caught in the brambles."

"Yeah, yeah... But Lord, why did you make my legs so long?"

The Lord answers, "The reason I made your legs long, my son, is so that when you're loping through the jungle in quest of the wildebeest and rhinoceros and the bull and the elephant, you would run very swiftly. Do you have any further questions?"

The colored fella says, "Yeah, Lord! What the hell am I doing here in Pune?"

No explanations help. No explanation ever explains anything. Now the Lord God must have been at a loss...

Man's reality is a mystery. There is no answer that can answer it because it is not a question in the first place. It is a mystery to be lived, not a problem to be solved.

And remember the distinction between a problem and a mystery: a mystery is existential, a problem is intellectual. A mystery is not created by the mind, so the mind cannot solve it either. A problem is created by the mind in the first place, so the mind can solve it. There is no "problem" in it. But the mystery of life – this existential mystery that surrounds you, these trees, these stars, these birds, people, you yourself – how can you solve them through the mind?

The mind is a very, very recent arrival. Existence has lived without the mind since the beginning. The mind is just an addition, it has just happened. Scientists say that if we divide human history into twenty-four hours, into one day, then mind came just two seconds ago: just two seconds ago! If this is going to be the measurement – twenty-four hours, the whole history – then mind entered only two seconds ago. How can it solve? What can it solve? It has not known the beginning, it has not known the end; it has come just now in the middle. It has no perspective.

If one really wants to know what this unknown is, one has to drop out of the mind, one has to disappear into existence. That is the Tantra way. Tantra is not a philosophy; Tantra is absolutely existential. And remember, when I say that Tantra is existential, I don't mean the existentialism of Sartre, Camus, Marcel, and others. That existentialism is again a philosophy, a philosophy of existence, but not the Tantra way. And the difference is vast.

The existential philosophers in the West have only stumbled upon the negative: anguish, angst, depression, sadness, anxiety, hopelessness, meaninglessness, purposelessness – all the negatives. Tantra has stumbled upon all that is beautiful, joyful, blissful. Tantra says that existence is an orgasm, an eternal orgasm going on and on and on. It is forever and forever an orgasm, an ecstasy.

They must be moving in different directions. Sartre goes on thinking about existence. Tantra says that thinking is not the door. It leads nowhere, it is a blind alley; it brings you only to a cul-de-sac. Philosophy is great if you are just fooling around; then philosophy is great. You can make mountains out of molehills and you can enjoy the trip. Just the other day I was reading a very, very philosophical piece. Meditate over it...

A most peculiar thing occurred to me, and I am going to tell it to you on the chance that it may have occurred to you too at one time or another, and on hearing me you will handle the situation better when it occurs again.

Yesterday I was in a restaurant and I ordered some lunch. I was with a small group of people around this table having a little lunch. It wasn't, you know, six, seven people around this table; I don't know, eight people, nine – about forty people having lunch: a small group of people.

With my lunch I ordered a glass of milk. Now, I like milk. You know how I feel about buttermilk, but milk I like. Milk I adore. I like fresh, cold milk. If it's warm: yuck! If I can taste it, I don't like it.

Anyway the milk came. And I was just about to drink it when I noticed that floating at the top of the milk was the littlest, teeniest black speck. And I am here to tell you that nothing in this world mattered but that little black speck! It became the most important thing in my life for the next few minutes. First of all, I wasn't gonna let that damn thing inside me, I'll tell you! You know, who knows these days what it was? It could have been a solid chunk of strontium 90, you know. Or maybe a large typhoid colony. Anyway I didn't want to swallow it.

Now, I've seen black specks before. I'm a sophisticated man, I've lived – and I'm sure you've seen them too. You can see them any place. However, I think you spot them mostly in sugar bowls. Once in a while you catch one lurking about in a bowl of flour. Oatmeal is loaded with black specks; I think oatmeal is mostly black specks, if you want to know the truth. But that's neither here nor there.

Now, the thing that bothered me about this black speck was that I didn't know where it came from. That's what bothered me. I knew where the *milk* came from – and that bothered me too, you know, but at least I knew where it came from. So I decided to get the black speck out of the milk.

Do you know how hard that is to do? Those black specks are smart as hell, they can smell a spoon a mile off! The minute you pick up the spoon they start running around the glass, don't they? You pick them up and they jump out. And you've got to be very careful or they get wise and they dive for the bottom, and you have to sit there like a fool waiting for them to float back up again.

Now there's one thing you can do: if you just take the tip of your finger and you touch the speck very gently, it'll stick to your finger along with a large blob of milk – and you'll have it out. But you know, when you're with a group of people you don't want to put your finger in your milk. You know, some wise guy is bound to say, "Say! How come you're putting your finger in your milk?" What are you going to say, "I'm trying to get a black speck out"? You know, you have no answer.

Now there's another thing you can do. You can drink the milk very carefully, keeping your eye on the speck all the time. The minute it starts to move towards you, you quit! You fool the little devil! But that's only possible if the speck is on the far side of the glass. In this case it was close to me, waiting, so what do you do? You twist the glass – and the damned thing stays right there!

Well, I'm going to tell you what I did, so that when it happens to you, you can handle the situation in a similar fashion. I got up and walked around to the other side of the table, and I drank it over there! He never even knew it!

Philosophy is creating mountains out of molehills. You can go on and on, there is no end to it. For at least five thousand years man has been philosophizing about each and every thing: about the beginning, about the end, about the middle – about each and every thing. And not a single question has been solved; not a single, not the smallest question has been solved or dissolved. Philosophy has proved to be the most futile of efforts, but still man continues – knowing perfectly well that it never delivers anything. Why? It goes on promising, but never delivers anything. Then why does man continue with this effort?

It is cheap: it does not require any involvement, it is not a commitment. You can sit in your chair and go on thinking. It is a dream. It does not require that you should change in order to see reality. That's where courage is needed, adventurous courage is needed. To know the truth, you are moving into the greatest adventure there is. You may be lost, who knows? You may never come back, who knows? Or you may come back utterly changed, and who knows whether it will be for the good or not?

The journey is unknown, the journey is so unknown that you cannot even plan it. You have to take a jump into it. Blindfolded, you have to take a jump into it, in the dark night, with no map, without knowing where you are going,

without knowing what you are going for. Only a few daredevils enter into this
existential quest. So Tantra has only appealed to a very few people, but those
were the salt of the earth. Saraha is one of them.

Now the sutras. These are the last four sutras of Saraha's *Royal Song*.

> *Once in the realm that's full of joy,*
> *the seeing mind becomes enriched*
> *and thereby for this and that most useful;*
> *even when it runs after objects it is not alienated from itself.*

The king must have told Saraha what people were saying about him. They
were saying that he was indulging in the senses, he was indulging in pleasures.
He was no longer a sannyasin; his renunciation was false, he had fallen.

He had asked permission of the king to become a Buddhist monk, and
he *had* become a Buddhist monk. He had lived the controlled and disciplined
life of a Buddhist monk. And then came this revolutionary woman, this arrowsmith woman, and she transformed his whole being, his whole life and his
whole style. She destroyed his character. She allowed him freedom – freedom
to be, freedom to be from moment to moment, with no past, with no future.

Naturally the ordinary common people started thinking that he had fallen
from grace, he had betrayed. And he had been a great brahmin and was a great
scholar; they had hoped for much from him, that he would bring some knowledge to the country, and now he had become like a mad dog. A thousand and
one stories must have been spread around the country about him, and the king
must have told Saraha what people thought about him. The king was hurt; he
had loved the man, he had respected the man – but the king was also of the
same world, his ways of thinking were similar to those of the people. He had no
insight into reality or into himself.

Saraha says to the king, "Once, even once, if you know what joy is, you
will forget all these stories. Once, even once, if you have any taste of what life
is, you will forget all this nonsense of character, virtue, respectability."

You can continue to live a respectable life only if you are dead, you can live
in a respectable way if you have not yet contacted life. Life is a radical phenomenon. It is a chaos – a very creative chaos, but it is a chaos all the same.

Saraha says: *Once in the realm that's full of joy, the seeing mind becomes
enriched...* But the question is of experiencing it.

Saraha says, "I cannot explain what has happened to me, but I can say this
much: if you taste it even once you will be transformed. The taste transforms."

"I am not going to convince you in any argumentative way, I have no philosophy," says Saraha. "I have a certain experience, I can share that experience

with you, but the sharing cannot be just from my side. You will have to move from your dogmatic standpoint, you will have to come with me into the unknown. I can take you to that window from which existence is clear, transparent, but you will have to hold my hand and come to that window."

That's what a master is meant to do: he holds the hand of the disciple and takes him to that opening from which he has looked into existence. In a metaphorical way, he lends his eyes to you. Once you have tasted, then there is no problem, then that very taste will go on pulling you. Then the pull is so tremendous that you cannot remain where you have been staying and vegetating.

Once in the realm that's full of joy, the seeing mind becomes enriched... But a seeing mind is needed to taste that joy – a mind which is not burdened with blinkers too much, a mind which is open.

Now, this is the problem with people who are too attached to philosophies, religions, scriptures, theories, dogmas: the problem is that they have too many blinkers, layer upon layer. Their eyes are lost behind curtains and curtains and curtains. Those curtains have to be peeled away just as you peel an onion. All those curtains have to be removed; then you have a seeing mind.

Right now, whatsoever you have is a non-seeing mind. It only pretends that it sees; it only says, believes, that it sees. Your eyes see not, your ears hear not, and your hands touch not – because you have lost that sensitivity, that flow which can make your eyes seeing eyes, which can make your ears hearing ears. That's why Jesus has to say again and again to his disciples, "If you can see, see it! If you have eyes, see it! If you have ears, listen to it, hear it!" He was talking to people who were not blind and who were not deaf. They had as much capacity to see as you have, and the capacity to hear as you have; they were normal people.

But why did he insist again and again, "If you have eyes..."? Was he always talking to blind people like you? But what did he mean when he said, "If you have eyes..."? Why this "if"? It is a great "if" because people appear to have eyes and yet they don't have. And that appearance is very dangerous because they go on believing that they have eyes.

Have you ever looked at anything without your thoughts coming in, interfering, distracting, interpreting? Have you ever seen a roseflower without language coming in, without your mind immediately saying, "It is a roseflower, it is a beautiful flower" – this and that? The moment you say it is a roseflower you are not seeing *this* flower. Then all the roseflowers that you have seen and heard about are standing in a queue, and this real roseflower is at the farthest end. The moment you say it is a roseflower, you are pulling a curtain over your eyes.

Language is the greatest curtain. Can't you see this flower just as it is, without calling it a rose, without even calling it a flower? What is the need? Can't you just look into this reality without any idea, without any cloud moving around you? Can't you be, for a moment, without language? If you are without language for a moment, you will have the seeing mind. Start trying it sometimes. Sitting by the side of a tree, just look at the tree and don't think what tree it is. And don't think that it is a tree, and don't think that it is beautiful or ugly; don't bring your mind in at all. Just watch. Whatever it is – X, Y, Z – let it be whatsoever it is. Don't judge.

Jesus says: "Judge ye not." Language is a judgment. With the judgment come all the prejudices. With the judgment comes your whole past. And whenever past comes in, you are removed from the present.

I was reading…

There was a man who owned a garage, and he had a cat. One day he was filling a customer's car with petrol when he spilled some in the cat's milk. The cat drank it all up and began to run round the place at sixty miles an hour. Then suddenly it stopped dead.

The customer said, "Has the cat died?"

"No," said the garage owner, "I think it's run out of petrol."

A garage owner has his language, his past, his prejudice. He understands things in a certain way. He says, "No, I think it has run out of petrol." And this is happening constantly.

It happened…

It happened while Sarvesh, our ventriloquist sannyasin with the talking puppet, was here and he was giving a show in the Radha Auditorium. The puppet was telling all sorts of jokes about different religions and races and everything. Then he said, "Well now, let's tell a joke about Germans."

So a German sannyasin – not Haridas, mind you – stood up and said, "I will not have you telling jokes about Germans! We are not as thick as you think, you know."

"Be calm, sir," said Sarvesh. "Please be calm and sit down. It is nothing personal."

"I'm not talking to you," said the German, "I'm talking to the little fella on your knee!"

Your mind is your mind. It is always there – thick or thin, good or bad, it is always there. Intelligent or unintelligent, it is always there. Knowledgeable or ignorant, it is always there. Educated, uneducated, it is always there. German,

Indian, American, it is always there. And reality is not German, and reality is not American, and reality is not Indian, so when you come with German eyes, with Indian eyes, with American eyes, with Hindu eyes, with Mohammedan eyes, with Christian eyes, you miss reality.

Start – this will give you a great preparation for the jump into Tantra. Start: whenever you are sitting, moving, walking, talking, try again and again to remain with the real, the uninterpreted, unjudged real. And slowly, slowly, doors open. Slowly, slowly, a few moments start coming to you which are not moments of the mind – non-linguistic visions of reality, non-mental visions of reality – and those will prepare you.

Says Saraha: *Once in the realm that's full of joy, the seeing mind becomes enriched...* So the first thing is the seeing mind, and the second thing is, don't avoid joys. Approach them with an open heart, with receptivity, with a welcoming being; absorb them. Wherever joy is, God is. That is the Tantra message in short: wherever joy is, God is.

And joy has three planes. The first is what we call pleasure. Pleasure is of the body. The second is happiness. Happiness is of the mind. The third is bliss. Bliss is of the spirit, spiritual. But they all share one reality and that reality is joy. Joy converted into the language of the body becomes pleasure, joy received through the body becomes pleasure. Joy received through mind becomes happiness. Joy received neither through mind nor through body – received without body, without mind – becomes bliss. These are the three layers of joy.

Joy is the only reality. Joy is God! Joy is the stuff which existence is made of.

Saraha says to be available to joy *wherever* it comes from. Never deny it. Don't condemn it. When it is of the body, so what? Then God is knocking at your body. When you are eating and you feel a certain joy, you enjoy your food, it is God; you are swallowing him. When you hold the hand of a woman or a man or a friend or anybody with tremendous love, and there is a thrill in your body energy, there is a dance, a deep dance in your body energy; when you are stirred –something vibrates like electricity, renovates, rejuvenates you, something which makes you more alive than you have ever been before – it is joy, it is God coming through the body. When listening to music you feel tremendously happy, it is joy through the mind. Looking at a flower without touching it and without bringing your mind into it, a moment comes when there is bliss – subtle, silent, profound benediction. But all are different manifestations of joy.

Joy is one of the most beautiful words in the English language. It covers the whole range of all kinds of happiness. Tantra says that the first thing is to be available to joy. You will be surprised: why this insistence. Are we not available to joy? It is sad to say, but it is so: you are not. Nobody is. We are more receptive to suffering; we are more ready to suffer than we are ready to be joyful; we are more available to misery than to joy. There is something in it.

Joy takes away your ego, and misery gives you your ego in a very strong way. Misery creates ego, and joy takes it away. Any moment of joy, and you are lost in it. The joy moment is not an ego moment; the misery moment is a very condensed ego moment. When you are miserable, you *are;* when you are joyful, you are not.

So let me repeat: because we are egoists, we are more available to suffering, misery, sadness, unhappiness. We create a joyless life around ourselves. We convert all opportunities of joy into sadness because that is the only way for the ego to exist. The ego can exist only in hell. In heaven the ego cannot exist.

You have been told down the centuries that if you become egoless you will enter heaven. I say to you: if you become egoless, heaven enters in you. Heaven is not a geographical thing somewhere, it is not that you go there. When you are egoless, you are heaven. When you are egoful, you are hell. It is not that hell is there somewhere at the bottom of existence and heaven is somewhere at the peak of existence – these are just metaphors. Heaven and hell are states of being.

When you are, you are in hell. When you are not, you are in heaven. And that's why if you are too attached to your ego and you want to feel yourself – that you are separate, different, unique, this and that – then you will remain miserable. Now the paradox: the ego creates misery – and the ego wants to be joyful. The ego seeks, is very greedy about joy; it wants to have all the joys possible – and the ego creates misery. Now you are trapped. The more misery the ego creates, the more interested the ego becomes in joy. But it cannot create joy: joy is not its function. This insight is a Tantra insight.

And one moment of joy, "Even *once,*" says Saraha, "is enough to change you, sir," he says to the king. "One moment, once, will be enough argument and proof of what type of life I am living, what type of being I am."

Once in the realm that's full of joy, the seeing mind becomes enriched... And mind is never enriched by philosophizing. By theories it is not enriched, by knowledge it is not enriched – only by experience. A rich mind means one which has experienced something of the real, something of the truth. There is only one richness – that is of truth. And there is only one poverty, and that is of lies. If you don't know the truth, you live in lies, illusions, projections, dreams.

...and thereby for this and that most useful; even when it runs after objects it is not alienated from itself. Why do people ordinarily run towards

objects? Somebody wants a car and somebody wants a house and somebody wants money and somebody wants power – why are people running after objects? What is the base, the fundamental reason for their hankering and hectic activities? You will be surprised. Tantra says they want to run away from themselves. They are not running towards objects, they simply want to run from themselves. Objects are excuses, they help you to turn your back upon yourself. You are afraid of yourself, there is great fear about yourself.

It happens here every day: whenever a person comes closer to meditation he becomes scared. Why? – because when you look into yourself, you will not find anybody there. Pure nothingness, abyss – abysmal nothingness. You start trembling, you are standing on a precipice; just a wrong step and you are finished. One starts running from oneself. People are running – not for things; people are running from themselves. They are not running *for* something, they are running *from* something. And that something is their own being.

So, whenever you are occupied, you feel good. Whenever you are unoccupied, you feel very restless, *very* restless. Nothing to do, you start falling upon yourself. If something is there to be done, you are engaged; engaged, you can forget that abyss which goes on calling from your inside. That abyss is what God is.

To come to terms with that abyss, to become friendly with that abyss, is the first step towards reality.

...and thereby for this and that most useful; even when it runs after objects it is not alienated from itself. Saraha says ordinary people are running after things because they want to avoid themselves. But a man who has come to know what truth is, even if that man is going towards objects, won't be deceived because he will also enjoy. In fact, he is the only person who will enjoy.

You are running after things because you want to avoid yourself. He has nothing to avoid anywhere, he is not escaping from anywhere – he can enjoy things. In fact, only he can enjoy things. How can you enjoy things when you are constantly afraid of your own being?

Saraha says that if you see a Tantrika enjoying a woman or enjoying a good meal or drinking wine, don't judge him because he looks just like any other ordinary man; he is not. The difference is very deep, the difference is very essential. On the surface they both look alike. How can you differentiate whether a man who is running after a woman is ordinary or a Tantrika? It is very difficult from the outside because from the outside they look almost the same.

Take a few examples: two dancers are dancing. One dancer is dancing only to perform, to feel the ego – that he is a great dancer. It is a performance.

He is looking into people's eyes to see what they are thinking. He is waiting for their applause, he is hoping they are going to applaud him. They will help his ego strengthen a little more. And there is another dancer on the same stage, dancing because he enjoys it. He is not performing. He not even bothering about whether people are applauding or not, whether people are there or not. He is absorbed, utterly absorbed in his dance? Will it be possible for you to make a distinction from the outside? It will be very difficult. More is the likelihood that you will not be able to make any distinction. It is possible you may even think that the performer is a great dancer because he is speaking the same language of the ego which you understand. The nonperformer may look a little crazy. The nonperformer will be so spontaneous that unless you know the language of spontaneity you cannot understand him.

To understand anything, you have at least to know the language. A Tantrika sitting by the side of a woman, holding her hand, and an ordinary man holding the hand of a woman – how will you make a distinction between the two? The ordinary man is trying to escape from himself. He wants to get lost in this woman so that he can forget himself. He himself is not in love with himself, that's why he is loving this woman – so that his reality can be forgotten. He is using this woman like an alcoholic beverage: this woman makes him drunk and he forgets about himself. It helps, it gives him a certain relaxation. He is, for a few moments at least, not in his usual anxieties.

And the Tantrika, holding the hand of the woman, is in tremendous joy. It is not that he wants to escape – there is nowhere to escape, and there is no one to escape. He is holding the hand of this woman just to share something of tremendous value with her.

You cannot share everything with everybody. There are a few things which you can share only in love, there are a few things which you can share only in trust.

People ask me why I don't talk to the masses. I don't talk to them because I have something to share, and that can be shared only in deep trust, that can be shared only in deep love. I can only talk with people who are in love with me. Otherwise it is meaningless: they will not understand, they will misunderstand. There is no way to make it understood. It can be communicated only when you are ready to respond.

When your hearts are ready, open, I can play on your hearts and a great music can be born. But if you come closed, untrusting, doubting, then I cannot create that music. It is impossible because you won't allow me to enter into your innermost core of being and play on your heart. If you won't allow me, then the music will not be created.

And then you want to know whether the music exists – and the only way to make you aware that it exists is to create it in you. You say, "Yes, I will trust if I can experience the music." The problem is that you cannot experience the music unless you trust. It has to be created, only then can you know that it is. But before it can be known, trust is a basic requirement.

The Tantrika is holding the hand of a woman. He can hold anybody's hand, but he will not be able to convey the energy that has happened to him; he can convey it very easily to somebody who loves, and it can be conveyed only in certain moments.

There are certain moments when two people come so close that the energy can jump from one to the other. You know those moments – if you have loved anybody, you will know – they are not there twenty-four hours a day. Even if you love a woman – your wife or your child, your husband, then too you know that for twenty-four hours a day those moments are not there; they happen rarely. Sometimes they happen – sometimes, something – and you fall together. Sometimes you feel that the other has moved very, very close, your peripheries are overlapping. That is the moment when something can be conveyed.

Now Saraha says, "If you look from the outside, sir, you will see us Tantrikas just as ordinary people hankering for things, the ordinary joys of life. We are not."

And, he says: *Once in the realm that's full of joy the seeing mind becomes enriched and thereby for this and that most useful...*

This is samsara, and that is nirvana. Saraha says that this enriched mind – enriched by joy – becomes useful for both this and that, for samsara and nirvana, for the outer and the inner, for the bodily and the spiritual, for the visible and the invisible. It becomes capable and useful for both this and that. This is a great statement.

Ordinarily, so-called spiritual people think that your mind can either be useful in the world, or in God. Their thinking is that of either–or. Tantra says that this thinking is dividing life into lower and higher, into material and spiritual, into samsara and nirvana. This division is wrong because life is indivisible. And really, if you are intelligent you will not only be able to enjoy God, you will be able to enjoy very ordinary things too. You will be able to enjoy a rock as much as you will be able to enjoy God.

See into this great, profound statement: When the mind is really intelligent and enriched by joy, you will be able to enjoy bliss, you will be able to enjoy happiness, you will be able to enjoy pleasure too because it all belongs to existence – the lowest as much as the highest. *...and thereby for this and that most useful; even when it runs after objects it is not alienated from itself.*

And Saraha says, "Even if you find me running, that running after objects is your interpretation. I am not running because there is nowhere to run and nobody to run." This state where one has attained to his inner clarity is such that one can enjoy everything from food to God, from sex to *samadhi*. There is no division; there should not be, there need not be.

Tantra gives you both worlds. Tantra is not an either–or standpoint, it is this and that both; it is very comprehensive. All religions look poor in that way because they take away the world and they force an unnecessary choice on you. They say: either choose the world or God. They put God in opposition to the world. Tantra is the only total religion – the *only* total religion. No religion has been born on the earth which has such a total vision.

Both, Tantra says. There is no question of choice – it is all yours. You can be in the marketplace, and you can enjoy the marketplace – and yet you can be beyond it, and you can enjoy the beyond too. It does not force you to choose. All choice is destructive. And because of these religions of the "either–or" standpoint, the world has remained worldly.

Who bothers about God? God is so far away, is not so real. And then one thinks, "Later on... One can postpone God, but life is running by – enjoy it first." These religions which have forced choice on man have forced man to remain worldly. Out of a million, one will become religious. An unnecessarily hard choice – he has to renounce the world, he has to move out of his family, away from friends; he has to go against all his love. You force him unnecessarily.

And then another problem arises. These people who are ready to choose God against the world are more or less perverted people who have failed in life somehow; who have somehow not been intelligent enough to understand life; who are somehow stupid, who are somehow sadistic, masochistic; people who are somehow neurotic, egoistic. They can escape from the world, they can start torturing themselves; that's what asceticism has been up to now. Torture yourself, be violent with yourself, kill yourself. Slowly, slowly poison your being. These people are not healthy people.

So, out of a million, one person becomes interested in choosing God. And out of hundreds of so-called religious people, ninety-nine seem to be neurotic. So, out of a hundred million, one person becomes a Buddha or a Christ or a Krishna. This is sheer wastage.

Just think of a garden where ten million trees are growing and only one tree flowers. Will you call that gardener a gardener? In fact, you will come to the natural conclusion that it is not because of the gardener that the tree has flowered; it must be in spite of him. He has planted ten million trees and only one tree has flowered and has become fruitful. It cannot be because of the gardener; it must be because it somehow escaped the gardener, the gardener could not destroy it. Somehow the gardener has neglected it, somehow the gardener has forgotten about it. Maybe… Ten million trees, and he has forgotten about it, so it has been missed and has flowered. Each tree is potentially fruitful, potentially capable of blooming; and each man is capable of becoming a God.

Tantra creates a totally new religion. It says that there is no need to choose: wherever you are, exactly there godliness can be experienced. Tantra is not against the world, it is for godliness. And its God is so vast that the world can be included.

To me it seems very, very relevant that the creation should be included in the creator. It should not be against. What type of logic is this which says that the creation is against the creator? If it is God who has created you, if it is God who has created your body, your sexuality, your sensuality, then it cannot be against God.

George Gurdjieff used to say that all religions are against God. And he was right – except for Tantra, he was right. All religions are against God. If you are against God's creation, you are indicating that you are against God. If you are against the painting, are you not saying that you are against the painter? If you are against the poetry are you not saying, in an indirect way, that you are against the poet?

If God is the creator, then the creation is his and must have his signature everywhere. Yes, it is there, and Tantra says that God's signature is everywhere. You just need seeing eyes, a seeing mind and a little receptivity for joy, and it will start happening.

> *The buds of joy and pleasure*
> *and the leaves of glory grow.*
> *If nothing flows out anywhere*
> *the bliss unspeakable will fruit.*

The key, the secret. These are the last sutras of Saraha. He is giving the ultimate touch to whatsoever he has said up to now. He is giving the final statement.

He says that pleasures are of the body. Pleasures are outgoing – pleasure needs the other, pleasure hankers for the object, pleasure is an extroverted journey. Good! There is nothing wrong in it. And then: joy is an introverted journey. Joy is more interested in oneself, joy is more subjective. For pleasure, the other is needed; for joy, you are enough.

Pleasure is bodily, joy is psychological. But they both remain buds unless the third, the ultimate in joy, happens: bliss. That bliss is the one-thousand-petaled lotus, the highest peak of your consciousness. When that opens, then all buds bloom.

Now, this has to be understood. An ordinary person can have only a very limited joy through the body, but a Tantrika will have tremendous joy through his body. It will not just be a bud, it will be a flowering. An ordinary person can have a certain joy in music, in meditation, in dance, but a Tantrika will have infinite joy. When you have known the last, the last starts being reflected in everything you do.

If you have known godliness, then wherever you walk, you are walking on holy ground. Then whatsoever you see, you are seeing godliness. Then whomsoever you meet, you are meeting God.

Always remember: your highest experience is reflected in your lowest experiences. Without the highest experience the lower is very mundane. That's the problem. That's why people cannot understand Tantrikas when they say that even in sex *samadhi* is possible. They cannot understand, and it is understandable why they cannot understand. They don't know *samadhi*. They know very ordinary, ugly sex. They know only frustration through it. They only know lust through it.

The English word *love* is very meaningful. It comes from a Sanskrit root *lobha*. *Lobha* means greed, lust. The ordinary love is nothing but lust and greed. How can the ordinary man understand that in love the ultimate can be reflected? But when you have known the ultimate, the highest, then the lowest is linked with it. Then anything stirs it, then anything becomes a message from it.

It is like this... You come across a handkerchief on the road; it is an ordinary handkerchief, not worth more than one rupee. But one day you fall in love with a woman, and you come across a handkerchief on the street – the same handkerchief, worth one rupee – but now it belongs to the woman you love. Now its worth is tremendous, now it is not just one rupee. If somebody were going to offer you one thousand rupees, you would not be willing to give the handkerchief away – it belongs to the woman that you love. Now this ordinary handkerchief has something which was not there before: it reminds you of your beloved.

It is exactly like that. When you have known *samadhi*, then even sexual orgasm reminds you of *samadhi*, then everything reminds you of *samadhi*. Then the whole existence becomes so full and crowded with godliness.

The buds of joy and pleasure and the leaves of glory grow. The buds are of joy and pleasure, and the leaves are of glory. But ordinarily you will just see leaves, unless the highest has happened. When the highest happens, then you see that even the ordinary leaves of your life are not ordinary leaves: it is through them that the ultimate flowering has happened. And now you know that the same sap flows to the ultimate flower, to: *The buds of joy and pleasure...* And to the leaves too the same sap flows. They all help together toward the one-thousand-petaled lotus.

Leaves of glory... means leaves of grace, gratitude. You start feeling the glory of existence; your life is glorious. It is no longer ordinary, it is luminous with godliness.

If nothing flows out anywhere... And when does this one-thousand-petaled lotus open? It opens when nothing flows out.

Now look: first, pleasure is when your energy is flowing out – bodily pleasure. Joy is when your energy is flowing in – subjective, psychological joy. And when does bliss happen? – when your energy is not flowing anywhere, it is simply there. You are not going anywhere, you are simply there; you are just a being.

Now you don't have any goals, now you don't have any desires to fulfill, you don't have any future. You are just herenow. When the energy has become just a pool, not going anywhere, not flowing anywhere; no goal to be attained, nothing to be sought; you are just here, tremendously here, totally here. This now is all the time that is left for you, and this here is all the space. Then suddenly this gathering of energy, which is not moving anywhere, not distracted by body or mind, becomes a great rush in you and the one-thousand-petaled lotus opens.

If nothing flows out anywhere the bliss unspeakable will fruit. And then comes the fruit. So, joy and pleasure are the buds, grace and gratitude and glory are the leaves, and this ultimate flowering of bliss is the fulfillment, the fruition. You have come home.

> *What has been done and where and what in itself it will become, is*
> *nothing...*

And now you know that whatsoever has been done *or* not done was just a dream. Now you know that karma, action, means nothing. You were just drawing lines on water; they go on disappearing. Nothing is left. Nothing really happens. All is. Nothing happens.

> *What has been done and where and what in itself it will become, is*
> *nothing...*

Saraha is saying, "Look, sir. What I am doing and what I have done and what has happened is all meaningless now that I know it is just a dream."

...yet thereby it has been useful for this and that.

But, he says, it is true – it has helped for this and that. Even while it was a dream, it was helpful; it brought me to this reality. I have stepped over that dream, but now I know it was a dream, now I know it was false. I have not done anything because nothing is ever done; it is all a dream, but it has helped – it has brought me to this ultimate fruition.

This samsara and that nirvana have both been enriched by that dream. The dream was not just futile, it was helpful, utilitarian. But not true.

Let me tell you one anecdote...

There was a hunter walking through the jungle and he met a snarling tiger coming towards him on the path. He reached for his gun. To his horror he saw that he had no bullets. The tiger was coming nearer, it was going to attack.

"What can I do? I'm going to be eaten up," thought the hunter, terror freezing him on the spot. Just as the tiger was about to spring, the hunter had a strange feeling. "I do believe all this is only a dream," he said to himself. "If I try hard enough, I'm sure I'll wake up." So he pinched himself hard and shook himself and blinked. In a moment the tiger was gone; the tiger had disappeared, the hunter was safe in his own bed. What a relief! He still trembled with fright, but now he laughed too. How real that tiger had seemed! Thank goodness it was only a dream.

When he felt calm again, the hunter got up and made himself a cup of tea. He still felt tired, so he sat outside his hut in a deckchair and smoked his pipe for a while. He really felt quite sleepy, so he tipped his hat over his face and closed his eyes. "I could sleep all day," he said.

After a time he heard growling. "Bless me," said the hunter, "I must have dropped off to sleep again. There's that tiger coming back. Go away, you silly tiger, I'm tired of dreaming about you!"

The tiger growled again, and came nearer.

"I'm not afraid of you. You're only a dream," said the hunter. Then he got up from his chair, walked up to the tiger, and punched it hard on the nose.

"What a funny man!" thought the tiger. "Men usually run away from me." And of course seeing this strange man, the tiger escaped.

As the tiger was escaping the man became alert to the fact that he was fully awake and the tiger was not a dream, it was a reality.

But what happened? The dream helped him even to tackle the real tiger. Naturally, the tiger must have become very puzzled. This has never happened! What type of man is this, that he gets up and hits me in the face just like that?

All is dream, but dreams can help to understand reality – even to over-come reality.

Says Saraha:

> *What has been done and where and what in itself it will become*
> *is nothing: yet thereby it has been useful for this and that.*
> *Whether passionate or not*
> *the pattern is nothingness.*

Says Saraha, "Whether you are living a life of passion or a life of no passion, those who know, know well that deep down neither passion nor nonpassion makes any difference. Deep down it is pure nothingness."

It is just like a movie projected on an empty screen. A beautiful scene is projected and you are thrilled with its beauty; a horror scene is projected and you start trembling. But Saraha says that the day you understand, there remain nothing but shadows on an empty screen. The sinner is a projection, so is the saint. The good is a projection, so is the bad. All is projected by the mind onto the empty screen of reality.

So Saraha says, "Sir, don't be puzzled too much by what people say. I *know* it is just an empty screen." Whether Saraha is a very great man of character or a characterless bum, whether Saraha is respected by people or is condemned and reviled does not matter – it is an empty screen, people are projecting their ideas.

I have come to know this nothingness. And this experience of nothingness, and the experience of the one-thousand-petaled lotus are two aspects of the same phenomenon. On the one hand you attain to ultimate bliss, on the other hand you know now that everything is just an empty dream. There is nothing to leave and nowhere to go; nobody to leave and nobody to go anywhere. It is not only that things are empty, you are also empty. It is all emptiness – inside, outside – just exactly like a dream. What happens in a dream? You create it, it is fantasy.

The last sutra:

> *If I am like a pig that covets worldly mire,*
> *you must tell me what fault lies in a stainless mind.*
> *By what does not affect one,*
> *how can one now be fettered?*

Says Saraha, "If I am like a pig, it is okay." If people say that Saraha has become a pig, a mad dog, that's perfectly okay. It does not make any difference whether they say that Saraha has become a great saint or they say that he has become: ...*a pig that covets worldly mire*...

...*you must tell me what fault lies in a stainless mind.* "What I do makes no difference; inside I know nothing, inside I know only nothingness. My purity is uncontaminated by what I do; doing does not affect my being at all. So you tell me, sir: ...*what fault lies in a stainless mind. By what does not affect one, how can one now be fettered?*

"And these things don't affect me this way or that. Neither am I detached, nor am I attached. I let things happen – whatsoever happens. I have no longer any plan, and I have no longer any style to impose upon life. I live spontaneously; whatsoever happens, happens, and I have no judgment. And I don't say, 'It should have been this way.' I have no 'shoulds,' I have no 'should nots.'"

Just meditate over this state: No "shoulds," no "should nots." no plan, no frustration, no repentance – because nothing ever goes wrong. How can anything go wrong when you don't have any idea of right?

This is ultimate freedom, ultimate liberation.

How can anything go wrong? Wrong can happen only if you have a certain notion of right. If you don't have any notion, you don't have any ideology, you don't have any ideals, Saraha says: *By what does not affect one, how can one now be fettered?*

And the last sentence of the sutra is of great beauty. When you really come home and you see what is, you will not feel that you have become liberated. On the contrary you will feel: "How ridiculous that I ever thought that I was not liberated!" The difference is great.

If, when you come home, when you come to know what is, you start feeling very, very enhanced and you are in a very great euphoria, and you say, "Now I have become liberated," that means you are not yet liberated. That means you still think the bondage was real, that means you are still in a dream – now in another dream. One dream was of bondage, this other dream is of liberation; but another dream again.

Saraha says that when you really become liberated – liberated from all right and from all wrong, liberated from all good and all bad – then you are not only liberated from bondage, you are liberated from liberation itself. Then suddenly you start laughing, "How ridiculous! The bondage cannot happen in the first place, the bondage had never happened. It was just a belief; I had believed in it, and I had created it through my belief. It was a dream, now the dream is over."

That's why the last sentence ends on a question mark. Have you ever seen any scripture ending on a question mark? This is the only one. I have not come across any other.

Scriptures begin with a question mark and end with an answer. That's how a logical treatise should go. The introduction can be a question, not the epilogue. But this beautiful song of Saraha ends on a question mark: *If I am like a pig that covets worldly mire, you must tell me what fault lies in a stainless mind. By what does not affect one, how can one now be fettered?*

He does not declare that he is enlightened, he does not declare that he is liberated, he does not declare that he has come home. He simply says, "I laugh at the very idea that I had gone anywhere. I had never gone anywhere. I have always and always been at my home. I have always been here and now. I was just dreaming, so the dreams created the illusion that I had gone somewhere. Now the dream has disappeared, and I am where I have always been." That's why he says: ...*how can one now be fettered?*

Nobody is there to be fettered, nothing is there to fetter. The bondage has disappeared, so has disappeared the man who was in bondage. When the world disappears, the ego disappears – together; they are part of the same game. Inside is ego, outside is the world. They cannot live apart, they are always together. When one disappears, the other disappears simultaneously. Now the ego is not there and the world is not there.

Saraha is propounding Buddha's greatest insight. Buddha says there is no substance and there is no self. Substance is not there, all is empty. And the self is not inside you, there too all is empty. To come to see this emptiness – awareness floating in emptiness; pure awareness, unbounded awareness... This awareness is emptiness itself, or this emptiness is awareness itself. This emptiness is luminous with awareness, full of awareness.

Tantra is a great insight into things as they really are. But finally remember, it is not a philosophy, it is an insight. And if you want to go into it, you will have to go not through the mind, but without the mind.

No-mind is the door to Tantra. Non-thinking is the way to Tantra. Experiencing is the key to Tantra.

Enough for today.

just a remembrance

The first question:

Osho,
Why is it that, whenever I leave your lecture, I quickly become disillusioned
with myself because I am unable to live up to the ideals you put forward in
your lecture?

What are you talking about? Ideals? – that's exactly what I go on destroying! I am not putting any ideals before you. I am not giving you any fantasies about the future; I am not giving you any future at all because the future is a trick to postpone the present. It is a trick to avoid yourself, a way to escape from yourself. Desire is a deception, and ideals create desires. I am not giving you any "should" or any "should not," either positive or negative. I am simply telling you to drop all ideals and *be*.

But I can understand your question. You make an ideal out of it, you start thinking, "How should I be?" You start thinking, "What should I do to be?" I am trying to take away the ideals and you make an ideal out of it: how to drop all ideals. You misunderstand me, you misinterpret me. You don't hear what I am saying, you go on hearing what I am not saying at all. Listen more carefully.

It has always happened. We don't know exactly what Buddha said because the people who reported were people just like you. We don't know what Jesus said because the people who reported were again people like you. The report certainly says what they heard, but it doesn't say anything about what he said. And these can be diametrically opposite things.

I speak a totally different language. You reduce it to some other thing – to your language; you come in and you start interfering.

You ask: "Why is it that whenever I leave your lecture I quickly become disillusioned with myself...?" You become disillusioned with yourself because you don't know who you are, and you have a certain image of yourself. That image is not you, that image cannot be you; that image is a mind construction. You have created an image of yourself – you think this is what you are. And when you listen to me and I start pulling your legs, you become disillusioned; your image is broken, your image is not left intact as it was.

But you are not broken. In fact the image is not allowing you to have space, it is not allowing you to *be*. The image has to be thrown out so you can have enough space to grow. The image has become too huge, too powerful; it has taken over your whole house and you are living on the porch, it does not allow you to come in. And the image which you have made out of ideals goes on condemning you, the creation goes on condemning the creator.

Look at the foolishness of it, the ridiculousness of it. You create an image, very beautiful – naturally, when you are creating you create a beautiful image – and then because of that image you start looking ugly in comparison. You create a very, very great image that you are a saint, and then you find yourself doing things which are not very saintly. Now you feel condemned. The image is yours, and against the image your act looks stinking.

What I am saying here, what Saraha is saying to the king, is that the image has to be completely dropped. The moment you drop the image and you forget about the image, then what is right and what is wrong? Then who is a sinner and who is a saint? Then you don't have anything to compare with. Then suddenly you are at ease. The comparison disappears and the condemnation disappears. The comparison disappears – and the ego disappears, the ego of the sinner and the ego of the saint. Without the ideal there can exist no ego at all. It exists through the ideal, via the ideal. The ideal is a must for the ego.

Either you think that you are a sinner – you create an ego, an identity – or you think you are a saint; then you create an ego, an identity. But both can only come into existence through the ideal. If the ideal is not there, who are you? Saint or sinner? Good or bad? Ugly or beautiful? Who are you? You are simply yourself, without any judgment, without any justification, without any condemnation. You are simply there in your reality; that's what I am calling "being."

Now you must be becoming disillusioned again and again, because your grip on the image becomes a little loosened. Whenever your grip on the image is loosened a little, you become afraid. The ideal is creating an illusion, and whenever I start taking the ideal away, you feel disillusioned. Be utterly disillusioned, and don't create the illusion again – the illusion of the ideal – and then see how life attains to a sublime silence. Then see how tremendous acceptance arises, how great benediction simply surrounds you for no reason at all. It is yours, just for the asking. You are not to do anything.

You are acceptable to existence as you are.

This is my whole message, and this is the whole of Tantra: you are accepted as you are. But you go on rejecting yourself. The ideal makes it possible for you to reject, the ideal makes it possible for you to be unkind to yourself, cruel, aggressive – to become a self-torturer. My effort here is to help you to become sane. This idealism creates insanity, it has turned the whole earth into a madhouse.

And you say: "I become disillusioned with myself because I am unable to live up to the ideals you put forward in your lecture." What are you talking about? What ideals? I am not saying, "You should do this." I am not saying, "You should be like this." I am simply saying, "Whatsoever you are, be." I am trying to take all "becoming" from you. I am trying to help you to see the point that you are already at home; you have never to go anywhere, and you have nowhere to go. It is already the case – existence is showering on you. *Samadhi* is already the case. Wherever you are, you are in nirvana.

This is enlightenment. This moment – with no ideals, with no desires, with nowhere to go; this moment – utterly relaxed in it, herenow – is the moment of godliness, the moment of truth.

But you listen to me and you start parroting, you listen to me and you start repeating words. You don't follow the meaning, you follow the letter and not the spirit.

I have heard...

A certain tough old sea captain bought a young parrot at a foreign port, being assured it was a marvelous learner, and hung it on the bridge. Coming back through the Bay of Biscay, a fearful black cloud came over and the skipper remarked, "It's gone bloody dark all at once!"

Soon after the cloud burst in a dreadful torrent and the captain said to the mate, "It's bloody pissing down!" The storm got worse, the ship lurched and developed a leak, so that one of the men called up, "What shall we do to be saved?" He got the reply, "Pump, you lousy shower! Pump, you poxed-up beggars! Pump!"

The ship and all were lost. A wet, swearing, washed-up parrot alone survived, and after some adventures finished up with a dear spinster, who was just expecting the vicar. As a precaution she threw a cloth over the cage, so that

the vicar was greeted with, "It's bloody dark all at once!" The lady was livid
and put the parrot immediately under the cold-water tap, at which he shrieked,
"It's bloody pissing down!"

"No, no, Miss Fantight! You mustn't be so cruel to God's creatures. Rather
bring him to church on the Sabbath and expose him to good influences." This
was done and the parrot behaved like an angel, even joining in the hymns. The
vicar, beaming at his own success, rose to announce his text, "Brethren, today
we ask: What shall we do to be saved?" and down the aisles rang the parrot's
clear tones, "Pump, you lousy shower! Pump, you poxed-up beggars! Pump!"

Don't become parrots. You can repeat what I am saying, but that is not the
point at all. Understand what I am saying. Repetition will create troubles for
you. A slight change of tone, of emphasis, a slight change of a single comma,
a full point, and all is lost. Listen to the meaning.

And there are different ways of listening. One way is listening from the
mind; then you memorize. And you have been taught how to listen through
the mind because all your schools, colleges, universities, teach you how to
cram. They give you a wrong notion – as if memory is knowledge. Memory
is not knowledge, memory is simply parroting. You will know the letters, you
will know the word, but it will be empty; inside there will be no significance, no
meaning in it. And the word which has no meaning in it is dangerous.

There is another way to listen, and that is from the heart. Listen through
the heart. Listen as if you were not listening to an argument, but to a song.
Listen as if you were not listening to a philosophy, but to a poem. Listen as you
listen to music. Watch me as you watch a dancer. Feel me as you feel a lover.
Then the word will be there; it will be used as a vehicle, but it will not be the
real thing. The vehicle will be forgotten, and the meaning will enter into your
heart and will remain there. And it will change your being, it will change
your vision of life.

The second question:

Osho,
How did Tantra grow out of Buddhism, which, as far as I know, views sex as
a hindrance to meditation?

It is related to the first question.

What Buddha said must have been misunderstood. Yes, he said that to
go into meditation one has to go beyond sex. Now, the people who heard him
thought he was against sex – naturally so: he said you have to go beyond sex.

They started thinking that sex must be a hindrance then, otherwise why do you have to go beyond sex? They started fighting with sex rather than going beyond it; their whole emphasis changed. They started fighting with sex, and Buddhism became one of the most ascetic religions of the world.

Can't you observe his tremendous grace in a statue of Buddha or in his pictures – can it come out of ascetism? Is it possible that this beautiful being, this graceful face, this love, this compassion can come out of ascetism? Ascetics are people who torture themselves, and when a person tortures himself he starts torturing others too, with a vengeance. When a person is in misery himself, he cannot see anybody else being happy; he starts destroying others' happiness too. That's what your so-called mahatmas go on doing: they can't see you happy, so whenever you are happy, they immediately come and say, "There must be something wrong, a happy person means a sinner."

You can observe it in yourself also because down the centuries your so-called mahatmas and saints have conditioned you to feel guilt whenever you feel happy. Whenever you are miserable, everything is okay. But if you are feeling great joy, you start feeling a little uneasiness – somehow it doesn't seem to be right. Have you not seen it in yourself? From where does it come? Happiness – and not right? And misery is okay. Something very antagonistic to life, very life-negative, very life-denying, has entered into the bloodstream of humanity. And it has come through those so-called ascetics. These ascetics are neurotic people: they are masochists, they torture themselves. Their only joy is in creating more and more misery.

Buddha is not a masochist – cannot be. Buddha looks so beautiful, so joyful, so happy, so tremendously blissful. Those who were hearing him have misunderstood somewhere. Yes, he says to go beyond sex; one has to go beyond it because it is only the first rung of the ladder. But he is not saying to go against it. Going beyond is not necessarily going against. In fact the contrary is the case: if you go against sex you will never be able to go beyond it. Going beyond comes only through going through. You have to understand sex, you have to befriend sex.

Something, somewhere, got misinterpreted. Saraha comes as a right interpretation of Buddha. And Saraha must have watched what a calamity had happened to thousands of people who were following Buddha: rather than going beyond sex they had become obsessed with it. When you are continuously fighting with something you become obsessed with it.

You can watch it: a person who believes in fasting becomes obsessed with food. Mahatma Gandhi was obsessed with food, continuously thinking about food – what to eat and what not to eat, as if what to eat and what not to eat seemed to be the only important thing in life. Ordinary people are less obsessed, they do not think about it too much. Do a three-day fast and think about what goes on in your mind. You will think about food continuously. Now going beyond food is good, but fasting cannot be the way because fasting creates an obsession with food. How can it be the way to go beyond it? If you really want to go beyond food, you have to eat rightly. You have to eat the right food, you have to eat it in a right way at the right time. You have to find out what suits your body, what is nourishing.

Yes, that will take you beyond food, you will never think about food. When the body is nourished you don't think about food. So many people think about food because in some way or other they are fasting. You will be surprised when I say that. You may be eating too much ice cream – that is a sort of fast because it is not nourishing, you are simply throwing rotten things inside you. They don't satisfy; they fill you but they don't fulfill you. You feel stuffed, but not contented.

Wrong food will create discontent, and your hunger will not be satisfied because hunger needs nourishment, not food. Remember, hunger is for nourishment, not for food. And hunger does not bother much about taste. The basic thing is whether it suits your body, whether it gives your body the needed energy. If it gives the needed energy, then it is okay. If taste goes with right nourishment you will be tremendously satisfied.

And remember, I am not against taste, I am all for it. But just taste cannot be nourishing. And just food without taste is unintelligent, stupid. When you can have both, why not? An intelligent person will find nourishing food, tasteful food. It is not such a big problem. Man can go to the moon and cannot find a nourishing food for himself? Man has done miracles and cannot satisfy his hunger? This does not seem to be the right situation. No, man has not looked into it.

There are people who believe in fasts – they destroy the body. And then there are people who go on stuffing any rubbish – they destroy the body. Both are in the same boat: both are fasting, and both are continuously obsessed. One is obsessed through indulgence, the other is obsessed through repression. Just in the middle is transcendence.

So is the case with sex, and so is the case with everything in life. Saraha must have become aware that the people who say that Buddha has said to go beyond sex were not going beyond at all. Rather they were becoming more and more obsessed with it and falling deeper into its mire.

There was a young nun who went to the Mother Superior in some distress, and after a great deal of beating about the bush admitted she was pregnant.

"Who was it? Who was this wicked, wicked man?" said the Mother Superior.

"Oh, Reverend Mother, I wouldn't commit a carnal offense with a man!" exclaimed the nun.

"Well, it wasn't fathered by a woman, was it?" said the Mother Superior, beginning to lose her temper.

"No indeed, Blessed Mother. It was fathered by one of the holy angels," simpered the nun.

"Holy angels! What is this nonsense?"

"Yes, Blessed Mother, he came down to me in the middle of the night in my sleep, and when I asked who he was he said, 'St. Michael,' and showed me his name on his sweatshirt to prove it."

Once you are against something you will find ways to get out of it, you will find some back door. Man is cunning. If you repress something, the cunning mind will find some other way. That's why you dream about sex; your saints dream too much about sex, they have to. In the day they can deny, but in the night... When they are conscious they can repress, but when they are asleep, then in the dream sex takes great, fantastic colors, it becomes psychedelic. And then in the morning they feel guilty, and because they feel guilty they repress more. And when they repress more the next night they have an even more beautiful dream of sex – or horrible, according to them. It depends on how you interpret it whether it is beautiful or horrible.

A "difficult" schoolgirl of fifteen was sent to the psychologist, who asked her a number of very personal questions. He was sure that sex lay at the bottom of the trouble and asked her, "Do you suffer from sexy or erotic dreams?"

"Certainly not!"

"Are you sure?"

"Quite sure," said the girl. "In fact I enjoy them."

It depends on you whether you call them beautiful or horrible. In the night they are beautiful, in the morning they become horrible. In the night you enjoy them, in the morning you suffer. There is a vicious circle created, and your so-called saint goes on moving in this vicious circle: the day he suffers, the night he enjoys. The day he suffers, the night he enjoys – and he is torn between these two.

And if you look deep down into yourself you will find it easily. Whatsoever you repress will remain there, you cannot get rid of it. The repressed remains, only the expressed disappears. The expressed evaporates, the repressed remains – and not only remains, it becomes more and more powerful. As time passes by, it becomes more and more powerful.

Saraha must have looked at what had happened two hundred years after Buddha: wrong interpretations. People were almost obsessed with sex. Out of that obsession of the Buddhist monks and nuns, Tantra was born as a rebellion – a rebellion against Buddhism, not against Buddha. Through that rebellion Saraha brought Buddha's spirit back. Yes, one has to transcend sex, but the transcendence happens through understanding.

Tantra believes in understanding. Understand a thing totally and you are free of its clutches. Anything not understood rightly will remain as a hangover.

So you are right. You ask: "How did Tantra grow out of Buddhism, which as far as I know views sex as a hindrance to meditation?" Precisely because of that. It is a rebellion against Buddhism, and it is for Buddha. It goes against the followers, but not against the master. The followers were carrying the letter, and Saraha brings back the spirit.

Saraha is a reincarnation of the same enlightenedness as Buddha was. Saraha is a buddha.

The third question:

Osho,
What does it mean: "The honeymoon is over"?

The honeymoon is over means that the fantasy part of your love is finished. Honeymoon is a fantasy. It is a projection, it is not reality; it is projected dream. "The honeymoon is over" means that the dream is over, and now starts the marriage, the reality. The higher the honeymoon, the greater will be the disillusionment. That's why love marriages don't succeed. Marriages succeed, but not love marriages.

The love marriage cannot succeed; failure is intrinsic to it. A love marriage is a fantasy, and the fantasy cannot win over reality. There is only one way to remain in fantasy and to remain always in a honeymoon, and that is to never meet your beloved. Then it is possible: you can have it for your whole life – but never meet the beloved, never meet your lover.

The greatest lovers in history were those who were not allowed to meet: Laila and Majnu, Shiri and Farihad – these are the great lovers. They were not allowed; the society created so many obstacles that they remained always in a state of honeymoon. It is just like when food is there but you are not allowed to eat it, so the fantasy continues. If you are allowed to eat it, then the fantasy disappears.

A love marriage cannot succeed. What do I mean by "not succeed"? In the sense that people want it to succeed, it cannot succeed. Marriage is successful, but then there is no love. That's why in the past all the societies of the world, out of experience, decided in favor of marriage and against love. Indian society is one of the most ancient societies of the world. It has existed for at least five thousand years, or more than that. Out of this long experience India decided for marriage without love: a marriage without love can succeed because it has no honeymoon part in it; from the very beginning it is very realistic, down-to-earth. It does not allow any dreaming.

In India, the partners themselves are not allowed to choose. The boy is not allowed to choose the girl, the girl is not allowed to choose the boy; the parents choose. Naturally they are more down-to-earth, more experienced. And naturally they cannot fall in love. They think of other things: finance, prestige, respectability, family. They think of thousands of things, but they don't think of one thing – love. Love is not brought into the matter at all. They go to the astrologer, they ask the astrologer and inquire into everything – but not love. Love must not become an ingredient in it.

Two unknown people, the man and the woman, are put together by the parents, by the society, and left together. Naturally, when you live with a person a sort of liking arises. But that liking is just like the liking you have for your sister; it is not love. You have not chosen your sister, neither have you chosen your brother; they were not chosen by you. It was accidental that you were born to the same parents – you have a certain liking. Living together for long, a thousand and one associations, and one starts liking – or disliking. But it is never love and never hate; it never goes to extremes, it is very balanced. The same is the case with marriage, arranged marriage. The husband and wife live together, and by and by they start feeling for each other.

Another thing the society does: the society does not allow any extramarital sex, so naturally the husband has to make love to the wife, and the wife has to make love to the husband. If you are allowed only one food to eat and no other food is allowed, how long can you wait? You have to eat it. This is the trick of the society. If extramarital sex is allowed, then there is every possibility that the husband may not want to make love to the wife, the wife may not like making love to the husband. Just out of hunger, and with no other outlet, they start making love to each other. Out of desperation they start becoming associated with each other. Then children are born – and more ties: religious, social ties. Then the children and the responsibility, and the family starts rolling.

A love marriage is bound to fail because the love marriage is a poetic phenomenon. You fall in love and you start dreaming about the woman or the man, and you reach to a peak, a climax of dreams. Those dreams continue until you meet the woman, until you meet the man. Then you come together, you become satisfied; those dreams start disappearing. Now for the first time you start seeing the other as he or she is.

When you see your wife as she is, when you see your husband as he is, the honeymoon is over. This is the meaning of the phrase "the honeymoon is over." And it does not happen only in marriage, it happens in many sorts of relationships. It happens here with me. You come to me and you can have a honeymoon, you can start fantasizing about me. I have no part in it, I am not a party to it. It is something that you do all alone. But you start fantasizing, desiring: this is going to happen and that is going to happen, and Osho will do this and Osho will do that. Then one day the honeymoon will be over. In fact, I always like to wait till the honeymoon is over, then I start working, never before it, because I don't want to become a party to your fantasies. I only start working when I see that now the honeymoon is over and you are back on the earth. Now something real can be done.

In fact, I always like to give sannyas when the honeymoon is over. To give sannyas during the honeymoon is dangerous, very dangerous, because the moment the honeymoon is over you will start feeling against me, you will start rebelling against sannyas, you will start reacting. It is better to wait.

In every relationship – in friendship, in a master-disciple relationship – in any kind of relationship there is a part which is of fantasy. That fantasy is just your mind: repressed desires are flying into dreams. In a better world, with more understanding, marriage will disappear, and with marriage, the honeymoon will disappear too.

Now listen. There have been societies, for example the Hindu society – it has killed the honeymoon by killing love, and only marriage exists. In America they are killing marriage and saving love and the honeymoon; only the honeymoon exists, not marriage – it is disappearing. But to me both are deep down in conspiracy. The honeymoon can exist only if there is some repression, otherwise there is nothing to project. And if there is something to project, then love fails again and again. Then the social pundits come in and they start making arrangements for marriage because love fails: it drives people crazy and does not help them to live their lives, it makes them suicidal, it makes them neurotic, schizophrenic, hysterical. So the social pundit has to come in, the priest and the politician have to come in and arrange for marriage because love is too dangerous. And that's how the society has moved between these two polarities.

Sometimes when people get fed up with marriage, as they have got fed up in America, they start thinking of love. When people get fed up with love, as sooner or later they will find – they are already finding it so – then they start moving towards marriage. Both are polarities of the same game.

To me, a different kind of society is needed where marriage and romance both disappear. Marriage disappears because to make two people live together by legal enforcement is immoral. To force two people to live together when they don't want to live together is against nature and against existence. Ninety-nine percent of social diseases will disappear if people are not forced.

Listen to this...

A man went to his lawyer and said, "I am very rich, so money is no object, but I want to be rid of my wife, who is a bitch, without being accused of murder. So tell me what to do."

"Buy her a strong horse and it may throw her."

A month later the man came back and said his wife was now the best horsewoman in the district.

"Try," said the lawyer, "buying her a Honda, and send her up the mountains in it."

The man did this, but she drove like Stirling Moss, putting in danger everybody but herself. The husband told the solicitor he was desperate.

"Then buy her a Jaguar."

The man was back in a week, delighted. "Name your fee," he said. "It worked."

"What happened, then?"

"Well when she opened the cage door to feed the jaguar, it bit her bloody head off!"

Marriage creates a thousand and one complexities and solves nothing. Yes, it succeeds: it succeeds in making people slaves. It succeeds in destroying people's individuality. Don't you see it all around? An unmarried man has a certain individuality and a married man starts losing his individuality; he becomes more and more of a type. The unmarried woman has a joy, something flowing. The married woman becomes dull, uninterested, bored. It is ugly to force people into boredom. People are here to be happy, people are here to enjoy and celebrate. This is ugly!

Marriage has to go. But if you choose fantasy and love, you will again fall into the same trap of marriage because love never succeeds, never succeeds the way marriage succeeds financially, security-wise, for children, for society, for this and that. Love never succeeds as marriage succeeds. So love is bound to create other kinds of troubles. And love exists because of repressed desires. When marriage disappears and desires are not repressed, love will disappear automatically.

A real society of human beings will not know anything of marriage and will not know anything of the honeymoon. It will know only of joy, of sharing with people. As long as you can share, good; if you cannot share, goodbye. Marriage disappears and with it disappears the ugly divorce. Marriage disappears and with it disappears the fantasy of the honeymoon.

When you are free to love, to meet, to be with people, the honeymoon will disappear. Laila and Majnu, and Shiri and Farihad will not be possible – nobody is obstructing the way. You can meet any woman and you can meet any man, whomsoever you desire and whosoever desires you; nobody else is barring the way. Then what is the need for fantasy? If all kinds of food are available,: whatsoever you want to eat is available, and nobody is standing there like a policeman or a magistrate or a priest, making you afraid and scared that if you eat this food you will go to hell, if you eat that food only then can you go to heaven – and the food you don't want to eat leads you to heaven, and the food want to eat leads you to hell... Anything that gives you joy leads to hell and anything that makes you miserable leads to heaven.

When nobody is standing in between you and your desires, when desire is free, there will be no repression. Without repression the honeymoon will disappear. The honeymoon is a by-product: it exists with marriage. It is like bait. You go fishing, you use bait. Honeymoon is a bait, it takes you into marriage. That's why women are very, very insistent about marriage – because they know. They are more down-to-earth, more empirical than men. Men have remained dreamers, they think of stars and the moon, and women only laugh at their ridiculous desires. The woman knows – she is very down-to-earth – she knows that within ten, twelve, fifteen days, two to three weeks, the honeymoon will disappear. Then what? She insists on marriage.

A man was asking his woman – he was in love – and he asked her in the night, "Love or something?"
And the woman said, "Marriage or nothing."
He asked again, "Love or something?"
And she said, "Marriage or *nothing*."

Love is not reliable, it comes and goes; it is a whim, a mood. If love remains, that simply means repression is still there.

Then in a different society there will be joy. *Love* will not be so important a word as *delight, celebration*. Two people want to share their energies; if they are both willing then there will be no hindrance. There will be only one limitation: if the other is not willing then it is finished, then it never starts. All other limitations should be dropped.

And now science has made it possible for the problem of children to be very easily solved. In the old days people were not so fortunate. You are more fortunate; the problem of children can be solved. You can stay with a woman until the day you think that now you have lived together long enough and your love, your joy with the woman goes on increasing, your joy with the man goes on increasing, and now there is no possibility of your becoming separate, you have found your soul mate – the day you feel that, you can have children. Otherwise there is no need to have children.

And in a better society, children should belong to the communes. The family has to disappear. There should be communes of people: a commune of painters, where painters – painter men and painter women – live together and enjoy their togetherness, a commune of poets, a commune of carpenters, a commune of goldsmiths; communes of different kinds of people who live together, rather than families. The family has been a calamity. It is better when many people live together who possess everything in common and who share their love with each other. But there should not be any restriction.

Love should never become a duty; only then is it joyful. The moment it becomes a duty it is dead, heavyweight, and it creates a thousand and one problems which cannot be solved directly. That is the whole situation in the world. You can go to the psychoanalyst, you can come to a master, you can meditate, you can do this and that – but your basic problem is not touched.

Your basic problem remains somehow connected with your sex energy, and you go on tackling it somewhere else. You go on cutting the leaves, pruning the leaves, and you never cut the root. People are miserable because people are fed up with each other. People are sad because they don't enjoy the company of each other. People are simply burdened: they are doing their duty, the love is not there.

Marriage and the honeymoon both come in the same package; they both have to go. Then there can be a non-repressed humanity, a fully expressive humanity, a fully expressive human being who knows nothing except joy, and who decides according to joy.

Joy should become the criterion. That's what Tantra is all about: joy should become the criterion.

The fourth question:

Osho,
I love a woman and I want her to be with me until I die. Is this a good last desire?

The first thing: no desire is the last if you are still living. No desire is the last desire if you are still living – who knows about the next moment? And how can you manage to know the next moment? How long you have known this woman? – a few weeks. Before those few weeks you had not even dreamed about her. If this can happen, it can happen again. After three weeks you may meet another woman.

Until you are dead no desire is the last desire; each desire creates another desire. Desire is a continuum. Only two things, death or enlightenment, stop desires. And certainly neither of them has happened to you yet – neither death has happened nor enlightenment.

It is good to understand desire. Each desire brings in new desires, one desire creates ten desires. It is just as out of one small seed comes a big tree, thousands of branches and millions of leaves. Out of one desire, the seed, many desires arise.

You cannot say anything about the future; you should not say – the future remains open. This is one of the greatest efforts of man – ridiculous, but man goes on making it. One: he wants to reform the past, which cannot be done. Whatsoever has happened has happened, there is no way to redo it; you cannot even touch it here and there. You cannot make it better, you cannot make it worse. It is simply beyond you. It has happened, it has become actual, and that which has become actual cannot even be touched. The past is finished, it is complete the way it is; you cannot go back and you cannot rearrange it. It is good; otherwise, if you could rearrange the past, if you could go back, you would go mad. Then you would never come to the present again; the past is so long.

It is good that the doors of the past are closed. But man, the stupid mind of man, goes on thinking of reforming, reformulating, doing something here and there. Don't you wish sometimes you had not said something, and you start thinking that would have been better? If you had not done something – would that have been better? And in your fantasy you try to say this or do that. But you are simply wasting time; now nothing can be done, it has slipped out of your hands.

The past cannot be reformed, and the future cannot be predicted. That too man goes on doing: he wants to predict the future. The future is that which has not happened. The future remains open; openness is what the future is. The future is indeterminate. It is not actual, it is only probable; nothing is certain about the future. There is no certainty about the future. But man is foolish: again he goes to the astrologers, consults the I Ching, tarot cards, shadow readers. Man is so foolish that he tries to find ways somehow so that he can know beforehand what the future will be. But if you can know about it beforehand, it is already past; it is no longer the future. Only the past can be known, the future remains unknown. That is the intrinsic quality of the future – unknownness. All is possible and nothing is certain – that's what the future is. All has happened, nothing more can happen – that's what the past is. And the present is just a passage from the actual to the potential, from the closed to the open, from the dead to the alive.

Now you ask: "Is this a good last desire?" You would like that it is your last desire, but then you would have to commit suicide, either actually or meta-phorically. You will have to commit suicide if you want it to be your last desire. Either go and jump in front of a train, or into the sea, or into an abyss – actually commit suicide – then you can have this as the last desire. Or psychologi-cally commit suicide, which is what many have done. Don't look at any other woman again; close your eyes, become afraid. Cling to whomsoever you love and don't go here, there, astray; don't even think, don't even dream: that is psychological suicide.

But in both ways you will not be able to live because you will not have a future to live. If you really want to live... And you want to live; in fact that's what you are asking: you want to live with your beloved. To live you have to be alive.

Don't think in terms of "the last desire." And why, why would you like it to be the last? Why can't you share your energies someday with some other women? Why be so miserly? Why be so inhuman? Are not other women as divine? Has not existence appeared in many, many forms, millions of forms around you? Why cling to one form? Why this clinging?

This clinging comes out of repression, because you have repressed your desires. Then one day you find a woman who is loving towards you and you cling. You are afraid to lose her because you know all those long nights when you were alone. If now this woman goes, again you will be alone. Now this woman is afraid of her loneliness herself: she clings to you. She is afraid that someday you may move towards somebody else; you may not look towards her, and she will be left alone. Long have been those nights of loneliness; now, no more: "We have found each other, we should cling to each other; we should possess each other and we should guard each other, so nobody goes anywhere."

But out of this guarding, look what has happened: people are bored. You want a lover, not a guard; you want a beloved, not a jailer. You want to flow, not to be imprisoned. Look at the contradictory desire: you want to live and love, but whatsoever you do disturbs your love, destroys your love, creates hindrances to the flow. You want to love and live, and you want to be joyously alive, but whatsoever you do goes against it, is against it.

Why should this be the last desire? I am not saying that this should not be the last desire, remember. Don't misunderstand me. I am not saying this should not be the last desire, I am saying, simply saying, why should it be the last desire? If it happens that you remain together, if it happens that you never find a more beautiful woman, a more loving woman – good, you are fortunate. If it happens that your beloved never finds another man who is more loving, more alive than you – fortunate. But if she finds a more loving man who can make her more joyful, who can bring her to greater peaks of ecstasy, then what? Should she cling to you? Then she is going against herself. Why should she cling to you?

And if she clings to you, she will never be able to forgive you because it will be because of you she had to miss that ecstatic man; she will always be angry with you. That's why wives are angry, husbands are angry. That anger has a natural base to it. The anger is not about mundane things; it is not about the tea not being hot enough, it is not that. Who bothers when you love a woman whether the tea is hot or not? When love is hot everything is hot. When love has gone cold everything seems cold. It is not that your slippers were not there where they should be when you got up. When you love a woman who bothers?

But when love disappears, that heat disappears. Then you are angry, and the anger is such that you cannot say it and the society does not allow it. The anger is such that you cannot be true about it. Maybe you have repressed it so deeply that you don't even become aware of it. You are not even conscious of that you are angry because now, because of *this* woman, other women have become unavailable to you; because this woman goes on surrounding you and is constantly watching you; because this man goes on watching you and does not allow you to move and have your life in your own way, the way you want it now.

Your past promises have become prisons. Then you are angry. And the anger has nothing to do with anything in particular; it is a general anger, so you cannot even say where it is, why it is, how it is. Then it jumps on any excuses – the tea is not hot, the food is not as you would like it to be.

This clinging creates anger. And we are not here to be unnecessarily in anger. Why? For what? For what purpose? If your beloved meets some beautiful person and suddenly feels that now she has found the right person, then what should she do? She should cling to you? She should not betray you? These words are ugly: *betray...* In fact, if she remains with you, she is betraying her own being; if she remains with you, she is betraying her love, she is betraying her joy, she is betraying existence. Now existence has called from another door; she is betraying it. And she will never be able to love you anymore; that is not possible. Existence has called from somewhere else. Some other eyes have become the doors and windows, some other form has become alive and attractive. What can she do now? She can avoid seeing that person, but how will she be able to forgive you? Now anger will start erupting. Now she will be angry for no reason at all, and the anger will destroy your love. It has already flown.

Remember, love is a breeze. Just see – there is no breeze right now, the trees are silent. What can they do? They cannot create the breeze. Whenever it comes, it comes. When it comes, they will dance with joy. When it has gone, it has gone. They have to wait. Love is like a breeze. When it comes, it comes – who knows from what direction, from what person, from whom.

This is the Tantra liberation. Tantra is a dangerous philosophy, it is a dangerous religion. It has not yet been tried on a larger scale; man has not yet been courageous enough to try it on a larger scale. Only a few individuals, few and far between, have tried it, and they have suffered very much because the society does not allow it, the society thinks it is absolute sin. But Tantra says that to live with a woman with whom your love flow has ceased, with whom you are no longer joyful, is sin. It is rape to make love to a woman you don't love. It is rape to make love to a man you don't love; it is prostitution.

This is the Tantra attitude about life. Tantra believes in joy because Tantra says joy is God. Remain true to joy and sacrifice everything to joy. Let joy be the only God, and sacrifice everything – whatsoever is needed. Remain flowing.

You say: "I love a woman. I want her to be with me until I die..." Are you thinking to die very soon? Who knows how long you may live? Why are you thinking about the future in the first place? To think about the future is to miss the present. You think that you are thinking great things – you have read such things by foolish poets. Poets are almost always foolish; they don't have a real experience of life, they only dream.

Now look: you think this is great love – that you want to live with her until you die. This is not great love, you are afraid. In fact, right now you are not enjoying it, that's why you are spreading into the future. Right now you are missing it, so you want to have it some day – maybe not today, then tomorrow, the day after tomorrow – that's why the fear arises. You would like to be with her for your whole life, so that somehow you can manage.

But why not now? If it can ever be had, it can be had right now. You don't know how to live right now, so you think about the future. And time is a great illusion. Only *now* exists. Tomorrow it will again be today. The day after tomorrow it will again be today. After one year it will again be today. It will always be today. God is always in the present. If you want to live, live right now. Why think of the future? Let your love be so intense, like a flame, that it burns you totally right now.

And now you are thinking "...until I die..." Who can say? At least *I* am not going to say anything about it because I would like you to remain free, and I would like your beloved also to be free. Meet as two free individuals, meet as two freedoms. And let the meeting be there while the freedom lasts. When your meeting starts corrupting freedom, separate; the time has come to say goodbye. Feel grateful for the days that you lived with the woman or with the man. Feel tremendously grateful that those days were made available to you through the other. Feel grateful for all that experience. But what can you do? With tears in your eyes, with gratitude, with love, with friendship, with compassion – separate. The breeze is no longer blowing this way. What can you do? Feel helpless, but become separate. Don't cling, otherwise you will destroy each other.

If you really love the other person, the moment love has disappeared you will make the other free. At least this much love is due: to make the other free, so that somewhere else, in some other pasture, love can flower and bloom. At least this much you can do for the other, that the love – if it has disappeared between you – can flower and bloom somewhere else with somebody else. Love is God. It is irrelevant where it happens, between whom it happens – between A and B, or C and D, or E and G. It is irrelevant where it happens. If it happens, it is good. The world has become so loveless because we cling to people when love stops. The world will be so full of love if people don't cling and remain free.

Be free in your love. Meet out of freedom, and when the freedom is destroyed, let that be an indication that love has disappeared – because love cannot destroy freedom: *love* and *freedom* are two names for the same thing. Love cannot destroy freedom. If freedom is being destroyed, then something else is pretending to be love – jealousy, hatred, domination, safety, security, prestige, social respectability – something else has come in. Before it enters and corrupts you and poisons you too much, escape from it.

The fifth question:

Osho,
I want to take sannyas and I have been waiting for it for years, but I am afraid I may get into some trouble because of it. What should I do?

I can only promise that you *will* get into troubles, I cannot say that you will not get into troubles. In fact, it is a device to create chaos in your life. But there are two kinds of troubles: destructive troubles and creative troubles. Avoid destructive troubles because they simply destroy. There are creative troubles which create, which bring you to a higher plane of consciousness. Troubles you have enough already. Certainly I am not going to add any more troubles of that kind.

It happened...

There was a woman in a railway carriage who was joined by a man who had with him a crowd of dirty and ill-behaved kids. Before they had gone very far, he gave one of his kids a fearful belting.

"Look here," said the woman, "stop beating that child or I'll get you into trouble."

"You'll do what?"

"I said, I'll get you into trouble!" the woman shouted.

"Listen, lady, my wife has run off with a black man taking every penny I've got; I'm on my way to leave these kids with a relative who drinks; the girl in the corner is fifteen and eight months pregnant. That kid over there has messed his pants, the baby has thrown the bottle out of the window, and the one I've just beaten has swallowed our tickets. For being off work, I've got the sack. Did you say you were going to get me into trouble – what *more* trouble?"

No, I am not going to put you into more trouble of the same kind you have been living in your whole life. I will introduce new kinds of troubles into your life. Be courageous.

And you have waited long – you say you have been thinking about it for years...

There was this football match between the mice and the insects. At half-time the score was six-all, and at the end it was eleven-ten to the mice. So the insects went to the centipede's cave and said, "Why haven't you been at the match?"

"I've been putting my boots on," said the centipede.

How long will you be putting your boots on? Soon the match will be over! Please do things faster.

The sixth question:

Osho,
Can't I take the jump myself, alone? Is a master absolutely needed?

Two fellows, Pete and Dave, are working on the scaffolding. A man comes past looking for new acts for the Variety Club, and he's just under the building when all of a sudden he sees Pete doing a triple somersault off the top of the scaffolding, followed by a backflip, another double somersault, and landing on his feet.

The fellow on the ground thinks that's tremendous, so he goes up to Pete and says, "Would you like to come and do an act for me?"

"Yes, all right."

"How much do you want for it?"

"A hundred pounds."

"A hundred pounds?"

"Well there's fifty for me, and fifty for Dave who hit me on the foot with a hammer."

You will not be able to go alone. You will need a master to hit you. The journey is so unfamiliar, the journey is into an abyss. Unless somebody really pushes you hard you are not going to take the jump, you will have to be hammered.

And the last question:

Osho,
What is nirvana?

Nirvana is this story – this ancient Buddhist story...

An exceptionally beautiful young woman, Enyadatta, enjoyed nothing quite as much as gazing at herself in the mirror. She was a little crazy too, as human beings are. When she looked into her mirror one morning, the figure in the glass had no head. Enyadatta became hysterical and rushed around yelling, "My head is gone, where is my head? Who has my head? I shall die if I don't find it!"

Even though everyone assured Enyadatta that her head was on her shoulders, she refused to believe them. Every time she looked in the mirror, her head wasn't there, so she continued her frenzied search, shouting and crying for help.

Fearing for her sanity, Enyadatta's friends and relatives dragged her home and tied her to a pillar so she wouldn't hurt herself. Enyadatta's friends continued to reassure her that her head was still on her shoulders and slowly she began to wonder whether they might not be telling the truth.

Suddenly one of her friends gave her a sharp clout on the head. She cried out in pain, and her friend exclaimed, "That's your head! There it is!" Enyadatta immediately realized that she had somehow deluded herself into thinking she had no head, when in fact she always had it.

So is nirvana. You have never been out of it, you have never been away from it. It is in you, you are in it. It is already the case, you have just to become a little more alert. You need a clout on the head.

The head is there: you cannot see it because you are looking in the wrong direction, or in a wrong mirror. You cannot see it because you don't have the clarity to see. Otherwise, nirvana is not some goal somewhere, it is not the afterlife, it is herenow.

Nirvana is the stuff you are made of. It is in each cell, it is in each fiber of your being. It is *you*.

Just a remembrance is needed. Just a remembrance...

Enough for today.

about Osho

Osho's unique contribution to the understanding of who we are defies categorization. Mystic and scientist, a rebellious spirit whose sole interest is to alert humanity to the urgent need to discover a new way of living. To continue as before is to invite threats to our very survival on this unique and beautiful planet.

His essential point is that only by changing ourselves, one individual at a time, can the outcome of all our "selves" – our societies, our cultures, our beliefs, our world – also change. The doorway to that change is meditation.

Osho the scientist has experimented and scrutinized all the approaches of the past and examined their effects on the modern human being and responded to their shortcomings by creating a new starting point for the hyperactive 21st Century mind: OSHO Active Meditations.

Once the agitation of a modern lifetime has started to settle, "activity" can melt into "passivity," a key starting point of real meditation. To support this next step, Osho has transformed the ancient "art of listening" into a subtle contemporary methodology: the OSHO Talks. Here words become music, the listener discovers who is listening, and the awareness moves from what is being heard to the individual doing the listening. Magically, as silence arises, what needs to be heard is understood directly, free from the distraction of a mind that can only interrupt and interfere with this delicate process.

These thousands of talks cover everything from the individual quest for meaning to the most urgent social and political issues facing society today. Osho's books are not written but are transcribed from audio and video recordings of these extemporaneous talks to international audiences. As he puts it, "So remember: whatever I am saying is not just for you...I am talking also for the future generations."

Osho has been described by *The Sunday Times* in London as one of the "1000 Makers of the 20th Century" and by American author Tom Robbins as "the most dangerous man since Jesus Christ." *Sunday Mid-Day* (India) has selected Osho as one of ten people – along with Gandhi, Nehru and Buddha – who have changed the destiny of India.

About his own work Osho has said that he is helping to create the conditions for the birth of a new kind of human being. He often characterizes this new human being as "Zorba the Buddha" – capable both of enjoying the earthy pleasures of a Zorba the Greek and the silent serenity of a Gautama the Buddha.

Running like a thread through all aspects of Osho's talks and meditations is a vision that encompasses both the timeless wisdom of all ages past and the highest potential of today's (and tomorrow's) science and technology.

Osho is known for his revolutionary contribution to the science of inner transformation, with an approach to meditation that acknowledges the accelerated pace of contemporary life. His unique OSHO Active Meditations™ are designed to first release the accumulated stresses of body and mind, so that it is then easier to take an experience of stillness and thought-free relaxation into daily life.

Two autobiographical works by the author are available:
Autobiography of a Spiritually Incorrect Mystic,
St Martins Press, New York (book and eBook)
Glimpses of a Golden Childhood,
OSHO Media International, Pune, India (book and eBook)

OSHO international meditation resort

Each year the Meditation Resort welcomes thousands of people from more than 100 countries. The unique campus provides an opportunity for a direct personal experience of a new way of living – with more awareness, relaxation, celebration and creativity. A great variety of around-the-clock and around-the-year program options are available. Doing nothing and just relaxing is one of them!

All of the programs are based on Osho's vision of "Zorba the Buddha" – a qualitatively new kind of human being who is able *both* to participate creatively in everyday life *and* to relax into silence and meditation.

Location
Located 100 miles southeast of Mumbai in the thriving modern city of Pune, India, the OSHO International Meditation Resort is a holiday destination with a difference. The Meditation Resort is spread over 28 acres of spectacular gardens in a beautiful tree-lined residential area.

OSHO Meditations
A full daily schedule of meditations for every type of person includes both traditional and revolutionary methods, and particularly the OSHO Active Meditations™. The daily meditation program takes place in what must be the world's largest meditation hall, the OSHO Auditorium.

OSHO Multiversity
Individual sessions, courses and workshops cover everything from creative arts to holistic health, personal transformation, relationship and life transition, transforming meditation into a lifestyle for life and work, esoteric sciences, and the "Zen" approach to sports and recreation. The secret of the OSHO Multiversity's success lies in the fact that all its programs are combined with meditation, supporting the understanding that as human beings we are far more than the sum of our parts.

OSHO Basho Spa
The luxurious Basho Spa provides for leisurely open-air swimming surrounded by trees and tropical green. The uniquely styled, spacious Jacuzzi, the saunas,

gym, tennis courts...all these are enhanced by their stunningly beautiful setting.

Cuisine
A variety of different eating areas serve delicious Western, Asian and Indian vegetarian food – most of it organically grown especially for the Meditation Resort. Breads and cakes are baked in the resort's own bakery.

Night life
There are many evening events to choose from – dancing being at the top of the list! Other activities include full-moon meditations beneath the stars, variety shows, music performances and meditations for daily life.

Facilities
You can buy all of your basic necessities and toiletries in the Galleria. The Multimedia Gallery sells a large range of OSHO media products. There is also a bank, a travel agency and a Cyber Café on-campus. For those who enjoy shopping, Pune provides all the options, ranging from traditional and ethnic Indian products to all of the global brand-name stores.

Accommodation
You can choose to stay in the elegant rooms of the OSHO Guesthouse, or for longer stays on campus you can select one of the OSHO Living-In programs. Additionally there is a plentiful variety of nearby hotels and serviced apartments.

www.osho.com/meditationresort
www.osho.com/guesthouse
www.osho.com/livingin

for more information

www.

a comprehensive multi-language website including a magazine, OSHO Books, OSHO Talks in audio and video formats, the OSHO Library text archive in English and Hindi and extensive information about OSHO Meditations. You will also find the program schedule of the OSHO Multiversity and information about the OSHO International Meditation Resort.

http://OSHO.com/AllAboutOSHO
http://OSHO.com/Resort
http://OSHO.com/Shop
http://www.youtube.com/OSHO
http://www.Twitter.com/OSHO
http://www.facebook.com/pages/OSHO.International

To contact OSHO International Foundation:
www.osho.com/oshointernational,
oshointernational@oshointernational.com